CURES *for* HUNGER

Also by Deni Y. Béchard

Vandal Love

CURES *for* HUNGER

A MEMOIR

Deni Y. Béchard

GOOSE LANE

Published simultaneously in the United States by Milkweed Editions.

Cover design by Christian Fuenfhausen.
Cover images from Shutterstock/Rido; Shutterstock/Kellis.
Author photo by Michael Connolly.
Printed in Canada.
10 9 8 7 6 5 4 3 2 1

Epigraph from the Penguin publication, *The Subject Tonight is Love: 60 Wild and Sweet Poems* by Daniel Ladinsky. Copyright © 1996 & 2003, Daniel Ladinsky and used with his permission.

Library and Archives Canada Cataloguing in Publication

Béchard, Deni Y. (Deni Yvan), 1974-
Cures for hunger / Deni Y. Béchard.

Issued also in electronic format.
ISBN 978-0-86492-671-5

1. Béchard, Deni Y. (Deni Yvan), 1974-.
2. Béchard, Deni Y. (Deni Yvan), 1974- — Family.
3. Authors, Canadian (English) — 21st century — Biography.
4. Fathers and sons. I. Title.

PS8603.E41Z53 2012   C813'.6   C2011-907732-9

Goose Lane Editions acknowledges the financial support of the Canada Council for the Arts, the Government of Canada through the Canada Book Fund (CBF), and the government of New Brunswick through the Department of Wellness, Culture, and Sport.

Goose Lane Editions
500 Beaverbrook Court, Suite 330
Fredericton, New Brunswick
CANADA E3B 5X4
www.gooselane.com

CURES FOR HUNGER

Because of our wisdom,
we will travel far
for love.

All movement is a sign
of thirst.

Most speaking really says,
"I am hungry to know you."

Every desire of your body is holy;

every desire of your body is
holy.

Hafiz (trans. Ladinsky)

But he who is outside of society, whether unsociable
or self-sufficient, is either a god or a beast.

Aristotle, Politics

CURES *for* HUNGER

PROLOGUE

My father died in a house empty but for a single chair. I never saw the property. I was told that it was heavily wooded, on the outskirts of Vancouver, and that a blanket of pine needles covered his car.

Two weeks before Christmas 1994, he'd stopped answering his phone. I was on the East Coast, so when I didn't hear from him by New Year's, I called the only one of his friends whose number I had. She didn't know where he was staying but offered to track him down. We agreed that the police shouldn't be notified; he'd had too many run-ins with them. A day later, she found his house.

I'd just turned twenty and was attending college in Vermont. A week before the second semester of my sophomore year, a police officer called with the coroner's report and told me that my father had taken his own life around December 16, a date that couldn't be confirmed since it was winter and the power had been cut off. His car had been re-possessed with what little he'd owned inside, and the public accountant had put his remaining cash toward thousands in back taxes.

But for a few phone calls, the death passed uneventfully, a quiet ending to a life that had spanned so much of North America, a childhood on the Saint Lawrence, in Gaspésie, and a poetry of names in his twenties: Montreal, the Yukon, Alaska; Montana, Las Vegas, Tijuana; Miami, Los Angeles.

Though I considered crossing the continent for his cremation, I was too broke. I might have gone in the spirit of his travels, bused or hitchhiked in a penniless homage, but I was unwilling to leave college. I'd fought for so long to be away from him that not even his death could bring me back.

And yet I hardly seemed to inhabit my rented room. I spoke to no one. I didn't see the forested road along which I walked to class, or the words scattered over the pages.

Often that winter I sat and stared at a paper on which I had printed three names.

Yvonne: the mother he hadn't seen since 1967; the grandmother I had never met.

Matane: the town in Quebec where he believed she and his siblings still lived.

Edwin: the name by which they'd known him.

In our last telephone conversation, he'd told me these three names. I'd grown up calling him André, and as for his family, they didn't know I existed.

I considered the names like keys to his past: the landscape of his youth, the face he'd worn as a boy. I'd never seen a photo of him from before he met my mother. Through his family, would I be able to make sense of the man whose reckless passions had shaped my life?

When finally I made the trip north to the village where he grew up, I found myself repeating the name they knew him by, as if preparing to tell them about a different father. His story belonged to me now, and in its telling he would return to those who had lost him.

part I

DAREDEVILS AND INVISIBLE FRIENDS

Racing trains was one of my favorite adventures. This was what we were doing on the day I first considered that my father might have problems with the law.

"Forty-seven, forty-eight, forty-nine!"

My brother and I practiced counting as my father kept up with the train.

"I'll push harder," he shouted. He thrust his bearded chin forward and bugged out his eyes and jammed the accelerator to the floor. His green truck heaved along the road, outstripping the train whose tracks, just below the line of trees, skirted the incline.

Almost instantly we left the red engine behind. He swerved past the few cars we came up on with shouts of "Old goat!" The road straightened and leveled with the tracks, and he shifted gears and kept accelerating, though the train was far behind. Then he braked, holding my brother and me in place with his right arm, the air forced from my lungs as he spun the wheel with his free hand. We pulled onto the crossing, though the warning lights on both posts flashed and bells rang.

With the truck straddling the tracks, he switched the motor off. He relaxed in his seat, looking out the passenger window, straight along the railroad.

As if on a TV screen, the train appeared in the distance, plummeting toward us. The engine broke from the shadow of the trees. Sunlight struck its red paint, and my brother and I began to scream.

My father turned the ignition.

"Oh no! It's not starting!" He was twisting the key but didn't give the engine gas. We knew the ritual and shouted, "Give it gas!"

He gave it gas and the motor fired. The truck shook but didn't move. The train engine was sounding its horn, filling up the tracks, its two dark, narrow windows glaring down at us.

The truck's wheels screeched, and we lurched and shot onto the road.

The train rushed past behind us, its iron wheels thudding over the crossing.

"That was a close call!" my father shouted and laughed like a pirate. But the color had drained from my brother's face. He turned to me, his eyes round as if to make me see just how close we'd come to being crushed. "We almost died," he said and swallowed hard.

I looked from his pale expression to my father, whose wild bellowing filled the cab. My fear had passed, and the air I drew into my lungs felt more alive, charged as if with a sudden, mysterious joy. I couldn't help but laugh with him.

Our yellow farmhouse faced the narrow road that ran the center of the valley. An apple tree and a row of blueberry bushes separated our back porch from damp fields, and the only neighbor my age was Ian, a dirty-faced farm boy with a mentally handicapped older sister—surely the victim of malnutrition, I imagined, given that my mother had explained how junk food destroyed the brain. Though I spent many afternoons with Ian, I never learned his sister's name. I simply thought of her as Ten Speed, because she raced up and down the road all day on what he referred to as "the ten speed." She had wide-set eyes and was always listening to a bulky black tape player clipped to her belt, its headphones holding her mess of brown curls in place.

Pine forest topped the mountains, large trees distinct like spurs against the sky in the hour before sunset. Many of the fields around our house grew Christmas trees, hundreds of neat rows of the pine, fir, and spruce that my father sold each December.

By the time we arrived home, he'd convinced my brother and me to keep our adventure between the three of us. His joyful mood had ended as soon as we pulled into the driveway, and he said he had to check the trees, something to do with an order for spruce. We were to go inside, but the thrill of train racing hadn't worn off, and I couldn't bear the thought of staying in the house. I begged to tag along, and he hesitated, then said, "Okay. Come on."

As the two of us walked the rows, I asked him to tell a story. He stared ahead, taking slow, deep breaths between his parted lips, and he stepped evenly, lightly over the wet, tufted earth that kept my attention. I had a specific story in mind. When I was younger, my mother had told me I'd someday grow facial hair, and I'd pictured myself, my face hidden in a dark, stinky beard as I showed up to class and sat in the back, terrifying the other kids. I cried, and my father laughed at me. I was so embarrassed and angry that he told a story about a fat bearded woman he'd lived with before my mother. She sat on him so he couldn't leave, and he wiggled from beneath her butt and ran away because he didn't want children with beards.

He stayed silent now, narrowing his eyes the way his dogs did when they wanted to run after something. He kept six German shepherds in a pen, and whenever he let them out, they sniffed the air and gazed into the distance, the wind ruffling their fur, and then they raced away so suddenly that I felt they were the happiest animals on earth.

But he just walked, and I followed him over the road to the Christmas tree fields on the other side. We stepped over sagging barbed wire and crossed a stream on a plank nailed with asphalt shingles for grip. I lingered to watch for trout in the dark pools beneath overhanging trees, but he kept on, and I ran to catch up.

"Tell me the story again," I said and reached for his hand. His fingers closed slightly, and he glanced down.

"Which one?" He'd been like this more and more — at first normal, making jokes, doing something fun and crazy, laughing wildly; then, a little later, silent, staring off.

"About the bearded woman," I said. I loved replaying the stories he told and didn't feel satisfied until I could see each detail, so I asked why he'd lived with her and what kind of woman she was. He nodded but didn't tell it at all. He just said, "You're lucky. If she'd been your mother, you'd have been born with a beard."

We came to where the fields gave way to tall tangled grass and huge weeds and forest. The mountain rose steeply above us, and we turned and walked along its base, the rows of Christmas trees running on at our sides. With each few steps another long, thin corridor appeared, descending out of sight.

Where the trees ended, there was a shallow, overgrown ditch separating the neighbor's blueberry farm from our land. The air smelled bad, like an alley trash can in the city, behind one of my father's stores.

"He got some bears. Let's have a look," he said and told me that our neighbor had set up bear traps. He waded into the yellow grass, crushing a path I followed. I pushed weeds aside and stretched my neck to see ahead. He'd often warned me to stay away from bears and their cubs, and he'd made me promise that if any came along when I went fishing alone, I'd get on my bike and hurry home. I'd seen them once, four dark spots near some distant trees, and I'd pedaled as fast as I could over the rutted dirt road, my fishing rod pinned to my handlebars. I felt a little nervous now, the stench of rotten meat stronger, but he was there, between me and the bears, and I wanted to show him that this was no big deal.

"Look." He stepped to the side and motioned me forward.

The dense grass came up past my elbows, and I walked ahead, my heart beating faster. Two large dark shapes lay on the earth as if crushed into it, their legs twisted awkwardly, one haggard carcass just before me, its jaws open, eye sockets hollow.

"You're not afraid?" he asked as I stood, measuring my breath, studying the second bear, sprawled on its side, a naked leg bone raised stiffly, claws struck into the rank air.

"No," I said. The bears were dead, and this wasn't a big deal, after all. I made myself go closer to look at the fanged, gaping jaws, the rotting fur like torn carpeting over the ribs. The smell made it hard to breathe, but I took another step.

He turned and said, "Let's go."

"I want to look at them."

He chuckled proudly. "Come on. You've seen enough."

I crouched. Two long curved teeth protruded from the top and bottom jaws. A few weeks earlier, in class, I'd read a story in my fourth-grade primer about the loup-garou, the werewolf. Because my classes were in French, we often read folktales from Quebec, but this one was my favorite. I'd tried to imagine the werewolf's mouth, its sharp teeth, and how my jaw would feel growing fangs as I stared at the full moon. I'd turned in my chair and made bug eyes and growled at the girl behind me, and she'd called out to the teacher, who'd threatened to send me to the principal's office as usual.

My father started walking, and I spun and jogged after him, through the crushed grass. As I followed him back across the rows, I told him the story, feeling a little breathless at the thought that what I'd just seen might not really be bears.

"There's this hunter who likes to hunt more than he likes to be in the village. He hunts all day long and he sleeps in his cabin, and he almost never goes home or talks to anyone. Then, one night, when it's the full moon, his uncles and cousins visit his cabin, but it's empty. They find clothes covered with animal hair, and there are huge wolf tracks in the snow."

Just describing this gave me goose bumps, and I rubbed my arms, picturing myself coming to the door and pushing it open and seeing my clothes on the floor, covered in black hair.

"I heard that a lot when I was a boy," he told me, his eyes serious, maybe a little worried.

I stared up at him, trying to match his pace. What would he look like as a loup-garou? His beard would spread over his entire face and neck and arms, and I pictured him standing at the edge of the forest beneath the mountain, dressed in torn fur, the bear skull on his head as he stared out at the valley through the ragged jaws. I knew I was seeing this wrong, that this wasn't like a werewolf at all, but my brain always played tricks on me. I'd look at something and minutes later I'd picture strange things, as if from a dream, and then I'd no longer be sure of what I'd really seen. I glanced up again. I'd expected him to say something about the story or the dead bears, but he was silent, eyes narrowed.

We made our way back toward the farm, past a few sheds that smelled of wet earth, and he stopped to look inside, as if he'd forgotten something.

"See," he said quietly. "Each year the sheds are smaller. They rot into the ground. The valley's moisture eats up the wood."

He spoke as if he'd already forgotten the bears, and he sighed, looking back at the rows. I couldn't remember him ever acting like this. He turned in a circle, as if to do something, glancing slowly here and there. But then he moved on, and I hurried after until we came to the ditch before the road and walked along it and crossed over a large culvert.

As we followed the asphalt, I heard the low whistle of a bicycle chain against its gears, and Ten Speed shot past with a sound like someone snapping a wet towel. Briefly, shouting voices blared from her headphones. I'd asked Ian about this, and he'd said that she listened to radio shows. We'd once found her sleeping in the hay of the barn, curled up, the voices clamoring from her frizzy hair. Then her eyelids popped open on large, dark, terrified pupils, and she sprinted past us, staying crouched low, and went down the ladder and out the door.

My father glanced behind us. A white car had appeared in the distance, and he stared, then turned and kept walking, looking straight ahead. He reached out and told me to hold his hand.

The car pulled next to us, and the darkening sky warped in the window that descended on two clean-shaven men. The driver, with eyes as blue as my mother's, said, "Excuse me. Can you tell us where André Béchard lives?"

My father squeezed my hand. He tilted his head to the side and looked at the man as if he didn't understand. Then he scrunched up his face.

"Who?" he said in a loud, ridiculous voice.

"André Béchard. Do you—"

"Oh, 'ey, dat guy. Yeah, I see 'im. 'E drive a big blue truck and 'e out drivin' in de city. Oh yeah, 'e out in de city. Dat's right."

The men stared as he gesticulated, and it was all I could do to stand perfectly still and make no expression.

"Oh, yeah, 'e come back later," my father was saying. "Dat's right, later."

The driver gave me a long, searching look, and I barely breathed, certain he could read on my face that my father was lying. But he finally shrugged.

"Okay," he said, his eyes like my teacher's when she was fed up with me. He drove off.

I gazed up, trying to understand why my father had pretended to be someone else, but he just laughed.

"I played a good joke on those guys," he said. "But don't tell your mother. She doesn't like jokes—not the way you and me like jokes."

I smiled and agreed, though there was a wincing look in his eyes, nothing like the wild joy of escaping the train. As we walked home along the asphalt, he stepped faster, and the hand holding mine felt hot and damp.

Often, after school, I wandered the fields alone, catching frogs and snakes, putting them in my pockets as I explored the woods along the stream. I couldn't stop thinking about the two men in the car. I was certain they were police. My father knew everything about police and had told me that they didn't always dress in uniform or drive cop cars. Whenever he saw them, he made fun of their clothes, especially the yellow stripe on one leg of their pants. He said he'd have joined the RCMP himself if their outfits weren't so ugly. Then he called them criminals in uniforms and told stories about the stupid pigs he'd fooled.

As I sat beneath the trees, a memory resurfaced: a night I couldn't place, that I was afraid to ask about. It seemed distant, like a bad dream after waking, but vivid, constant in my recollection. There was a house where we'd stayed, at a river ferry crossing on an Indian reservation. My father and mother had spoken in hushed tones. Was this years ago? I'd wanted to know what was happening, and he'd told me that a man was coming to fight him.

"I want to fight, too."

"You're too little."

"No! Let me fight."

"Okay. Maybe. You just wait inside. Maybe you can help me."

"You promise?"

"Yeah," he said, smiling at me. "All right. I'll probably need your help."

I sat on the couch as he paced the small living room, stopping only to draw back the curtain and look out at the gravel driveway and the dark road to the ferry landing. The man who was coming had worked for him and wanted money he didn't deserve. My father had told me stories about fighting. He always made it sound fun, and I was desperate to hit the man, too.

"He'll be here soon," my father said and prowled back and forth, hunched like an angry dog. His rage burned into the air so that I breathed and tasted it.

But then I was opening my eyes, lifting my face from the cushion, rubbing my cheek.

He'd come in the door, dark red gouges on the skin around his eyes, the collar of his shirt torn. He picked up the telephone's black receiver. Blood covered his knuckles.

"He's knocked out," he told my mother. "I knocked him out."

"What happened?"

"She jumped on my back. His girlfriend—she tried to scratch my eyes."

"She's out there?"

"I broke her jaw. I didn't mean to. She jumped on my back."

My mother just stared.

"I wanted to fight," I shouted and began to cry.

She hurried to the couch and lay me back against the pillow.

"Go to sleep," she told me, her voice stern. There was a tension in her face that I knew from my father's rages, when he was angry at her, though he wasn't now.

"I didn't mean to," he kept saying. He was holding the phone.

I understood that outside the man and his girlfriend lay on the dark gravel.

My father dialed and spoke into the phone, telling what had happened, that two people had come onto his property.

Then I was waking again. Red and blue lights flashed outside, rippling in the folds of the curtains. My father was putting on his jacket, the door opening, cold night air and the smell of the river washing into the room.

After the fight by the ferry, there'd been a visit to court, my brother and I neatly dressed, our mother grim and silent, trying to keep us quiet, giving us the candy she usually forbade, rotting out our teeth and bones, turning us into retards.

Maybe the police had come to the valley because he'd beaten someone up again. Or the train engineers had complained. But now that I was listening and watching, I realized that something had changed, my mother withdrawn, my father—when he was home—like a watchdog in the seconds before it snarled. If I could read minds, I might make sense of the shouting that woke me at night, the slammed doors, my mother crossing the house, naked but for a blanket wrapped around her, telling him to leave her alone.

Sometimes the fights were obvious: he got angry when she cooked strange meals like boiled oranges and rice, or he told her to stop nagging him for having shared his vodka with me. He'd let me have a swig on a fishing trip, and, proud of how much I could handle, I'd snuck more, the bottle lifted above my face, a shimmering bubble rising with each gulp. My brother called out to my father, who snatched it from my hand. I became drowsy and passed out, but at school I bragged that my father had let me get drunk. My mother turned the color of chalk when she heard me say this, and my father later reminded me that drinking was one of our secrets. But everything was becoming a secret. Even most of their fights were mysterious. They just had to look at each other and they started yelling.

So maybe she knew. Maybe she'd discovered he was in trouble. I wondered how long it would be before the police returned.

We were driving to get the mail, the five of us, my father at the wheel, my mother holding my sister on her lap, my brother and I wedged in between.

Large, distant mountains stood at the horizon, the highest already white. A few rusty leaves still clung to the roadside trees, and as we drove, sunlight broke in along the clouds, flashing over the hood of the truck.

The post office was a two-story building next to the muddy slough near where I was born, just outside the valley. A brass bell rang when we opened the door. The owner, a soft-looking, bespectacled man who lived up a set of creaky stairs, was reading the paper. He got up from his stool, pushed his glasses high on the bridge of his nose, and gazed at the wooden pigeonholes on the wall. He took down a sheaf of letters.

I followed my father back outside and down the steps. He stood in the sunlight as he tore the envelopes open. One held a flowery card. He stared into it. I'd never seen him get mail like this, and I stepped in close but still couldn't make out the words.

"What is it?"

My mother laughed. "It's from his other family."

The skin of his neck flushed. He didn't appear to breathe.

"What other family?" I asked. I had no idea what she meant, and I looked up at him, trying to see inside the card. He never talked about his parents the way she talked about hers. But he didn't respond, and she stared at the ground and sighed. "It was just a joke. I was just joking."

He folded the card and put it in his jacket pocket, and we got in his truck and left. But I couldn't stop wondering what had made him so angry. We often received cards from my mother's parents in Pittsburgh, but this was the first time I'd seen him get one. Though I knew he was from Quebec, he almost never spoke about where he'd grown up, other than to say, "My brother and me, we beat up all the kids in our village, so you and your brother should stick together." And then he'd look a little angry, probably because of all the fights he'd been in.

It was frustrating. I knew almost nothing about him. Why hadn't I realized this before? Did he keep secrets from me the way he did from her? The only time I thought about where he came from was at school, because that's where we spoke French and often read about Quebec. My mother loved French but didn't speak it, and she told me that my father grew up speaking it even if he almost never did now. He claimed it was useless, but she insisted on making us learn it. Though

French classes weren't offered when my brother started school, they were the year I began.

That evening, as I did my homework, I couldn't stop trying to make sense of the card and his other family. I approached the chair where he watched TV.

"*Est-ce que tu peux m'aider avec mes devoirs?*" I said. If he checked my homework and spoke in French, I might figure something out. Maybe there were questions I could ask in French that I couldn't in English. Besides, I was always curious to hear his voice change.

"Okay, *viens*," he told me, but as soon as my workbook came into his big, dark hands, he furrowed his brow. His eyelids drooped, his expression guilty, as if he'd lied. He hunched in his chair as I rattled away, explaining the assignment. When I stopped, he made a suggestion on how to write a sentence, but I was pretty sure he was wrong, and I corrected him.

He lowered the book and stared at the TV. Black smoke rose from an aerial view of a city. He seemed upset, as if this were a place he knew. All around him hummed familiar danger, the electric buzz of his irritation, and I didn't move or speak.

When he switched to English and said, "This isn't a good time," I felt relieved.

My mother had clear blue eyes, not dark like his, and silvery stripes in her light brown hair that, when she pulled it back in a ponytail, reminded me of the markings on a cat.

"Whose eyes do I have?" I asked. We were alone in the kitchen while she made goat cheese and I pretended to do my homework, my brother and sister watching TV, my father gone. I spoke as if the question weren't a big deal, though my teacher had made us read about eye color and told us that to have blue eyes the genes had to come from both parents. My mother said that mine were probably from her, unless someone in my father's family also had blue eyes, but she didn't know. I didn't bother to explain how it really worked and asked, "Why don't you know?"

"Because I've never met them. He's not close to them anymore."

"Why not?"

"I don't really know. He didn't get along with them. He doesn't like to talk about it."

"Oh," I said, grudgingly, surprised that even she didn't know much about him. I fiddled with my pencil and considered my workbook. "And whose hair do I have?"

"I had blond hair when I was younger."

"And my nose." She'd often told me that I was lucky not to have her small nose. She called it a ski jump, though I saw nothing wrong with it.

"Your nose is your father's. You have his real nose."

"His real nose?" I repeated. "His nose isn't real?"

She was always doing this—telling me shocking things.

"He had his real nose smashed in a fight. Doctors rebuilt it and gave him a new one that's smaller and very straight. I never saw his real one, but I'm sure you'll have it when you grow up."

I looked down at my workbook. I was sitting at a picnic table, the kind you saw in parks but never in other kids' houses. My life was nothing like other kids'. I never said "Mom" and "Dad," but "André" and "Bonnie," and no one I knew had changed homes so often. Every winter, we used to move to places with heat, rundown houses where my father got electricity using jumper cables, clipping the ends above and below the meter after stripping away the rubber. Summers, we'd stayed in a trailer on blocks in the valley, goats and German shepherds in pens outside, my first memories sunlit days and broken-down motors, the mountain just above us, no electricity or running water, and our drinks in wire milk crates set in the stream.

From my mother's stories, I knew she'd gone to art school in Virginia but had run away with a draft dodger. I pictured a guy really good at dodgeball, but, as if angry, she said he was dodging war, not balls. She met my father in Vancouver while working as a waitress, an encounter that—because he'd once described it to me as "She served me ham and eggs, and I left with her"—made me hungry whenever I thought about it. After that, they'd traveled British Columbia, living out of a van and fishing, an existence I fantasized about—mornings waking up and going straight outside to the river, no bedroom to clean, no school to worry about. But they'd decided to settle down and have children, and my perfect life ended just before I was born.

Whenever I asked her questions—about war or why it's wrong—she answered carefully, explaining with so many details—Vietnam, corrupt government, the loss of individual freedom—that I didn't understand much. She never talked to me like I was a child, but as if I were a very old and serious man, and so I sat and listened, trying to remember the big words she used. And then, to let off some steam, I asked her to retell *The Little Engine That Could,* and she did, though she seemed much less interested in this than in the world's problems.

As opposed to my mother, whenever I asked my father about his family, he barely answered. "Why don't you like to speak French?" or "What did your parents do?" earned me few words: "There's no point," or "He fished. She took care of the kids." And then he'd tell me how he'd traveled cross-country to Calgary and gone to a party and got in a terrible fight over a beautiful woman.

"This bruiser," he said, "was two or three times as big as me. We were throwing each other across the room. We broke the table and chairs and knocked all the pictures off the walls. There wasn't anything we didn't break. That guy was really tough, but I just didn't let myself get worried. You get worried in a fight, and you've had it. So I kept hitting him, and pretty soon everyone at the party started cheering me. They were originally his friends, but he was arrogant, and I was the better fighter. They could see that, so I guess they wanted to be on my side. Each time I got him down, I'd say, 'Stay down,' and everyone else would shout, 'Stay down,' but he'd get up, and then I'd hit him five or six times, and he'd fall on his ass again, and everyone would yell, 'Stay down.' I tried to be nice, but that guy was really big, and he kept shaking his head and trying to get back up and then I'd have to hit him again. It wasn't easy, but I finally made him understand."

By this point I no longer remembered my original question, and I asked him if he'd had worse fights, and he told one story after another. His confrontations with bruisers, this being one of his favorite words, often had strange endings.

"The bruiser was so strong I had to bite his nose to win. We were on the docks, by the fishing boats, and I got him down and bit his nose and just hung on until he started crying. Sometimes you have to do things like that to win a fight."

He told me about journeys, from Calgary to Tijuana in a truck without brakes, or driving an old Model T along Alaskan railways to get to towns not connected by roads. Whenever a train came, he swerved off the tracks, and afterward he and his friends hefted the Model T back on.

My favorite was the time he and a friend were driving through Nevada and picked up a Mormon. He drove so fast that the Mormon prayed in the backseat and wept to the Lord until my father, racing at over a hundred miles an hour, slammed the brakes. The Mormon flew onto the dash, his back against the windshield so that the car was briefly dark and all my father saw was his screaming face. The friend kicked open his door and they chucked the Mormon out. The man grabbed at the earth, kissing it—"Like the goddamn pope," my father said.

I didn't know what a Mormon was, but I'd seen the pope on TV, descending from an airplane and kissing the ground.

"I bet dogs pissed all over that ground," my father had told me and changed the channel.

Neither Mormons nor the pope could be too bright or brave. Hearing his descriptions, I forgot about my questions and his secrets. Reckless speed and the thought of untamed distance thrilled in my blood.

The proof that his stories were true was his madness. He raced through traffic or hit large puddles with such speed that his truck appeared to have wings of muddy water and sputtered until its engine dried. Watching TV, he contemplated Evel Knievel, who, dressed in his cape and the shirt with crossed lines of stars, jumped his motorcycle over buses. Though he calculated how difficult this would be, he preferred Houdini. Having seen a documentary on him, he discussed ways of escaping handcuffs, live burial, and torture cells.

Yet many of his exploits had involved not escaping torture but subjecting us to it. In the mall, when I was four, he'd hidden, standing with mannequins in a window, arms lifted and motionless, head cocked at an angle as he stared into space. He blended in perfectly, his posture so convincing that my brother and I walked past him repeatedly, crying as we called out his name. Only when a woman stopped to help us did we see the mannequin in the display leave its place and hurry toward us, laughing.

Or once he took my brother and me to a store that he intended to rent. Though he ran Christmas tree lots each winter, he also had three seafood shops in the city and wanted to open more. But while we snooped in back, he locked us in and hid outside. My brother was six or seven and, having taken on the role of voicing our terror, pounded on a window until it cracked. My father loomed in the broken glass. His key ring jangled against the door right before he threw it open and spanked us for acting like babies. But as he tried to strike me, I struggled and shouted, "I wasn't crying!" Even afterward, following him back to the truck, I was enraged, yelling, "I wasn't crying!" until he turned and glared at me and said, "Okay. That's enough!"

Train racing was more frequent and always fun, though he did it rarely now, unlike when I was little. Sometimes he didn't stop, just raced in front, swerving past the gate, striking the embankment like a ramp and sailing to the road with the clatter of rusted shocks. Or he waited on the tracks, though under normal circumstances his battered truck was known to stall or refuse to start. He even got out once, pocketing his keys after telling us to wait. We screamed as the train heaved into sight. We beat on the windows and called, "André! André!" until he hurried back and jumped behind the wheel and pretended to turn the key, yelling, "It won't start!" But finally the engine fired, and we screeched from the tracks.

Only later did I wonder why we loved danger so much, why my mother hated this feeling that made me happier than anything else.

Usually when I woke up, my father had already gone to his stores, and he returned after I was in bed. But some mornings before school, if his truck was in the driveway, I searched the misted rows of pines through our windows. His figure passed between them, followed by the swift movement of his German shepherds, all soon obscured by rain.

The November of my fourth grade, while he worked his tree lots, I worried that the salmon runs would end and checked spawning dates in the books I'd hoarded from the school library. He and I used to fish often, in the streams between the fields or in the reservoir outside the valley, but he had less and less time and often wasn't even around, so I couldn't ask. I lay in bed, looking at pictures of fish—the toothy great barracuda or the gaping goosefish with its antennae. Their mystery riveted me, the way they appeared from the deepest, darkest water and vanished again, how they belonged to a different world. I wanted nothing more than to catch one, for my father and me to go to the river the way we used to and stand together and then laugh over what we'd caught.

When I woke, my face was on the book, the page glued to my cheek. I carefully peeled it off and sat up. He was shouting somewhere downstairs.

I got out of bed and opened my door. No one was in the kitchen at the bottom of the stairs, and I crept down, gently setting my foot on each step so that it wouldn't creak.

I went to their door and listened. My mother was crying.

"It's all bullshit," he said.

"I saw it. It was as real as you standing here. I was lying there dead, and my body rolled over, and half of my face was rotted. It was me from a past life."

My hand fit against the edge of the doorframe, my cheek to its cold, painted wood.

"Stop going to those things. What's wrong with you?"

"I'm not stopping. I need to figure this out. I want to know who I used to be."

It was unfair that he didn't want her to learn more. Her description was thrilling, like a mystery in a novel. But maybe he was protecting her. That happened in stories, too. All this was confusing. I'd thought she was angry at him, not the other way around. I was so frustrated by all I didn't understand that I stomped back to my room, not trying to be quiet at all.

The next day he was gone, and she made us sit with her on the living room carpet. She wanted to teach us something special she'd learned. We sat cross-legged and closed our eyes, and she told us to calm our minds and look inside until we saw a white light. The white light was our soul. This, she said, was called meditation.

I rolled my eyes in the dark, then opened them. My brother and sister sat, my mother, too, eyelids settled, faces smooth. The sun descended against the mountains, the fields already in shadow, the last flare of daylight in the dirty window glass. I closed my eyes again, and there it was — the glow, a pale thumbprint in the dark substance of my mind.

That night, when she came to say good night, I told her.

"I saw my soul. I saw the white light."

Tears came into my eyes, not from sadness but the spinal thrill of mystery — all that could be known and discovered. She knelt by my bed and stroked the hair from my face.

"I'm proud of you," she said. "I want you to keep looking inside yourself and to tell me everything you see."

My mother often talked about purpose.

"You all have one," she said, driving us home from school, staring off above the glistening, leaf-blown highway as if we'd keep on toward our purpose and never return.

She told us that our gifts helped us to understand our purpose. Since my brother's and sister's report cards held stars mine lacked, they were clearly gifted in school. In particular, my sister's gifts were singing and, when necessary, punching boys, and my brother's were math and behaving. He was also gifted with an obsession for space travel and Choose Your Own Adventure novels, and he played so many hours of *Tron Deadly Discs* on his IntelliVision that his thumbs blistered.

Though I'd tried my hand at creating sculptures from trash and even made dolls with my mother's old maternity underwear, stuffing them with cotton and twisting them the way clowns did with long balloons, none of this was appreciated. The sculptures returned to the trash, and the dolls, shortly after I gave them to the neighbor's toddlers, unraveled and were left on the roadside so that it looked as if a pregnant woman had been carousing the valley night after night.

As we were nearing home, I asked my mother why I had a purpose.

"So you can do something great for the world," she said.

Maybe this was why I always felt unsatisfied or craved to see something amazing. Whenever I learned about anything new, I couldn't stop thinking about it—meditation or fishing, the police or my father's other family. My mother had once told me how society had become corrupt and might end, and I'd thought about this until it seemed as if the destruction should happen any minute now. It would be the greatest story ever. There would be no more school, and I'd live in the mountains and fish and meditate forever, unless this wasn't my purpose after all.

"But how can I know?" I practically yelled.

"What?"

"What my purpose is?"

"Just ask inside yourself," she said. "All the answers you'll ever need are inside you."

I sighed. Something had to happen right now, like in a novel. I wanted the sun to burn up the mountains, the sky to dissolve into the fields, the earth to melt into crystal blue water. But along the road, dead autumn grass resembled a dirty shag rug. Ten Speed appeared in the distance and zipped past, turning her head to take us in with her wide, empty eyes. And then the road before us was clear. A few naked trees leaned this way and that, hunched and bent and reaching, like old people.

"Do you have any invisible friends?" my mother asked.

"What do you mean?"

"Are there people you talk to?"

It seemed like a dumb question. I talked to everything—to stuffed animals and books, to my pillow and the trees. I walked across the fields talking.

But my brother was eager to explain. "Not real people," he said.

"Spirit guides," she interrupted. "Your brother and sister have one. How many do you have?"

I looked out the window. Ten Speed had made a U-turn and was trying to pass us, her chin to the handlebars. I watched her a moment, giving my mother's question some thought.

"Twelve," I said.

Briefly, no one spoke.

"Well then," she told me, "you should have no problem finding your purpose. Just ask. I'm sure at least *one* of them will tell you."

Novembers were disappointing. My father was gone, running his sea-food stores or selling Christmas trees. My birthday passed while he worked, and that Friday, at school, the kids sang "Bonne Fête à Toi," though I wouldn't actually turn nine until Sunday. As they yammered, I mourned the few remaining weeks of salmon season and that my father was too busy to take me. The teacher told the class my age, and they all asked, as they did each November, why I was a year younger. I explained how my mother had thought kindergarten was a waste of time and made me go straight to first grade. They told me kindergarten was fun, and I said it was for slow learners, which she'd also said, though from what I'd heard, it did sound fun.

The next morning, when my father was saying good-bye to my mother in the kitchen, I got up and grabbed my book on salmon and ran downstairs.

"The salmon runs are going to end," I whined and showed him the dates. "Can't we go for my birthday? It's tomorrow. You were going to forget it. You always do."

He'd just finished putting on his rain gear by the door, and he sighed.

"We can't go fishing," he said after a moment, "but how about I take you to work for your birthday? There's a spare bed. I'll bring you back tomorrow."

I said, "Sure, okay," as if I didn't care, though I planned to harass him about salmon fishing and make him feel bad about not doing something more special for my birthday. Even on our way into the city, as I tried to bide my time, we passed a shallow river where Native Americans stood in the current, spearing salmon that splashed between the rocks. My father had long ago explained why they were allowed to fish this way and catch as much as they wanted, and I'd been jealous. I couldn't help but mutter, "I wish I was Indian" as we drove past.

My father sold Christmas trees near downtown Vancouver, on a parking lot rented from the Pacific National Exhibition, which had closed its rides for the winter. He'd put up fences and turned the space into a maze of pine, spruce, and fir, and he'd been sleeping in the mobile home that served as an office and a warm-up place for his employees, the young men who hauled trees and flirted with Helen, a pretty blond with fringed bangs who ran the till. She played Christmas music over the speakers until the last customer left, then put on the Eurythmics or Duran Duran, and everyone gathered in the cramped living room to drink and talk, the trailer floor creaking and grinding against its cinder-block supports.

Though his workers all had yellow rain jackets and pants, my father wore green, as if it were a general's color. Yellow was ugly, he told me, and he pointed out that you called cowards yellow. In green, he blended with the trees, so that sometimes I didn't notice him watching as I wandered and talked to myself. I'd look up suddenly, seeing the faint figure, his eyes still and dark as unlit windows.

Even though I was actually proud of going to work with him, I couldn't stop worrying about the salmon runs. Each time I reminded him, he sighed and said, "Okay. I'll think about it. Stop asking, will you?" Then he turned back to speaking with customers or giving commands.

By that night, I was starving. On the couch, I huddled in my jacket,

trying to read *Mystery of the Fat Cat,* wishing I had enough friends
to form a gang or that I lived someplace with interesting creatures
like rats and cockroaches. My stomach clenched and gurgled, and I
pictured myself sinking my teeth into Helen's arm as if I were a fam-
ished rat. What had changed? I never used to worry about food. Was
it something my father had done, or my mother's dreams? I was feeling
sad and frustrated, as if I might cry, and this only made me angrier. I
hated myself when I wanted to cry. I threw down the book and went
outside.

Misting rain drifted over the lot, gauzy halos around the hanging colored bulbs. No one stood near the trailer, the music turned low,
Perry Como crooning softly as if from far away. Pine needles covered the
asphalt, and I walked into a dark row of trees, hundreds tied in twine
and leaned against two-by-four supports. Voices reached me, rising and
falling, like the ocean from a distance. The corridor of trees became so
dark that I froze, trying to see ahead, my senses overpowered by the
smell of pine sap.

"André . . . ," I called, but my voice broke, and I swallowed and tried
to make my throat work. "André!" I shouted. Footsteps scuffed past beyond the trees and stopped.

"Hey, André!" a man barked, his voice nasal and angry. "Your kid's
looking for you."

The footsteps scuffed off, and I pictured big rubber boots on indifferent feet, dragging through pine needles.

"Where?" my father called.

"Just over here," the man barked again. "Over there."

My father called my name, sounding tired. His silhouette appeared
at the end of the corridor, his sou'wester gleaming faintly. He didn't drag
his feet but stepped quietly until he stood before me. His beard seemed
black, his eyes lost beneath the rubber brim.

"What is it?"

"I'm hungry," I said, trying to keep my voice under control, though
it sounded too loud and whiny and on the verge of tears.

"It's late. You should've told me before." He spoke slowly, as if to hold back his anger, and I forced myself to swallow and answer as calmly as I could.

"I didn't know," I said. "I just realized."

He sighed as if relieved that I hadn't started crying, and the tension seemed to release from around him. Hazing rain gathered on my face as I tried to read his expression. I'd always felt that he liked having me along. We used to laugh together, and he'd tell stories whenever I wanted, but that almost never happened anymore.

"Come on," he said. "I'll order you a pizza."

I followed him back between the trees, and in the space before the trailer, with the colored lights and chrome coffeemaker, the music and the blue tarpaulin tied up above the door, he shouted to Helen and told her to order me a pizza.

"What kind does he want?" she called through the slit in the sliding window.

"Whatever. He'll eat anything."

He looked down and tried to smile, lines around his eyes. He hesitated, then said, "Why don't we get your room set up?"

We went inside, down the narrow hall of fake-wood paneling, to a flimsy door. A mattress lay on the floor, an upside-down plastic milk crate next to it, a lamp on top. He flicked the space heater on, and its front began to glow red. The air smelled of burned dust.

"Is this okay?"

"Yeah," I said.

"You can read in here. Helen will bring your pizza. Then you can sleep."

"Okay," I told him, concentrating on keeping my voice steady and unbothered.

He stared down, not looking into my eyes, just seeing, as if I were something he'd found on the roadside and he didn't know what to do. Then he forced a big smile.

"Goddamn it!" he said with the exaggerated enthusiasm he used when he flashed money or bought employees beer. "We should decorate your room, shouldn't we?"

He looked around, and in the closet, on a shelf, found a battered magazine. He opened it, and a long piece of paper, with a picture of a woman, folded out from the middle.

"Why is that page so long?" I asked, and took an easy breath, feeling that he might be normal again, that we were about to do something fun, and that if I were patient, there'd be another chance to ask about going salmon fishing.

"It's called the centerfold," he said and pulled the page free, the paper popping off the staples. There was a nail in the wall, and he pressed it through the top of the centerfold and stepped back.

A dark-haired woman wore a long blue shirt. It was open in the front, and her nipples stared out from the white skin where she wore her bathing suit. There were shelves behind her with old, serious-looking books.

"Do you like it?" he asked.

"Yeah," I said. "Is she in a library?"

He leaned close, furrowing his brow. "I guess so."

"It's strange that she's in a library, isn't it?"

"Well, I never thought about it . . ."

"What books do you think she's reading?"

One lay on the floor, next to a blue sandal that had fallen off her foot.

"I don't know. Anyway, she can keep you company tonight."

"Can I take her home and put her up in my room?"

"Ah . . ." He lifted a hand and scratched his beard. "I don't know if that's a good idea."

I understood. My mother wouldn't like it. This would definitely have to be a secret, too. So I hesitated, then asked, "Do you think we can go salmon fishing for my birthday?"

He stared down. "You don't give up, do you?"

"It's because I really wanna go. It's important."

"Okay," he said. "Okay. We'll go salmon fishing."

"You promise?"

"Yeah, I promise. Look, I have to get back to work. Helen will bring your pizza."

After he'd left, I stared at the centerfold, wishing I had a library like the naked woman's. The books appeared expensive, with covers as thick as those on encyclopedias, but when I tried to make out the names on the spines, I couldn't read a single one.

The night before our fishing trip, I could hardly sleep. Then, as soon as I did, my father was waking me. It was still dark out. My brother and I huddled into our clothes in the cold room. We followed him to the truck.

He drove slowly, yawning, drinking from a thermos, looking straight ahead, hushed music on the radio. I liked the dim glow of its dial, the yellow headlights tunneling through the valley dark, the way steam washed through his beard as he drank, the fragrance of coffee.

Normally, he drove like a maniac, yelling at slow drivers and telling us to watch for lazy pigs who sat in patrol cars doing nothing. He had gory stories about boys who stuck their heads out the window, as I did, catching the wind in my mouth and feeling it whip through my hair. My mother used similar techniques for seat belts, describing me soaring through the windshield and skittering over asphalt. "No more skin," she'd say. "You'd look like raw meat and have broken bones and a concussion, and you'd never think right again." Though my father's seat belts didn't work, his stories were better than hers, my favorite that of the man who liked to drive with his head out the window. A passing truck knocked it off, and, lacking eyes to find it by the roadside, he had to drive home without it.

Now, though, there were no stories. My father yawned, rubbing his face, or he drank from his thermos. My brother was asleep. I turned in my seat.

Behind us, in the center of the lane, rode Ten Speed, kinky hair hidden by a dark hood, her face lit red from our taillights, her wide-set eyes unmistakable. I couldn't believe it. She took the mountain turns faster than we did, her legs pumping like the bars on my mother's sewing machine. She neared and lagged and neared again, keeping up because we weren't going fast. I thought to tell my father, but he looked irritated and sleepy, and it was fun to watch her. I figured we'd lose her on the highway, and we did, though she kept up much longer than I expected.

After two hours, we followed a narrow asphalt road into the mountains, then gravel paths, and finally parked. As soon as we opened the door, the stench was unbearable.

"Goddamn it," he said. Dawn lit the treetops as we followed him through the forest to the river. Water rushed past boulders and gravel bars. Everywhere, all around us, large, brilliantly colored salmon with hooked jaws rotted. I'd studied them in books—had in fact stolen the best one and scissored out the pages that showed it belonged to the school library—and I knew that as salmon spawned, their jaws became curved, their teeth canine, their backs humped, and their coloring no longer silvery blue but a bruised red.

A few bloated, moribund salmon still worked their way upstream, moving through the current with the laborious motion of an old dog wagging its tail.

We'd waited too long. The season was over. Still, we pretended to fish, standing in the cold, testing our waders against slippery rocks and rushing water. I didn't let myself show disappointment, and he didn't either. I glanced to where he stood, his face a little haggard, dark lines beneath his eyes as he stared at the swirling current. He breathed through his parted lips, his jaw slightly pushed forward, and I imitated this look, feeling instantly tough. If I took away his beard would he be me, just with dark hair and eyes, and someday would I no longer be me, but him, with his real nose, so more him than he was himself? Though I liked the thought, it was confusing and quickly faded. I breathed the cold air blowing down over the river. There was so much I'd never know, and I stopped thinking about it. Maybe we'd race a train every now and then, but nothing else would be the same. The good times had ended forever for reasons I couldn't understand.

We caught nothing and left early, stumbling in rubber waders back to the truck. As he drove, I talked. I'd decided that as much as I liked fish, mental powers were more interesting. I explained this and told him how when I'd meditated, I'd seen my soul, and also that if I was quiet and listened, I could hear the advice of my invisible friends. He was silent, the day ending, the sky gently streaked like one of his old faded shirts.

"Your mother told you all this stuff?" he asked.

"Yeah. I can even read people's minds if I want. Did you know that's possible?"

He didn't answer, just clutched the steering wheel until his knuckles turned white. My brother looked out the side window, not speaking, and I realized that I'd been repeating things that enraged my father. The truck gained speed, swerving along the narrow road until we came to the highway. It careered through the junction, wobbling. The tires screeched and then caught, and we surged forward.

"Goddamn it anyhow," he said.

My brother and I sat, pretending nothing had happened. Was my father angry about not catching any salmon, or because I'd repeated my mother's words? Should these things be secrets, too? Sitting at his elbow, I watched the stark motions of his hands guiding the wheel, the way he hunched, narrowing his eyes as if aiming at something far away, just as she had, speaking of purpose.

Beyond the windshield were the last smoky colors of sunset, the sky ragged above the trees as if torn from a picture book. I gazed at it, not thinking, not wanting to, and after a while, as if pushing against the density of night, the truck slowed and I fell asleep.

A week later, Ian told me that his sister had gone missing. She'd ridden to the highway on her ten speed and traveled so far that she hadn't known how to get back. The police had found her watching the traffic, crying because the batteries in her black tape player had gone dead.

LEVITATION CLUB
AND THE END OF THE WORLD

The way my mother described the end, it didn't sound bad. Nature would prevail, and those who'd chosen to return to it would survive. Though I pictured war and the destruction of cities, I'm not sure she mentioned these things. The end, as I understood it, came to me through how she spoke of chemicals and machines and our denatured lives. She seemed at odds with a force I couldn't identify, resentful of what she heard on the radio. But the two things she most hated were Christians and processed foods.

"See that?" she said in the supermarket. A fat man trundled down the aisle. "He eats foods made of chemicals." She pointed at bloated bags of chips, leering cartoon faces on boxed cereal, or candy bars like turds in brown wrappers.

"Sugar corrodes your bones. Your teeth turn brown and fall out. Your muscles get weak, your brain stops working, and your skin begins to sag. The human race is becoming stupid because of all that unnatural junk."

I considered an ancient man with his walker, bald head speckled and seamed like a nut, then another, hands crabbed up beneath his chin as he stepped awkwardly with the plodding motion of an injured insect.

Back at home she made us drink the beery milk from her goats. My brother and I cramped our fingers around the glasses and chugged the frothy white sauce. We spoke of the end of goat milk season the way we did about the beginning of summer vacation.

"I can't wait for cow milk," he said.

"Me, too," I agreed, though I knew that goat milk might be my salvation.

Even if I missed holes when I buttoned my shirt and didn't notice if my shoelaces came untied, I managed to draw a small following at school. We met beyond the playground, on the blustery slope where our teachers weren't likely to catch us speaking English, and I told them about the powers of the mind, telepathy, and telekinesis.

Watching TV, I'd seen Marco Polo spy on a Buddhist monk practicing levitation, and my mother had confirmed that peaceful men in faraway places could float and even speak with their minds. So I began practicing. Lying in bed, I let myself become as light as air, attempting to rise from the thin foam mattress. When this didn't work, I tried with something small. I lay a sheet of paper on my dresser and stared at it. I put it on the floor and squinted over it with rage. I propped it against the wall and tried to help it slide down, which eventually it did, though I wasn't sure how much of this was my doing.

"You just have to focus," I told the other children, feeling inspired by my own words, as if the experiments I'd failed at until then were obviously possible.

"You let your eyes close halfway," I said. "You look at the paper, and it will start to float. You can even do it with yourself. In bed. You can levitate."

A scrappy boy named Matthieu stared, his mouth agape. He had a scar like he'd been operated on for a harelip, though he insisted a kid had thrown a stone, and he'd beaten him up.

"You did that?" he asked. "You floated?"

I shrugged. "Only by accident. I was sleeping. I fell down when I woke up."

Testing myself as a budding cult leader was risky. I was far from popular, bad at sports, and a pet for the girls who took turns tying my shoes. I often forgot to zip my fly, and after school, when I climbed into my mother's van, the first thing she'd do was realign the buttons on my shirt and tuck the untucked side in or pull the tucked-in side out.

"You have to try," I told them.

"Why?" asked Guillaume, big and awkward and freckled, with a blushing face the mean kids called *la tomate.*

"Because the world is going to change. We have to be ready."

The children nodded. There was a hardy evangelical community near the school, and they'd heard this before. A few gave their own testimonials. One thought he'd floated ever so slightly in bed because he'd heard the plastic rustling beneath his sheet. Guillaume had caused a paper propped against the wall to slide to the floor. Everyone was impressed.

Back in class, Mme Hans jabbered, making us do grammar exercises. As I conjugated the verbs in a story about sugar cabins and ice skating in Quebec, I couldn't imagine why my father had left a place where everyone ate sugar and skated around all day, even if they did fight a lot, a fairly important fact that the story didn't mention. But Mme Hans cared only about verbs. She had short gray hair and a chest like a longshoreman, and she was probably a good fighter, too. Staring at her, I thought of a barrel wearing women's clothing. I pictured it going over Niagara Falls. She repeated: *j'étais, tu étais, il était, nous étions.* Why did we have to learn how to speak when we already could? I closed my eyes and felt my body growing light. Soon, I'd no longer need grammar. I'd rise, passing through my desk unseen, and slip through the wall into the fresh air outside. Then I'd run like hell. But for now I was still dissolving, becoming mist.

"*Reveilles-toi!* Wake up!" Mme Hans said and slapped the back of my head.

This was her warning, for which I referred to her—to the other students—as "Mrs. Hand," thereby breaking the most important rule, that of not speaking English.

During reading period, I asked to go to the library. But when the librarian saw me, he made himself look busy, ducking into his office and fussing about, pausing to rub at his mustache. I'd been hounding him to find me books on ESP and psychic powers.

I pulled out a chair and sat and slumped. The elbows of my red checkered shirt had holes that my mother would patch as soon as she noticed. The tabletop felt cold through them.

In a few days, school would let out for Christmas, and I needed enough to read. My parents rarely spoke, and the mystery of his simmering rage and her muted fear dug at me. Whenever my father left, my mother went through papers or made phone calls in the hushed voice of a TV villain. I'd definitely need a lot of books to get through the break. I couldn't sit still without one. Even sleep was impossible without a story first.

I went to the shelves and stood the way I did before the open refrigerator. I'd planned on giving up reading about fish, so maybe I could take the novel about mutant telepathic children living after a great war? I'd drawn on it for my recess sermons, telling grim stories about the future.

But there was also a volume I loved on prehistoric fish, so I walked to the section of fish books. It was empty, and I realized that I'd checked them all out, and they were at home.

Just before dark, my father's truck crunched into the driveway, and my brother went out to say hi. I sat in the kitchen, reading about coelacanth, a prehistoric fish rediscovered off the coast of South Africa when it was caught by a fisherman. This made me wonder what ancient fish might accidentally be in my father's stores. Outside, the pulse of my brother's words sounded light and quick next to the slow, somewhat gravelly voice of my father.

My mother was helping my sister in her room, so I got up and looked out the door. The gray sky sagged into the valley, promising cold rain and not the snow I was hoping for.

"Sh," my brother whispered. He was peeking from behind the shed, the bangs of his brown bowl cut in his eyes. "Hurry up!"

I hustled behind the wall. My father was there, grinning through his beard, and seeing him, I knew that we'd do something bad and very fun.

"Don't tell your mother," he said. "You promise?"

I nodded as he took a long, curvy bottle of Pepsi from his jacket. He popped the cap and it hissed. My brother lifted his shoulders and dropped them and sighed nervously.

"Just a little drink," my father was saying. "It's going to burn."

My brother held the bottle in both hands and tipped it back. He shook his head and swallowed, looking as worried as I felt, though we both tried to smile. This wasn't a joke at all. My mother had always warned us never to drink pop, and I never had.

"Good, huh?" My father passed the bottle to me. I hid my fear and took a swig. The cold liquid fizzed on my tongue, burning gas rising into my sinuses. Permeating sweetness followed, chemical in its intensity, and I gave the Pepsi back. Though I stood as if nothing were unusual, I could feel my bones corroding just beneath my skin.

"You'll learn to like it," he told us and raised the bottle, draining most of it in a few gulps. It was a miracle he was still alive. He wiped his mouth with his sleeve and told us to promise again. Even as he smiled, his eyes became still and menacing. We promised. Then he sent us back inside.

My mother was standing at the stove and looked at us suspiciously. "Have you done your homework?"

"I'm almost finished," my brother told her, but I just took my backpack to the living room and dumped it, then crouched as if I'd come upon strange droppings. Sometimes only by misbehaving could I hide previous misbehavior. The composition manual with three ducks on the cover lay before me, and I kicked it about as if playing soccer. The cover fell off, and my heart seized. Wasn't it clear that I wasn't made for school?

"Deni's acting weird!" my brother complained. My mother came in, and without looking at her, I opened the mangled manual. This was just another thing that would make me stand out in class. I closed my eyes to squeeze back my frustration. I was always the weird kid. The others had colorful backpacks and new clothes while my brother and I had big flannel shirts with brown patches on the elbows and patched pants that hid our shoes. Our backpacks were made by cutting a leg off my father's jeans, chopping it in two, sewing one end shut and putting a drawstring on the other. All the kids had pointed and said, "What's that?" and the next morning my father had walked into the kitchen with one naked leg, hollering, "What the fuck happened to my jeans?" My mother had turned red with strangled laughter and told him, "Oh, I thought you didn't use that pair anymore."

Now he'd undressed by the kitchen door and prowled into the living room. He glanced about like an animal in a box, and my mother retreated to the stove. He sighed and sat in his chair and turned on the TV.

"You should pay attention to the news," he told us, interrupting our homework. "It'll teach you everything you need to know."

We joined him in learning how America could deploy nuclear missiles from thousands of underground shelters joined by tunnels beneath the desert. The commentators discussed the importance of surviving a first strike and what had changed since Brezhnev's death. My father grumbled and said, "Things were getting better until he screwed it all up."

A little later, he proclaimed the ayatollah "a mean son of a bitch" and said, "Maybe Reagan can clean up the mess Carter made. That guy didn't know what he was doing."

"If World War III starts," my brother asked, "can we capture a tank and can I live in it in the backyard?"

My father turned sharply and looked to where we lay before the TV.

"Well," he said, "okay, I guess that's fine." But he kept studying my brother.

I tried to picture the camouflage tank beneath the apple tree and wondered if I should ask for one, too, but I could tell from my father's face that he thought my brother's request was weird. I'd been compiling a list of all that I shouldn't mention to him, levitation being at the top. That was the good thing about what was in my mind: no one else could see it, so I couldn't get in trouble. Still, I often worried that my mother could tell what I was thinking just from looking at me. Or maybe it was because I knew that she believed in telepathy. My father didn't, so it was easier to make him happy.

I carried my book into the kitchen and sat across from my sister, who was coloring horse pictures. She wore bell-bottoms and a plaid shirt, her blond hair in a barrette. My mother glanced at me with those blue eyes that saw right into my head. Instantly, I wanted to confess, but my fear was stronger. She'd be angry, and my father would be angrier.

Pepsi, which she'd forbidden, seemed far worse than alcohol. How could she accept that he drank it?

"What's a nuclear missile?" I asked to distract her.

"Oh, that's hard to explain," she told me. "It's a terrible, terrible thing, and it could kill all of us. It will probably destroy the planet someday."

But she didn't explain the way she usually did. She paused, staring into the bubbling spaghetti sauce as if seeing this future.

"The world," she said more quietly, "is a terrible place. It's not so bad for boys, but girls have to be strong."

My sister looked up. She was six, and I wanted to tell my mother to be quiet.

And yet I longed to see the fierceness of the world revealed, to witness it at last.

The entire class was laughing at me. It was the day before Christmas break, but they still made fun of the lunches my mother packed. Usually, to hide my sandwiches, I ate them from inside my brown lunch bag, like a wino swigging from a wrapped bottle.

"Show it," they were saying. They had chips, PB&J, and cookies. I took out two dark, crumbly slabs of bread with six inches of lettuce and tomatoes piled between.

"Oh," I said as the tomato slices slid free and the bread broke and the lettuce spilled onto my desk. The children howled. To make my accident appear intentional, I lowered my head and snuffled about like a cow, gobbling from my desk. Kids were falling out of their seats. I sat up, making bovine eyes and working my jaw with a ruminating motion.

Mrs. Hand swatted the back of my head.

"*Cochon*," she scolded, and the students fell silent.

During recess, when I spoke about levitation, the kids looked doubtful, having seen me imitate a cow. Only Guillaume was enthusiastic. He was getting better at moving sheets of paper propped against the wall. He talked until his face turned red and spit gathered at the corners of his lips, and even I wanted to knock him down.

I explained that my mother had said I should build mental powers slowly, by meditating with a candle. She'd set one up for me, and when I'd concentrated, the flame had wavered considerably. Guillaume sputtered that he'd try it, though his parents didn't let him play with fire.

No one else cared. They were looking at my unzipped fly, my lopsided shirt, my shoelaces trailing in the dirt. They trickled away as I rambled— great wars, mutations, superpowers. I felt that if I talked enough, something amazing would happen.

"You have to focus," I said. "It takes time." I said all sorts of things.

"Maybe you aren't the right type," I told Matthieu as he turned away.

"The right type of what?"

I had no answer, and he snorted and wandered off.

Normally, I'd be excited for Christmas break, but home wasn't fun these days. For the rest of recess, I followed the path around the playground, walking backward, closing my eyes when I could, just breathing, not letting myself be angry, not thinking anything at all. Each time the wind gusted, I leaned back into it, trying to see if it would hold me up.

On Christmas Day, my father returned, smelling of pine sap. He'd shut down his lots and stripped his rain gear at the door without speaking to my mother. He turned up the heat that she kept low since, as I'd heard her complain, he didn't give her much money for gas and we'd once run out and had to warm ourselves around the stove. He sat in his chair wearing boxers, and stared at the TV as the anchorman mentioned the anniversary of the Soviet invasion of Afghanistan. Briefly, there was a clip showing men outside a church, all wearing sandwich boards printed with The End Is Near.

At least when the end came I wouldn't have to go to school, and my life would be like *The Chronicles of Narnia*. Maybe I'd do things my father had, catch huge salmon that took hours to reel in or drive a truck without brakes, crashing into things that people no longer needed.

"Did you like school?" I asked him.

"I didn't go for very long," he said, eyes on the TV. "I had to work, but my brother and me, we'd walk my sisters to school and beat up kids who bothered them on the road."

"Where are your sisters now?"

He looked at me, then stared off and sighed. He seemed uncomfortable, the way I did when my mother made me put on too many winter clothes, but he had only his underwear on. He sat tensely, as if he might jump out of his chair and run forever.

"Can I stop going to school and work with you?" I asked.

He smiled faintly, almost sadly, and said, "Someday."

I wanted him to tell me a story about what we'd do. If I could think about the future when everything would be different, then each boring day at school wouldn't be so bad. But he said nothing, and I sprawled on the rug and watched the news, which felt more serious even than school. With his eyes locked on the screen, he inhaled slowly through his mouth, the way I did when my nose was plugged, and I wondered if he breathed like this because of something to do with his nose.

"Bonnie said your nose isn't real," I told him.

"What?" He glanced down at me.

"She said doctors gave you a new one. How did it get broken?"

He hesitated, cheeks scrunched up as if he might become angry, though I kept my face curious and unafraid. It wasn't easy, but it worked.

"Someone hit me," he said.

"Why?"

He shrugged. "It's a long story. I was coming out of a . . . a bar, and they were waiting for me, and they . . . they hit me in the face with towing chains."

"What's a towing chain?"

"You use it to pull cars." He glanced back at the TV, but I had the sense that I was missing a pretty good story. After all, who just went and hit someone in the face with chains?

"What did you do?" I asked.

He stared down at me where I lay on the rug. "Well," he said and cracked a grin, "I gave them the worst beating of their lives. They cried like babies and ran away."

I was waiting for the story to go on, but he yawned and focused back on the TV. When had he stopped telling stories the way he used to? He said nothing, and I grew so bored of the man's head droning away on the TV screen that I left to read at the kitchen table.

After dinner, I asked my brother what would happen if there was a nuclear war. How did it all work? He focused his large brown eyes on mine, nodded seriously, and took a breath. Then he described a future of cannibalistic humanoids in caves who'd hunt down good humans. The monster humans would eat people because there'd be no animals left. The good humans, though, might not eat at all. Given that I could eat endlessly, it occurred to me that I might become a monster human.

Later, in bed, I couldn't bear not understanding all that was happening—the way my parents ignored each other and rarely laughed. I stared at the dark ceiling until the house became quiet and stayed that way for so long I thought I might fall asleep. Then, downstairs, footsteps slowly crossed the wooden floor and just stopped, as if someone was standing and thinking, not sure where to go or what to do next, as if too afraid to move. Even now, without my knowing, so much could be happening. I might wake up and find the world changed—sirens and detonations forcing us underground, faceless creatures capturing me, tying me to a table and brandishing knives.

In a dream, I crossed a yellow field, running toward my mother, who appeared gray, caught in motion, a colorless snapshot—her hand extended, floating before me as I reached. In the center of the sky appeared a black shape like a fighter jet. It began to spin as, from every horizon, darkness rose, and there was no more light.

In the morning, my father was gone, and after breakfast my mother said that we were going into town. A bag held her presents, and if ever there were proof of the nonexistence of Santa, it was this: my mother with her receipts, leading us into the mall to return everything my father had bought her.

Outside the clothing store, she put my brother in charge while she went inside. My sister sang quietly to herself as we watched the crowds surge past Boxing Day signs.

A slouching woman stopped and stared. After glancing around, she came closer. She had blond, frizzy hair and a long jacket that reminded me of burlap. She asked if we were alone.

"Our mother is just over there," my brother told her, repeating the words that my mother had drilled into us.

The woman's big eyes rolled from one side of the mall to the other. Instantly, I knew she'd do something repulsively sexual. Both during school assemblies and by my mother, I'd been warned about perverts.

She slipped three pamphlets from her purse and gave one to each of us.

My brother blanched. "We can't," he told her.

"It's all right. Your mother won't mind," she said and hurried off, not having exposed her naked body from beneath the jacket after all.

He stood, hunched, as if he'd returned home with a bad grade. The pamphlet showed two abandoned-looking children in saggy diapers waiting in a doorway as Jesus approached along the sidewalk. He'd probably change their diapers. No, whatever he'd do had to be bad if my mother hated Christians so much. Maybe he'd feed them processed foods. She'd never explained why, if proselytizers came to our house, she slammed the door in their faces.

She snatched the pamphlets from us.

"Who gave these to you?" She made a constricted huff like a growl and went to a trash can and tossed them. As she led us out, she searched faces, asking if we recognized the woman. My brother said he didn't, and I could no longer recall what she'd looked like.

"Why were you so angry?" I asked her that night as she was tucking me in. I wanted to hate the woman who'd given us the pamphlets, but I didn't understand why I should.

"I don't want you to grow up with that garbage in your head. When I was a kid, I had to go to church. I imagined God was some big, mean guy staring down, and I was afraid to do anything, afraid to be myself or have fun."

She told me about her father, how strict he was, as if this were also God's fault. She said she'd wanted her freedom. The way she told me this—the look in her eyes—made me feel that she was still struggling to be free. She seemed as if she were going to tell me something else, and an expression like pain came onto her face, but she said nothing.

"Who is God?" I finally asked, just to make her speak. She sighed and explained how some people believed in an all-powerful, judgmental geezer who saw everything we did. Her description was so convincing that I forgot what we'd been talking about before and became a little jealous of this old man's mental powers. Above all, I was angry at the thought of being spied on, and I told her that I never wanted to take a bath again.

My sister was lying on her belly with a book, the blinds drawn, her room so dark I didn't know how she could read.

"Want to hear a story?" I asked and flopped down next to her.

"Okay," she said and turned onto her side. I wasn't sure why I was bothering her. Vacation had ended and winter dragged on, my parents fighting, all of us busy with our own things, books or music or video games.

I began to describe a future in which everyone could levitate, but she said, "Tell me about how Bonnie and André met."

"Well, she's from Pittsburgh," I said and thought of all she'd shared over the years. "Grandma's mom is German, and Grandpa's from some-where else. He made steel. Bonnie didn't like them because they be-lieved in God, so she ran away to live in nature. Since André grew up really poor, he could do everything—farm and catch fish and even . . . deliver babies." This expression always sounded funny to me, as if he were a mailman, but now the story I'd been struggling to find became clear. It was about my birth, and I repeated the version he'd often told me. "I was born on the living room couch. André delivered me. The cord, was around my neck."

"What cord?"

"Babies are born with a rope. Sometimes it feeds them, but some-times it strangles them. He took it off and blew into my mouth, and then I began to breathe."

"Oh," she said quietly, as if expecting something else, but I couldn't think of what came next. My story seemed to have started well, but what happened after my birth? Feeling vaguely irritated, I got up and walked away. The next day, after school, she asked me to tell another story, but I said I was busy and left her in the musty silence of the house.

As I crossed the frozen fields, I wished for spring and that first breathless warmth that was no warmth at all but seemed it after so long in the cold. Dandelions would bloom, like when I was very small and everything was perfect.

I sat in my favorite place, a grove of oaks that were larger than the other trees. The ground beneath was without weeds, soft and dark and always in shadows in the summer, though now I stared up through the naked branches at the colorless sky. Everyone I knew had died. The house had burned down. The school had been incinerated. I was the hunter, the loup-garou transformed by the forest and the animal power of solitude. In nature, I would survive. The world would end, and when it began again, I'd still be here.

But when would that happen? My brother liked *Dungeons & Dragons*, and his *Monster Manual* described lycanthropy, which turned men into werewolves. Though I'd thought of my father when I read it, I knew that it was too simple—that nothing, not even the end of the world, would happen the way I wanted it to.

Eventually it grew dark, and my mother's voice called across the valley from the back porch, my name echoing off the mountains. I started home.

The snowmelt came suddenly, flooding drainage ditches, covering the fields, water gathering toward our backyard until it shone in a crescent around the slight rise where our house had been built. The sun blazed day after day, and I forgot my frustration and boredom and loved the sense of expectation and change, of possibly having to survive a natural disaster.

I'd read a book about young people who bonded after society's collapse. The abandoned cities sent shivers up my spine, the vines that grew through cracked concrete and broken windows, the mountains where the youths sheltered beneath overhangs, staring out over the desolate landscape for a flicker of light.

Reading made me feel as if I'd swigged my father's vodka. Did my brother or sister experience this? My brother loved video games, and my sister sang constantly so that her location in the house could be determined according to her volume. My mother always told us to read, but did she know that books made me want to run outside and breathe the air rolling off the mountains, smell the wet fields and drying mud, hear the crunch of onion grass under my feet? Stories seemed like paths. If you went outside and looked, there was the world, just the world, but if you went and looked after reading a story, there was a world where anything could happen, as if beyond the mountains were a hundred countries to which I might go, a hickory cane over my shoulder and my few possessions tied in a red bandanna.

But there would be no escaping this time. The flood hemmed us in, our house like a frog on a lily pad. Neighbors put out sandbags, and in a few places the water on the road was so high that my father had to drive through it very slowly, afraid of shorting out his engine.

My mother had gotten two horses a few years earlier and checked on them and on her bedeviling goats. She cooked restlessly, baking crumbly bread in coffee cans so that each loaf came out with the can's seams printed on it. She made flat, hard cookies that looked like very wet mud thrown at a wall.

As I studied the flood, imagining all the ways to cross it, she joined me on the back porch.

"We're going to leave soon," she told me, and my heart beat with an excitement so involuntary, so sudden, that it ached.

"Where?"

"We're moving. Just you and me and your brother and sister."

"What about André?" I asked, realizing something terrible was happening to my family, though I had no word for it.

"He's staying here."

"When will we come back?"

The wind gusted in her hair as she stared beyond the smooth surface of the water to the mountain, her expression like my brother's as we rushed the train track.

"We're not coming back," she said, her voice almost breaking.

"Ever?" I didn't understand. Though I loved the idea of setting out, I couldn't imagine never seeing the valley again. It was the one place we were sure to return to after our many temporary homes, and I'd never known spring or summer anywhere else. What would we do if we were separated from my father, gone away somewhere strange and new?

My mother stared off, lips slightly parted so that I thought she might say something else, her eyes narrowed as if to glare past the limits of the sky.

The next morning, I checked on the flood. I walked out to where the water began. Beneath the surface, the grass appeared distorted, like the bottom of a swimming pool, undulating. Far off, the red-ribboned tops of a few Christmas trees showed, and then there was simply the smooth surface of the deluge, stretching on toward the mountain.

I wanted to worry that we were leaving, but it seemed impossible — not just because of the flood, but because my parents often said crazy things that never happened. Besides, just before going to work, my father had made a comment that now obsessed me.

"I bet carp are swimming up from the rivers, right through the fields," he'd said. "If we take the boat and shine the flashlight in the water, we'll see them."

I couldn't think of anything but carp—gliding out of the river, nestling in the branches of submerged trees, riding currents through the beams of flashlights.

The rowboat lay upside down in the shed, and I discussed with my invisible friends whether we should take it and do some exploring. Eleven of them were in agreement, making me suspect that I had eleven invisible friends but maybe only one spirit guide. The guide was concerned. In fact, he sounded a lot like my brother later did.

"We're not allowed," he said.

"Come on. Just for a little while. There are carp out there."

"No. We can't. We'll get washed away by the river and die."

In the past, my father had been more open to ideas like this, but I suspected that convincing him to do something wild might not be as easy as before.

"Can we go out in the boat?" I asked him that evening,

"I'm busy."

"But we can see carp."

"That's true," he said, nodding to himself. "There might be carp out there."

I hesitated, knowing what I had to say next.

"Do you think it would be *really* dangerous?"

He looked at me and grinned as if he'd just woken up and was himself again, not that person who cared only about his business.

"Okay," he said, "we can go later on tonight."

After dark, the moon shone against the water, turning the flood into a silvery plain. In the rowboat, we crossed the hidden fields of Christmas trees as my brother and I took turns aiming the flashlight through the luminous surface. My father kept letting go of the oars and taking it from us, saying we were using it wrong, but he couldn't find any carp either.

As he peered down, we sat on the opposite side, trying to counterbalance. His edge of the boat sank dangerously close to the water, but he didn't seem to care. Did he know we were leaving him? He didn't show it. Sitting there, saying nothing, I felt what a relief it would be if the end came now, the three of us in the boat, with no choice but to find a new home.

He shone the light on the eerie shapes of drowned Christmas trees and worried that if the water didn't go down soon, they would die. We'd had floods before, and afterward, I'd followed him along the rows as he'd pulled up yellow yearling pines, their dead roots slipping from the earth.

"I'm going to lose a lot of money," he said, peering over the edge, the oars dragging in the rowlocks.

Then he shut off the light and we just sat, gazing along the gleaming surface to the mountains, the water still, the moon full and blazing all around us.

A week later, when the waters went down, my father hired a helper from a nearby farm, a young man with a fuzzy, lopsided mustache and bulging biceps who, as a boy, my mother once confided in me, had jumped from the roadside bushes to make cars swerve until he caused a grisly head-on collision. I'd spent a recess describing crushed vehicles, bodies plunging like divers through windshields and flailing over the road, beheaded and skinless, and just the sight of him now made me shiver so badly that my joints rattled.

But rather than cause more deaths, he helped my father replace the tractor bridge. They finished at sundown and returned to the back porch and each drank a beer. My father was telling him how quickly floods could begin, that he'd seen rivers triple their size in seconds and had almost been killed like this in a Yukon mining camp.

"I'd just finished my last shift and had a few days off, and there was no way I was going to stay in camp. I wanted to get out and drive into town and have some fun. But a gorge with a river in it separated the camp from the main road where our cars were parked. A wooden footbridge went across, but the snow was melting in the mountains and it was raining so hard the gorge had almost filled. There was a narrow point farther up, not too far upstream, and the water was coming through in surges. I was standing in front of the bridge. I really wanted to leave, but each surge that came through was higher. The water carried uprooted trees that almost hit the bottom of the bridge. I remember watching. I had a bad feeling. I counted the seconds between the surges. One passed, and the water shook the bridge, and then I sprinted. But halfway across I realized I'd waited too long. I heard the roar of the next surge, and I jumped just as the bridge snapped in half. My chest hit the earth, and I dug my fingers in and pulled myself up and ran, because the water was starting to come over the edge."

He coughed into his fist and cleared his throat. His helper bobbed his head self-consciously, then took a drink of his beer and licked his lopsided mustache.

"It was a dangerous thing to do," my father said, a hint of anger coming into his voice, his gaze unfocused as if he were alone—"but I didn't regret it. I hated that camp. The men there just talked about women and what they'd do when they got out. It was no different than prison."

Though his telling was gripping—the rising river, the shaking bridge, his bold dash across its planks as the water descended—it wasn't this that haunted me. It was the way he'd spoken about the camp, reminding me of all that I didn't know about him. I reran that line over and over in my head, how he said it, the intensity and anger in his words: "It was no different than prison."

Beyond my window, a pale splotch in the low clouds showed where the moon hid.

Shouting had woken me.

"You can't go! I won't let you!"

My heart knocked at my ribs as he swore, his words banging about the house, thudding against the walls like one of the outside dogs gotten in and running from room to room as quickly as possible, just to see this strange inside world.

"You can't stop me!" she shouted. Her footsteps crossed the living room.

"You're fucking crazy!" he yelled and slammed a door so that the house shook.

I stared at the ceiling, trying to make sense of all this, to will my brain to do more than listen to the battering of my heart. There was a secret at the center of our lives. It was like something from a dream, a shape that I glimpsed but couldn't remember, then saw again another night; I woke knowing I'd seen it, but not what it was or meant. In the dark, I couldn't sleep, certain that someday this thing would reappear, as a man or a place, or just a feeling, the awareness of danger I had before I turned my eyes and saw. It would reappear and I'd have known it would but without any power to stop it.

I might have slept, drifting in and out, sensing a subtle change like a snowfall in the night, the gradual silencing of the outside, though now the season's shift was within our walls. Who had made this world up? Who had created all this for me? It was as if my life were important and I had to be ready to face something, but that moment never quite arrived.

In the morning, I slowly went down the stairs, more tired than ever, yet vividly aware of the changes in the house. My mother was packing, hurrying about. My father's truck was gone.

"I don't have time for questions," she said. She told us only that we were moving across the Fraser River to a town called Mount Lehman. She shoved everything in boxes, occasionally pausing at the window.

My brother sidled close, puffy dark circles under his glassy eyes. He hadn't slept either, and the strangeness of his gaze shone in a way that made me want to run to the mirror. He said he had something to ask, and I knew from his expression that he'd readied one of the strange questions he used to torment other kids. They often involved World War III, and his favorite was, "If America dumped boxed cereal on the USSR, why would it be chemical warfare?" He then had to explain in minute detail our mother's words about chemical foods.

Now he said, "If a nuclear bomb strikes a mile away, do you run toward it or away?"

I let myself see this. My gut ached. A wall of blinding light approached, melting cars and incinerating Christmas trees and cooking human flesh from the bone. Though I knew he'd trick me, I blurted, "Away! I'd run away!"

"Wrong," he said, loudly but without inflection.

My chest felt tight. I went to the kitchen door and outside, over the wet grass, past the apple tree.

I wanted someone to tell me what to think or hope, but there was just the waterlogged fields and the windy silence of the valley and, like a music far away, from a distant car window, the threat of nuclear extinction.

The packing and dumping of boxes revealed how little we owned— blankets and clothes, worn-out books, and some binders of school papers—but the moving still took all day. We carried boxes out to the van for her or helped unload. Now, as we returned for our final trip, she drove up to the house slowly, craning to see whether my father's truck was in the driveway. It wasn't, and she sighed, then sped onto the gravel. She told us to wait in the van.

She loaded the spinning wheel she'd bought in hopes of making everything, even our winter clothes, from scratch. Then she filled several jugs with water. We asked why and she said that the water in the valley was from a spring and we would miss it. We pulled out of the driveway, each of us holding a shimmering jug in our lap. My sister had her hair pinned back, her forehead high and pale, her chin lowered to her collar as she looked out the window. My brother stared straight ahead. What were they thinking? I could hardly make sense of everything in my own mind. What would my father say when he knew I'd left without him? Would he understand that it wasn't my fault?

We passed Ten Speed where she'd stopped on the roadside, one foot on the ground as she watched, her head thrust forward, eyes full of fear for us, dark and wide and flashing with refracted light as our van drove by.

I took a breath and stared out. I made myself stop thinking and just looked at everything. I was seeing all this for later, for the rest of my life. I knew this with an unmoving wisdom that made me feel that someday I would indeed be someone else.

And then I was no longer in my seat, in the van, but on the mountain where my father had once taken me. I could see the entire valley, its fields and streams, the curve of the road whose presence alone, each day after school, gave me a sense of certainty. It descended past wet rocks and old, gaunt trees, then leveled and turned and gave onto the straightaway. Past a few farms and the fields of Christmas trees or sod, it rose back along the mountains and returned to where it entered, beyond rock faces lit with quick, brittle streams.

Just outside was a service station where carpooling parents waited. If we turned right, we headed to my school in Abbotsford or to Vancouver. Left led toward Nicomen Island, that piece of muddy earth where my father got his mail and where I was born.

Mountains stood against the distance, larger and whiter than those of the valley, the flat, humid, windy ranges washed down from them over millennia and called prairies by those who'd chosen to stay. This was the shape of the world. As a child, I could have drawn it with a crayon: that damp sheet of alluvial land hemmed in by the horizon.

And now we were gone.

PRAYERS, MANTRAS,
AND HOW TO SWEAR

On the paper there was a tree, the trunk split in two, and each of those branches split in two, and so on. At the top were the words *arbre genéologique*, and at the trunk and each fork stood empty boxes. I'd been trying to act normal, but I couldn't stop yawning, and now there was this. Other kids were filling in the boxes. I couldn't concentrate. It had taken me a while even to write my own name on the trunk. In the two boxes on the branches above, I printed *Bonnie* and *André*. But the highest boxes were the problem. Mrs. Hand told me to write the names of my grandparents—"your father's father and mother." When I said, "*Je ne les connais pas*," she said, "*Ta grand-maman et ton grand-papa?*" as if I hadn't understood. But I couldn't even remember the names of my mother's parents. My head hurt. I'd met them once, years before, but no memories remained. Mrs. Hand told me to take the sheet home and fill it in, but I forgot and accidentally sat on it for hours while reading a novel. The next day I got an F+.

Normally, when I had really bad grades, my mother marched into school and grilled my teacher. Sometimes this embarrassed me, and sometimes it was fun to watch. But when I showed her this grade, she just sighed. Even I was too exhausted to ask the usual questions about why I was the only kid who didn't know anything about his father's family.

The boredom of school stretched out beneath an overcast sky. How was it possible to survive twelve years? Without my father, life became as silent and tense as a classroom during a math quiz—no driving fast, no stories about bruisers and close calls. Just thinking about him

made my heart speed up—its throbbing in my chest, its slippery bumping against my ribs like a panicked frog in my fingers.

I was sure I'd never see him again, but then, four days after my
mother took us to the new house, I woke to find him eating breakfast,
my mother silently preparing our lunches on the counter. He just said,
"Hi" and smiled. His empty suitcases were in her room, so he must have
come in the night. I sat across from him, and he told me about a lobster
at his fish store that was the size of my arm, and how he'd saved it so we
could eat it together. I asked if maybe it was prehistoric, and he nodded
and said, "Maybe."

Over the next few days, I expected fights, shouting, or slammed
doors, but he moved in naturally, as if it had been planned, and I soon
gave up trying to make sense of it. Our family always seemed on the
verge of disaster, and then the danger passed, and very little changed.

That Friday, he picked me up from school shortly after my mother
dropped me off.

"I'm taking you fishing," he said, his face lined and grim, as if our
outing were a form of punishment. "We'll come back in the afternoon,
and I'll leave you in the playground before she gets here. Just pretend
you went to school. You won't tell her about this, right?"

I nodded, this lie by far the most extreme ever. I loathed the idea
of standing in the playground as the other kids stared and wondered
where I'd been all day. It seemed like a lot to make me do in exchange
for a little fishing, but I felt guilty for having left him. I also wondered
if I might get special treatment, and after a few minutes on the highway, I asked for a lesson in swearing—something I had requested fairly
often—and amazingly, he agreed.

"*Fuck,*" he said, "well, *fuck* means a lot of things. *Fuck off* means go
away right now. *Fuck you* means I really hate you. *Fuck* just means you're
angry. You know what *shit* is, and *damn,* well, *damn*'s not that bad."

"What about *cocksucker*?" I asked.

"You should probably stay away from that one," he told me, then
was silent, as if thinking up more vile types of profanity. I was eager to

learn them. Swearwords gave me the feeling that good stories did, a sense of disembodiment, of being carried away, beyond rules, beyond everything. But instead he said, "Your mother wants to leave, you know."

I looked at him. His eyes were glued to the traffic ahead.

"She wanted to abandon you guys. I barely convinced her not to."

He glanced over, checking my expression, then looked back at the road.

"If she has to go," he said, "she can take your brother and sister, but you can stay with me. We'll get a motor home and travel the country and do nothing but fish."

Maybe this was why he'd moved in with us, because she'd decided she'd had enough and was planning on running away. I tried to console myself with the idea of fishing trips and that he might like me best. He rarely spent time with my sister, and my brother didn't care for fishing. I wanted to smile, but the muscles of my face tensed up as if they were doing the thinking.

"What about school?"

"You can take a year off. It won't change anything. You never liked school, and I didn't either. Look at me. I didn't need it."

He pushed his jaw forward confidently, then shot another glance my way.

"You don't let yourself get picked on at school, do you?"

"No," I lied.

"Because," he said, "if you stay with me, I'll make sure you're one tough goddamn kid."

"Really?"

"I'll teach you how to fight. I was a good fighter. I could've been a boxer. I just had no direction. But I'd give you direction. I'd teach you how to kick some ass."

An image of me came to mind, my fists swirling like bugs around a lightbulb as all the school bullies fell. My father once tried to teach me and my brother to box, making us put on gloves in the living room, but my mother had been furious and he'd relented, a strange, almost embarrassed look on his face. It was the only time I'd seen him surrender to her anger. Could it really be possible that she was leaving? Though he was fun to be with, I couldn't imagine a day without her. My clothes would stink and my grades would all be Fs and I'd starve to death. But then again, life with him might be very, very fun.

"Even if I learn to fight," I asked, "can we still travel and fish?"

"Yeah. And when we're not fishing, I'll teach you to be tough. You should get started now and make sure no one fucks with you. If someone does, you let them have it, okay?"

"Okay," I said, but I was picturing our motor home climbing a mountain road, then pulling onto the gravel above a shimmering river.

He exited the highway and we soon arrived where we often fished, off the broken rocks near the Lions Gate Bridge, where everyone tried to snag salmon while keeping a lookout for the warden. He gave me my rod, but once fishing, I kept catching the lure in seaweed because I was watching the others or trying to see salmon in the water.

A damp, irregular wind blew in along the rocks. I drew my chin down and breathed into my collar. The gray sky appeared low, the towers of the bridge trailing mist.

A man hooted and everyone turned. I reeled in my line and climbed onto the rocks. He'd hooked a salmon, and as he brought it close, the fish fighting wildly in the shallows, he asked my father to use a metal gaff lying near a tackle box.

My father took it and crouched at the edge of the water. He swung it as the fish thrashed. He swung three or four times to get the hook to stay. A chunk had fallen out of the salmon's head. The man swore and for the first time I sensed real danger in those words, not for my father but for the other man.

"You didn't have to ruin the fucking fish," he yelled. He was big, with veins on his face and a fat nose, the sleeves of his black sweater rolled up. I was pretty sure he qualified as a bruiser.

"I didn't ruin your fucking fish," my father said, and though he was smaller, he swore much better, not chewing his words like the bruiser. Each time he roared *fuck* his size doubled so that he soon towered over the other man, his back curved and puffed up, his arms bowed out, fists like bricks. "You fucker, you shouldn't have asked if you didn't want me to hook it." He spun and threw the salmon and gaff into the water.

The bruiser seemed ready to drop his rod and fight, but he hesitated. The men along the shore watched, fishing rods lifted like antennae. I had no idea swearing could do this, and I was sure there was no way the bruiser would attack, though I was a little excited to see him try. He glanced from my father's face to me, where I crouched on a rock. He looked down and turned away, swearing under his breath.

As we drove home, the cloudy sky was so dark that headlights shone like flares against the wet streets. My father clutched the wheel, glaring past the cars in front. He hadn't fully returned to his normal size, and I knew he'd do something wild and impatient. I held on to the seat as he tore past a yellow light and swerved through an intersection, tires screeching.

A siren wailed. Police lights flashed behind us. He looked into the rearview mirror.

"Motherfucker," he said, his shoulders drawing in. Had the police caught him at last? He pulled over, and I turned to look through the back window at the officer getting out of the car.

With him, police were never like they were with my mother. They asked about work and where he lived and what he'd done that day, then they stayed a long time in their cars with his driver's license. Once, when we'd all gone to dinner, he'd been pulled over and we'd waited for so long that he told us the cop was deciding whether to arrest our mother. He said that one time they tried to take her away and that he held her legs while they pulled her arms, and that he finally hung on and got her back for us. She remained silent, looking out the passenger window, and he forced a smile in her direction. But she hadn't been driving, and I'd known the police were interested in him.

"Why do they ask you so many questions?" I said.

He rubbed his face and sighed as if letting out all the air he'd ever breathed.

"Because they like me," he mumbled. "They like how I drive."

My brother and I never had much in common. He started school the year before French classes were offered, so we lived a strange playground phenomenon, each of us in his own language group, as if we'd grown up on opposite sides of an ethnically divided city. His friends were well behaved, and one of them, Elizabeth, invited him to parties where kids rode around her lawns and gardens in an electric train. Now that I no longer talked about levitation, my friends seemed increasingly like ruffians. We discussed deep-sea fishing and creatures such as sharks and electric eels. Those who'd grown up in Quebec taught us French profanity. The words and the way they were rhythmically strung together—*crisse de câlice de tabarnak!*—reminded me of how my father swore in English. But when I practiced them, I didn't get the same heady feeling as with *fuck* or *goddamn.* Still, each time we learned a new insult, we ran toward the students from the English classes, shouting it at their helpless faces.

Now, in our new house, my brother and I shared a room for the first time since we were toddlers. After my mother tucked us in, we switched on our flashlights and played *Dungeons & Dragons,* working through modules, *The Keep on the Borderlands* or *The Lost City.* Magic and endless journeys and the satisfaction of easy violence were so attainable that each morning I woke and looked around, surprised that I had to go to school, that my life could actually be this boring.

And while we wandered catacombs, listening for predators, my mother delved into past lives. She attended a psychic church where there was no religion, she assured us; they just used a real church for meetings. Prayer, she said, was a way of talking to invisible beings who existed in nature and who cared about us. She taught us to repeat *om,* which was relaxing and sounded like *mom.* She'd learned to do it at the church, and otherwise the members sat around and shared experiences. She told us how one man had teleported himself while riding on a bus. He'd wanted to be somewhere so badly that suddenly he was there. The next day he boarded the same bus and the driver said, "Hey, I saw you get on last time, but I didn't see you get off."

I watched her closely, trying to see signs of whether she might leave us, but she kept baking bread and flat cookies, and driving us to school with lunches so hard to chew they made my jaw ache. Maybe she was planning on teleporting away, or just vanishing, moving on to her next life. More and more it became clear to me that anything was possible.

One Saturday, while she was at the psychic church and my brother

and sister were with friends, I again went with my father to work. The
night before, he'd been arguing with her, and I'd pretended to go to the
bathroom. It didn't sound like she was leaving, but rather as if he was
trying to convince her to leave me behind. But all I overheard clearly
was him saying, "Deni's like me. He doesn't need school." This was how
he started in as soon as we left.

"You and me, we like being in nature and fighting," he said and
cited his own frequent battles as a child, sounding angry, as if the fights
hadn't been fully resolved and somewhere there was a brutish nine-year-
old with whom he still had to get even.

"If I stay with you and we travel together," I asked, "can we go to
other countries, too?"

He glanced over. "What do you mean?"

"Can we travel around Africa?"

"Africa?" he repeated. I'd read a story about the descendants of
dinosaurs surviving in the interior of Africa, deep in isolated lakes, and
I told him about it.

He stared at the road. "That's probably not a good idea. There are
lots of snakes in Africa. Don't you think it's nice to go camping and not
worry about getting bit?"

As he spoke, he paused between each few words, as if to catch his
breath. I pictured snakes coming through the windows of our motor
home while we slept, but I was more afraid of him losing his temper.

"I guess," I said and shrugged, wondering if he was scared of snakes.

He changed the subject to how hard it was to keep his seafood
business going, and I made a mental note to check the display in his
store and see if any prehistoric fish had accidentally been caught. My
mother, he told me, didn't care if the economy was bad or that the cocksuckers at the bank were making work hard. I pictured bankers throwing rocks, his employees ducking while trying to sell fish. But things
couldn't be going so badly. He'd bought a briefcase and explained how
important it was for a successful businessman, showing me its cylinder
lock and the tag that said Patent Leather. Besides, if he no longer had his
stores, that would be better since we were going traveling.

At his fish market, I didn't see any lack of money or any cocksuckers.

Everyone was nice, and customers were shoving ten- and twenty-dollar bills over the counter.

He checked that his employees were doing their jobs, and he took a wad of cash from the till and put it in his jacket. Then he sat me on a stool with a book, under the watch of the two men who worked there, and he disappeared for an hour with a young, very pretty Chinese woman who also worked for him and whose name I could never remember.

I questioned his employees about whether they might have accidentally cut up any strange, very ancient-looking fish, but they said they hadn't, so I looked for myself. Inside two bubbling tanks, crabs and lobsters clambered over each other, their pincers held shut with rubber bands. In the display were prawns, speckled trout, thick halibut steaks, silky salmon fillets, bags of fist-size clams, and red snappers with surprised-looking eyes. The creatures on the ice always made me realize how big the world was. Staring at them, I pictured the deep, ancient, glistening dark of the ocean. I began telling the employees how someday I planned to travel around Africa and find the lost descendants of dinosaurs.

"What are you guys up to?" my father asked when he returned alone, the shoulders of his jacket flecked with rain.

"We're talking about dinosaurs," I said, then told the employees, "André and I are going to travel and do nothing but fish after my mother leaves and he goes bankrupt."

Both men blanched and glanced away, but my father's face became so red it looked painful. In his truck, he grabbed my arm.

"You can't say those things!" He tried to catch his breath. "You're lucky. My father would have thrown you through this window."

I sat perfectly still, showing no emotion, because if I got upset when he was angry, he got even angrier. He let go of my arm and gripped the steering wheel as if to tear it off. Briefly, I pictured him lying in broken glass and wondered about his father.

"It's okay," he told me. "You didn't mean to. You just need to stop talking so much."

As he began to drive us home, I considered his words. I talked constantly and had never thought this might bother him, that there were things about me he didn't like. Until now I'd been feeling pretty special since he was spending more time with me the way he used to.

After a while, he said, "I hate those fuckers. I hate the bank." He told me that he'd planned his revenge. He would rent a safe-deposit box and put a package of fish inside. "I'm not sure, but I don't think they can legally take it out no matter how bad it smells."

Later, waiting at a red light, he pointed to a bank and an armored car in front of it.

"You see," he said, "they bring the money on Friday. That's when people get paid. They bring their paychecks, and the bank has to have lots of money for everyone."

I nodded, not sure why this mattered.

As we were nearing home, I began talking again. I'd managed to stay quiet for most of the drive until my tongue began tapping back and forth against my teeth and prodding the roof of my mouth, which tickled. It needed to speak, and I'd been thinking about how my father didn't like my mother's spiritual ideas. I wondered how he felt about an all-powerful god staring down on him, knowing everything, even his adventures and other family.

"Do you believe in God?" I asked.

He shrugged. "Life's a big joke. God's playing a joke on us."

To me, this made it sound as if God was a bit like him. I asked if he prayed, and he said, "I hate church. I grew up with those fucking priests. I'd never go back."

"But Bonnie said you see things sometimes."

"She said what?"

I repeated a story she'd told me. "One time," she'd said, "he woke up and saw a bright white light above him, and he couldn't move. He was paralyzed all night."

"She told you that?" he shouted as we pulled into the driveway. I'd done it again. I'd talked too much.

I cranked the door handle and dropped to the ground and clomped inside.

My mother had just returned with my brother and sister, and they were watching a TV show about amazing people. My father loved *Ripley's Believe It or Not!* and *That's Incredible!* and he often called us in to explain what was being shown, the chain saw juggler or the parachuting escape artist. This time the host discussed the yogis of India, men who not only could stop their heartbeats but controlled every function of their bodies.

"This is the sort of stuff we talk about at the church," my mother told us.

I sensed my father's interest, a lull in the anger he'd brought into the room. He sat shifted forward, as if he might learn something about this mysticism business.

The host explained that to clean their intestines, yogis swallowed long strips of linen that they worked through their digestive tracts. The TV image switched to a small, mostly naked brown man who was feeding linen into his mouth, his Adam's apple moving laboriously. He looked as if he were trying to eat a very large spaghetti noodle, and he rolled his belly with each gulp. The host said it took hours for the linen to reach the yogi's intestines. Then the yogi would draw the linen back through his body. The last shot was of him pulling it from his mouth. He smiled as he held it out, black from its journey into his bowels.

My father sat stock still, mouth open.

"That's shit. That guy's pulling shit out of his mouth. That's disgusting!" He picked up the small black book he kept his business numbers in and hurled it at the TV.

"Go to bed! All of you, go to bed!" he shouted. "That's fucking disgusting!"

Lying beneath the covers, I wondered what about the yogi had made him so angry. The little man's actions hadn't seemed magical at all, but rather like a difficult and time-consuming form of flossing, which I despised.

Summer came and went, my mother and father rarely together, my brother and I reading and playing so much *Dungeons & Dragons* that we hardly noticed anything else. Then school started again, and we mourned the loss of our free time.

Now everything was definitely changing. My mother and I sat in Baskin-Robbins, and as I ate my ice cream, she explained that she wouldn't be with my father much longer. She said that she loved me and never wanted to leave me.

"But how do I know what I should do?" I asked and licked a run of melting chocolate off the waffle cone. I had forgotten how good sugary foods could be.

She considered this and, as if choosing her words with care, spoke slowly. "The world is both physical and invisible," she told me and described how thoughts and moods hung about us like clouds. We shared subtly in the lives of others by crossing paths with them, by breathing the same air. Truths could also come to us like this.

I licked some more of my Rocky Road and gnawed on the cone. Was she telling me that by sitting next to my father and taking deep breaths, I'd know what was best?

"You just need to meditate on the right choice," she said and smiled, as if, were I to do so, the white light of my soul might flare up like a neon sign in a bar window, spelling out not Budweiser or Molson but Go with Your Mom!

Her hair was graying quickly, and it reminded me of when she'd once picked me up from school after getting a perm. I'd neared our van, then seen the woman with the curly hair and turned away. She'd laughed and called to me, but I'd been afraid. If she left without me now and I didn't see her for years, maybe the same thing would happen.

"But André and I are going to travel and go fishing," I told her, suddenly upset, letting the chocolate drip over my fingers.

"What?" she asked, the gentleness emptying from her eyes.

"He's going to get us a motor home, and we're going to live in it."

"That's bullshit," she told me. "He's going bankrupt. He can't even afford to make payments on his car. He's lying to you. He lies to everyone."

Day after day, I tried to think of what else he might lie about. There had been the afternoon that the two men stopped us on the valley road and he lied about not being himself. The police hadn't come again, so maybe he'd tricked them. I denied the bad things I did, so why wouldn't he? And he misbehaved even more. The list was long.

He drove like a daredevil.

He'd been in lots of fights.

When we lived by the ferry, he'd knocked a man unconscious and broken a woman's jaw.

When he was angry, he yelled at my mother.

She'd tried to run away, and he'd just followed her.

Often, he made cruel jokes.

How could I know whether I should stay? If I did, I might starve, since he ate candy bars and Pepsi the way a gerbil lived off brown pellets and water. And yet he was wild and didn't care what others thought. I couldn't take my eyes off him. An exciting new disaster might happen at any moment.

I especially loved the stories he used to tell, the way he spoke rhythmically, words transformed, punches and fallen bodies in their syllables. "I kept hitting and hitting this bruiser," he said, "ducking his punches and jumping up and hammering him, but he had a head like stone and my hands were starting to hurt, so I tripped him. He might've been tough, but he went right down."

And I loved the tricks he played. He called everything an old Indian trick, so that I pictured an old brown Indian telling him, "Don't forget to blow on a fire to get it to start," or "If you're losing a fight, kick him in the balls, then in the face. Who gives a shit if he's down. Kick his teeth out. It's a fight."

"This," he said, "is my favorite old Indian trick." He was storing the chain-link fencing he used each winter at his tree lots, and after he stood the rolls on end, he propped cinder blocks on top, just out of sight. If thieves tried to steal the fencing, the blocks would fall on their heads.

Once, on his big lot downtown, he discovered that someone was climbing the corner of the fence each night and stealing a tree.

"Here's a good old Indian trick," he said and emptied a bag of dog shit on the ground. He rolled a tree in it, then he propped it in the corner where the thief had been. The next morning, he took me outside the fence to where the tree lay near the road. We laughed long and hard about the thief who'd gotten smeared with shit.

But sometimes his antics didn't make me feel that good, as when he caught a long-legged spider on his dashboard. We were waiting at a light. It was summer, the windows down, and he said, "Look at that old goat!" In the car next to us, a geezer with thick glasses hunched over his steering wheel as if it were a book in the hands of a nearsighted reader. My father leaned past me and threw the spider onto his bald head.

Now I had to decide. I was sitting on the couch. Hinges creaked in the mudroom and footsteps crossed the kitchen. My father stood in the doorway, the skin on either side of his mouth slack, his gaze too still.

"Is that for school?" he asked.

A Jules Verne novel lay on my lap. It had enraptured me, the idea that a land existed beneath the earth — and why not? How could scientists know for sure? But I said nothing, seeing that this wasn't the father who wanted to travel and fish, but the one who cared only about his business.

"You read too much," he said. "You should get some exercise."

As I tried to think of what to say, a feeling of loneliness, still beyond words, dawned. I'd stopped talking about levitation and mental powers and invisible friends, but I hadn't considered there might be other things about me that he didn't like.

"I got in a fight today," I told him.

"You did?" He raised his eyebrows, then yawned, lifting his forearm to hide his mouth. "That's good. I'm glad you're standing up for yourself."

I'd been trying to be tough at school, using *fuck* and *goddamn* to swear kids to tears and run them off. When Matthieu had pulled on my jacket, I'd called him a fuck banana. He'd appeared so dazed that I'd taken the opportunity to punch him.

"Good. That's good," my father said, eyeing me as if I might be lying. "You really let him have it, huh?"

"Yeah, I let him have it pretty good." Hearing myself, I felt that my

victory was far grander than it had seemed in the moment, though I wasn't
sure I'd used the swearword right.

My father leaned against the doorjamb, still looking at me, but
yawned again. He went into the kitchen. The fridge door opened, bottles clinking.

"Goddamn it," I heard him say, "there's nothing to eat."

I closed my book. I had to make up my mind. Maybe I should leave
with my mother. My father definitely wasn't as fun as he used to be.

He came back, anger all around him, like the smell of cigarettes
on a smoker's jacket. He sat and put the peach-colored phone on the
armrest, then lifted the receiver. He swallowed hard and pushed his jaw
forward and began to dial.

Seeing his expression, I knew that he was going to swear at someone. The sadness eased from my throat, and an odd feeling of lightness
came over me. What was it about words, or the way some of them could
contain so much force? No·one could swear like him! It was his gift.
Each insult came from his stomach, not like a belch but like the sudden
act of vomiting, a sound that catches in the throat and burns in the
sinuses like bile.

The faint ringing from the earpiece reached me, and a tired tinny
voice said, "Hullo." My father didn't even introduce himself. He shouted,
"Don't you fucking play games with me!" Then he took a breath so deep
I could see all his teeth and the dark lines of his many fillings and the
red of his throat. He yelled, stringing words together, "Motherfucking
cocksucking piece of shit, I'll kick your stupid fucking ass!"

Wanting to sound like this, I forgot I had to decide, and without
realizing it, I jumped up and danced on the carpet in victory. He grabbed
his black book and threw it at me.

The end would be like a fishing trip, a long drive through the night, dark
mountains and washed-out roads, to a dawn over a river where all that
mattered began.

I went into the woods and closed my eyes and turned in circles with
the intention of getting lost. I had to hone my survival skills. Wandering,

I looked for tunnels under bushes and imagined magic portals beneath the low branches of trees.

And then I just sat. There was something I couldn't understand, that made it hard to breathe, my throat thick with sadness. My father had always told me I was like him, and I did my best not to cry in front of him. But I noticed how my mother watched me sometimes, her brow furrowed, a wetness in her blue eyes, as if just seeing me race through the door might make her cry. She liked it when we talked and I read books, but what did my father want me to be? Crazy sometimes. Quiet at others. It was confusing. It wasn't fair.

In novels, something bad happens so that the hero has to travel and change, but my life just dragged on. Only when I read did the pressure in my chest go away. As I turned pages, I felt a rush of vertigo, tingling along my arms and face. Even telling stories at school, I became transfixed, sailing further and further into the air, toward the sky, more and more distant from the truth. And once I'd told a story, no matter how outlandish, how embroidered with magic, I knew it was true. I had only to glance at photos from my parents' first years together to see the past, and the scene that unfolded—that I told everyone—I never doubted.

To my classmates, I bragged about my father, the immense salmon and steelhead trout that he reeled from icy rivers, standing deep in the current, almost swept away. They listened, but at some point—when the salmon bit his leg or gashed his hand or wrapped the line around his boot and tried to drag him downriver—they snorted and called me a liar.

What they didn't realize was that their stories stank because they thought too much about time. There was too much walking, too much opening and closing of doors. They didn't see that two shocking events years apart, on opposite ends of the country, longed for each other the way a smiling girl across the room made me want to sit next to her. Hearing my father, I forgot the slow march of minutes. A dog had once tried to bite him, and he'd also reeled in a forty-pound salmon, so it seemed natural that the injured fish would bite him, too. Minutes and hours had to be done away with, the thrilling moments of life freed from · the calendar's prison grid.

Soon, I told myself as I walked home through the forest, my life would be a story, and I'd be free.

School let out for Christmas. The autumn had been mild, but the weather finally changed. Snow fell in the naked forests and turned the ditches to ice.

We moved again, to a smaller farm, this time to be closer to my father's stores. My mother barely unpacked. She no longer paid much attention to food, making slapdash sandwiches and rushing off to meet friends from the psychic church. Though she still had two horses, the years of goat home brew were over.

On Boxing Day, she took us to the mall. My father had given each of us a hundred dollars in loose change. We'd spent Christmas counting, huddled like misers over stacks of coins, but at the mall I noticed that my brother didn't buy anything.

I sidled up to him. "What are you going to get?"

"Nothing. I gave my money to Bonnie."

"You did? Really?"

"She needs it. It's important."

I shuddered. In my backpack, I had rolls of pennies, nickels, dimes, and quarters, and I couldn't believe that my parents' stupidity might deprive me of the pleasure of spending them. As I bought a book of mystery stories, my mother stood off and watched, her expression that of tried patience, as if enduring some classroom humiliation. My heart went out of shopping.

As I walked back across the parking lot next to her, she stared into the distance, searching for something, an answer from her own invisible friends, a way to bridge the annoying, relentless minutes in which nothing at all happened, so that she could connect two pieces of her own story. I knew she'd need my money to do this, and that I'd give it to her.

When we got home, my father's new cargo minivan was in the driveway, and he was back on the farm preparing a burn pile. He'd been busy closing his lots and wasn't around more than a few hours on Christmas.

He began walking toward the house. I went to my room and lay on the bed with my new book.

The fighting began just outside, and I rolled off the bed and went to the window. I wondered what they'd said to start the argument, but I was getting angry, too, and yelling might have felt good.

"I'm sick of this nonsense," he tried to bellow, but to my surprise, the dark fields and night silence didn't seem to care, and a wind blew through his voice, hollowing it.

"It's none of your business," she shouted back, drowning his words. This startled me. She spoke with such force, his force, as if she'd put on his boots and jacket and glared at him with his dark eyes, and he stood naked in the field, wanting his things back but too tired to take them.

"I can't believe it," he said. "You talk to . . . to some psychic and now you think Vancouver is going to be destroyed by an earthquake."

"I'm sick of explaining myself!" she told him. The clouds cleared the moon, and the dark thinned so that the stars pulsed once, all together, and withdrew like barnacles.

She said a few more things, about him not respecting her wishes or giving her space to grow, and her voice remained loud, something exploratory in the way she raised it to new heights, as if only now discovering this could be done.

Her van started up, and its taillights flared and scorched off along the driveway.

The night lulled, and a fire began on the back of the property. He was burning hundreds of leftover Christmas trees, the light blurring in the frosted window glass. Ever since I could remember, he'd loved building fires: garbage on the property, tires and old appliances, wood from rotting sheds, and once a camper that fit on the back of a truck. He'd piled branches and dead pine and spruce on top, then doused it all with so much gasoline that he'd had to pour a long thin trail of it far away just to light it safely. We'd crouched together, and he'd dropped the match. The flame zipped like a shark's fin across the grass and the heap burst skyward, the air sucked in and up, sudden heat against my face. It got so hot that Christmas trees turned to ash before our eyes, and the metal of the camper sagged and collapsed. He'd stood with his hands on his hips and laughed, and I had no idea why burning things felt so good, like yawning or stretching in the middle of class. Maybe he was trying to feel that way now, all alone burning trees.

I went to the mudroom and put on my boots and pulled the door from its warped frame. Frozen air spilled over me, and I followed the hard earth of the driveway back.

'Halfway there, I came to a ditch, the spine of the buried culvert visible where big trucks carrying trees had passed. Beyond that was the tossing light of the fire. The cold stung my face, the night silent but for cars on the road. I hadn't had time to get used to this farm, the sheds and barn unexplored, the forest scant and far away, beyond a frostbitten field.

I glanced back. My heart clenched and thudded as the world came unstrung. The lights of the house drifted out toward the road. The rising moon slipped a little higher in the sky, bumping over the stars.

I took a few more steps and stopped, my rapid breath misting, the smoldering center of the fire a red eye. I couldn't see him. Sparks rushed up through the chill air, planing as they cooled and died. When the wind shifted, the heat warmed my face.

He called my name.

Fear released from my chest, and I continued over the baked earth. He was just beyond the fire, his arms crossed, and I stood next to him.

"She's upset," he told me.

I made myself appear as calm as possible, and I was proud of how I stood next to him and watched the fire, asking matter-of-factly, "What are we going to do?"

"I don't know," he said, as if he might want my advice. "Maybe we can all go on a trip. Sometimes, when you go on a trip and come back, things are better. Sometimes that's all it takes."

I pictured this, a long journey, days and days looking out the window at trees and mountains, and then him saying, "This is far enough." We'd turn around and return, ready to start over. But would he change?

Firelight shone on his cheekbones but hid his eyes, and though I worried that he might tell me to go back inside, he didn't.

"Things will be better," he said, and in his voice I heard my mother's, the sadness and uncertainty and fear, and I knew that something had changed.

I lost track of the days. I read or played *Dungeons & Dragons* with my brother, my fears vanishing like fish descending through a dark current.

One night I fell asleep reading on the couch and I heard my parents come in the front door after arguing. They walked into the living room, and I didn't open my eyes. I sensed them above me, looking down, silent as if surprised that I existed. My mother said she'd take me to my bedroom, but my father told her that he'd do it. He lifted me, my cheek against the coarse fabric of his shirt, my arm hanging. I could have opened my eyes and said I'd walk, but I sensed in his gentleness that he wanted to carry me. I breathed the odors in his shirt, pine sap and coffee, gasoline and sweat, but I felt no comfort. My heart didn't slow. I didn't drift asleep in this safety. I watched, starting to get angry, surprised to be this little boy, one arm folded against his chest. I felt like I was remembering, as if this moment were a photograph and I were seeing how things had once been.

After he'd closed the door, I turned on my lamp and read. It was the only way to feel calm. In the novel, kingdoms clashed, and at some point I dozed and was swinging a sword at faceless, blurring enemies until I sensed danger and turned, a dark shape closing in. I woke, gasping, then lay awake until the sun rose.

At my new school, I jostled through the morning crowd, kids turning and saying, "Hey, watch it!" I fell asleep in class. I forgot my homework. When kids talked about the presents Santa had brought them, I said Santa didn't exist. "Only babies believe in Santa," I told them. "Get over it."

A girl began to cry. I heard someone say he hated the new kid.

During recess, I explored the sprawling grounds. I despised everyone. I couldn't talk to others without wanting to hurt their feelings. As I turned the corner, five boys appeared before me.

"Hey, it's the new kid," Tom said. He was in my class, tall and blond, his bangs neatly brushed back.

The kids formed a half circle and began closing in.

Years ago, when I started first grade, my father had given me talks about fighting, as if I weren't heading off to elementary school but to become a mercenary. He'd warned me never to show fear and said that I should terrify my enemies.

"Fuck you, dog-shit-faced cocksuckers!" I howled.

The boys backed away, but Tom broke from them and ran forward and kicked me in the balls. I dropped to my knees, the air gusting from my lungs.

"Run!" he shouted to his friends. "This kid's crazy!"

They raced off while I held myself, waiting for my lungs to work.

Back in class, Jamil approached me. He was a swift, dark East Indian boy I'd seen that morning near the entrance to the school. He'd pushed down another boy and farted in his face, then sped off. He glanced at the dirt on my knees.

"I don't believe in Christmas either," he told me. "It's a bunch of crap. Do you want to be friends? We can beat up Tom after school."

"Yeah," I agreed. "Let's beat him up."

Until now swearing had been as good a defense as my fists. Prayers and mantras might reach the invisible world, but profanity was the power of words brought into this world to lay low my enemies. And yet I'd been kicked in the nuts. My father was right. I needed to get tough.

As Jamil passed the information through class that I was challenging Tom to a fight in the alley between two brick buildings, I could hear myself describing the victory to my father. But an hour later, walking into the alley, I began to tremble.

Tom was waiting with his friends, their shirts rumpled, dark with the interminable winter drizzle. Every detail appeared mapped out against the brick wall, their nervous faces drawn on graph paper. Rain beaded along Jamil's hair as he stood at my side, saying, "Go! You take him!"

Tom shoved me in the chest. I got him in a headlock. We stumbled against the wall, the bricks rasping our clothes like sandpaper.

His friends tried to jump in, but Jamil blocked them. He kept slapping them in the face, dancing from side to side as if guarding a volleyball net.

"What's wrong, pussy?" he shouted. "Tom can't fight for himself?"

Tom popped out of the headlock. From behind me, he tried to dig his fingers into my eyes. I rammed him backward into the bricks. I threw my body against him again and again until his head struck the wall with a wooden sound.

I spun and punched him three times. He just stared, his nostrils too large and dark. Blood began to drip from one of them. His eyes teared up. He ducked and grabbed his backpack and ran. He disappeared along the alley, his jacket flapping.

I had blood on my lip where one of his fingernails had dug in.

I hurried to the pickup zone. My brother was waiting on the sidewalk. His eyes went to my face and then, like a switch, dropped to my mouth.

"What happened?"

"I got in a fight."

Kids gathered around, pushing between us. They told him about it, speaking quickly, pointing here and there.

My mother's brown van appeared from the traffic and pulled to the curb. I got in, and she reached across the space between the front seats and took hold of my chin.

"Are you fighting?"

Her blue eyes glared at my cut as if seeing the one thing she most hated.

"I had to."

"Fighting is wrong. You don't fight. You talk to people. And if you can't resolve the problem through talking, you tell your teacher. You tell the principal. You tell me. Do you understand?"

I just sat. It was pointless to argue. What she was saying would ruin me at school. I'd have to fight constantly.

My brother spoke from the seat behind us.

"Everyone said that Jamil helped you."

"What?" she asked.

"It's not true," I shouted. "He just made sure no one else hit me."

I tried to meet her gaze but felt blinded, as if looking at sunlight flashing on seawater.

"Listen," she said. "I don't want you to fight again, but André is going to ask what happened. When he does, don't tell him that you got help. He's not going to like that."

My father was so busy that we hadn't seen much of him, but that night he was taking my brother, my sister, and me to dinner. By the time he picked us up, my mother had already left for one of her meetings. My father hardly spoke, not even in the restaurant. He called for coffee, then noticed my lip.

"Did you win?" he asked, his eyes suddenly still.

I glanced at my brother. "Yeah," I said.

"You did?"

I nodded, trying to hide my anger. The story was almost perfect. The confrontation in the alley, the kids gathered to watch, the rain falling along the narrow slice of sky. As far as fifth-graders went, Tom was a bruiser. But with my brother sitting across from me, I couldn't tell the story right.

"What was it like?" my father asked.

I glanced once at my brother, then avoided his eyes and hesitantly described how I'd knocked Tom into the bricks, then spun and hit him three times and gave him a bloody nose.

"That's good," my father said.

I risked another glance at my brother. He was watching me, his face nervous and confused. My father looked between us, and I dropped my gaze to my hands, but it was too late.

"What is it?" he asked. "Why are you looking at him like that?"

When I didn't say anything, he turned to my brother.

"Come on. Let's have it."

My brother shrugged. He could never lie. I was doomed.

"Deni got help," he finally said.

"No I didn't," I shouted. My tongue curled in my mouth, *son of a bitch* caught in it, trying to get out as I clenched my jaw to keep it in.

"What help?" my father asked.

Reluctantly, my brother explained, but he was telling it wrong. He hadn't even been there, and all he described was Jamil protecting me.

He had the details right, but the way they went together wasn't. Tom had almost clawed my eyes out! I'd banged his head against the bricks all by myself. It was a close call!

My father glared at me. "From now on, you stand up for yourself. You can handle a couple of kids, you hear me?"

I wanted to remind him how he and his brother had watched each other's backs in their village. But there were dark creases beneath his eyes, and the bones of his skull seemed close to the skin. A look came into his eyes, like that of a dog about to bite.

"Anyway, we all know you're not too smart," he said, his lips smiling thinly, showing his upper teeth. He began to say something else, but my tongue came loose and I yelled, "Shut up!"

The room tilted and blurred. I had blood on my lips again. My brother and sister stared into their plates. I felt dizzy and didn't speak. I wouldn't look at him.

As we were leaving, he kept sighing and rubbing his face and glancing over at me, but I refused to return his gaze. What he had taught me, I knew, was what I had done. If I could have told the story my way, he'd have understood.

"That fucking bank," he said to himself. "It's ruining my life. I'm going to dump a load of manure on their steps."

I sat near the window, cold radiating from the glass. If the end was inevitable and there was a new beginning, why not pray for it? Why not get it over with? I'd had enough of their rage, of them crying out like animals in the dark.

The next day, I told my mother that I wanted to leave.

She packed our lunches, but instead of taking us to school, she drove us to the house of one of her friends and told us to stay there and play *Dungeons & Dragons*.

When she returned, it was almost noon. Everything we owned was inside the van, boxes and blankets crammed to the walls, her favorite German shepherd lying between the seats. Her white horse trailer had been hitched up, both horses inside.

She hurried us into the van, saying she'd explain soon. We drove to the border.

On the interstate, she told us that we would stay with our aunt in Virginia.

My sister began to cry. She said she'd never see her friends again, and my mother told her that she would someday. My brother remained silent, sitting in the back, arms crossed as he stared at his feet. But my rage had been released, and I felt as if I were waking from a long sleep, empty and open, eager to see the world. When we drove through Seattle, I pointed out the Space Needle.

"Who cares," my brother said, "we're not here to look at things."

As I watched the darkening highway, I felt an excitement I couldn't explain. We were traveling, and maybe someday, when I saw my father again, I'd tell him this story, of leaving, of discovering a new life. We wouldn't be angry anymore, and he'd tell me everything he'd done after we'd left. He'd laugh and describe how he'd driven into the city and gone to the bank, a salmon in his briefcase. He paid for the safe-deposit box, took the key, and locked the fish inside.

I tried to picture him wild and victorious, the way he'd been when I was little, always laughing, always playing a new trick, but suddenly I was angry again.

The gray dawn reached us as we crossed the mountains east, scars of snow on the roadsides, blue ice on the rocks. The moon was still out above the far, fading lights of distant towns. This wasn't the journey he'd told me about, the one from which we'd return and start over. And yet I felt the freedom of movement, of newness, the thrill that moves from the heart along the limbs, the desire never to stop, never to be held again in one place.

part II

GHOSTS OF THE CIVIL WAR

Early in their relationship, my father wouldn't let my mother drive. He didn't believe women should. Though my brother could walk to the valley's five-grade, two-room schoolhouse, she insisted on a better school thirty minutes away. My father, having discovered the demands of driving children, gave her an ancient box truck he'd used to sell fish at intersections before he opened his stores. Its panels were leprous with rust, and the only seat was the driver's. My sister sat on a wooden stool next to my mother, but my brother and I were happy on the floor because of a rusty hole.

"Get away from it," my mother told us. Each day, I collected lumps of chewing gum from the playground to see how they thwacked against the asphalt. Even when she yelled, we remained on our hands and knees, studying the blurred, passing grain of the road, pleased when we changed lanes and the broken yellow line flickered past.

In 1980, my father brought home our first new vehicle. The GMC Vandura was earth brown, a three-quarter-ton, and, to my five-year-old eyes, a mountain. It had a cream corduroy interior with four swiveling captain's chairs, a shag rug, two tables on posts, small ceiling lights like those in airplanes, and a couch that opened into a bed, lit by lamps in plastic shades. Between the front seats, a cover unlatched to reveal the glistening engine, and on the back, a chrome ladder joined a roof rack printed with maple leaves. That first day, I practiced climbing around the van, looking for fingerholds, counting laps without falling, until I grabbed the antenna and that was it for FM radio.

My father found the van difficult to navigate through traffic, so he let my mother use it and bought himself a Ford Bronco, which, a few years later, he exchanged for a minivan newly on the market, one stripped for hauling cargo. But she fell in love with the brown conversion van, its V8 capable of pulling a horse trailer with ease. She said she wanted it and stood her ground until he signed it over and let her make payments.

She drove us kids, as well as our German shepherd, everywhere. High above the road, offering a vantage on the traffic, the van swayed, sailing on its shocks so that we had all, including the dog, vomited on the rug in the days before we got our sea legs. She used it to haul hay and goats, and we took it on road trips, parking on gravel washouts in the mountains where we fished, or to Barkerville to see gold panned by bearded men who my father referred to as winos. She hated these trips, her van back under his control, and while he fished, she packed, unpacked, cleaned and readied the food, demoted from captain to stevedore.

But eventually she completed her mutiny. She drove us across the border and headed east, rushing through that first night.

I slept on the floor, lulled to sleep by the engine's vibrations, but at dawn, I woke and sat next to her. She studied each passing car, glancing in the side-view mirror often.

"Why are you so afraid?" I asked.

She sighed, the first rays of sunlight in our eyes.

"He's angry," she said in a measured tone. "I don't know what he'll do. He didn't want me to leave, and . . ." She hesitated, searching for words, then finished her thought all at once, as if she couldn't hold it in any longer—"I don't trust him. He's dangerous."

As the sun rose, I also glanced behind us, at the dim faces that became visible when a car pulled close. Why should we be so afraid? How bad was he? He'd talked about nothing worse than driving fast and getting in fights. But then I recalled the night at the ferry, the blood on his face and hands, the knowledge that two people lay unconscious on the gravel driveway. Could he do this to us, too?

At a rest stop, as she walked us to the bathrooms, she looked at every vehicle, at the shadows behind misted windows.

"Stay close to the van," she told us. "Watch out for strange people. He might have sent someone after us. The van sticks out like a sore thumb."

But those January days in the mountains, the van was the only comfort we had.

After we crossed Washington, she bought us plane tickets east, sending us to our aunt. There, we waited, often sitting on the porch, afraid that he'd caught up. A few days later, we were ecstatic to see our mobile mountain pull into the driveway, glittering with dust.

At our aunt's, we slept on spare mattresses and foldout beds. The phone rang often, and if my mother answered, he shouted so loudly that I could hear the crickety jabbering from across the house.

Days, I roamed the woods, catching crayfish in streams banked with red clay, or I read whatever I found—novels about voodoo and murder. But though the future seemed more exciting than ever, sometimes I began to cry for no reason. Deep sobs that I couldn't fathom took over, and I wept until my aunt grabbed fistfuls of her blond hair and pulled it so taut that the dark roots looked like a strip of paint.

I didn't understand why we'd come so far. I'd felt I was the most like my father, and yet I hadn't cried when we'd left. At night, the phone jangled down the hall, and I awoke, staring at the dark window. The couch creaked in the living room as my mother got up to unplug the phone. Where was he? What was he doing now that we were gone?

Everyone in the family got an unlisted number, but an air of tension remained, as if at any moment he might arrive and hurt my mother and take us away.

We enrolled in school, and he called there and spoke to my brother, who, under the scrutiny of the secretaries, couldn't answer his questions and had to hang up in tears.

At the new school, the principal, a former drill sergeant, strode the halls with his chest puffed up, his hips so wide that his pants looked like jodhpurs. The cafeteria had a traffic light (green for talk, yellow for whisper, and red for silence), and in my fifth-grade class, two white boys with incipient beards got in a fight with two big black boys.

My peers, the white ones, called themselves Rebs. We were study-ing the Civil War, and they wrote "The South will rise again!" on their folders. Our teacher praised the merits of Robert E. Lee and lowered her voice to confide that the war hadn't been about slavery.

When the yellow bus finally took me home, I read, hunched low, knees against the seat in front. The ruckus of shouting kids kept dis-tracting me from *Taran Wanderer*, which I'd found in the library. I would read three lines, Taran setting out on his journey, and then I'd begin think-ing about what my father was doing and why everyone was so afraid.

"I fingered her," a sixth-grader behind me was telling another kid, practically shouting. "That's right. She let me. She was so tight I could only git my little finger in . . ."

I narrowed my eyes, trying to stay with Taran. But what in the hell was he talking about? Was fingering like thumb wrestling or mercy? Either way, it sounded like the girl had won.

The bus creaked to a stop and the door flapped open. My brother and sister and I and our oldest cousin, a tall girl with wavy brown hair, climbed down the high rubber-coated steps to the sunlit blacktop. The gravel driveway rose through a corridor of trees, and by the time we reached the carport, we were panting.

Behind the house stretched sunburned yard, sparse woods between it and the green, sprinkled lawn of the neighbor boys, both blond, the elder athletic and protective of his brother. He'd just come through the trees, a red rubber ball under his arm, and was calling. We dropped our backpacks and joined them for kickball, tawny dust puffing around our feet.

My uncle's silver truck rolled in, and I ran to see him. My mother referred to him as a local boy, and he towered over me, with a scruffy beard, a receding hairline, and a beer belly that pressed his overalls, out-lining the carpentry pencil in the front pocket. He worked in aluminum siding and once showed me a copperhead he'd killed with a piece of firewood. This time, the bed of his truck held two dinosaurian snapping turtles that he'd hooked in a forest pond and brought home to stew.

"They'll bite your finger clean off," he drawled as I climbed onto the back bumper.

I definitely wasn't going to finger these turtles. Both were bigger than hubcaps, their stout heads moving side to side as their clawed feet feebly paddled the puddle of dirty, sunbaked blood. I prodded one with a stick, but it took no interest.

"Can we go fishing sometime?" I asked and jumped down, but he'd turned away as if busy. He often took my cousins fishing, and I didn't see why I couldn't go, too.

"Here, catch!" he said and tossed a small brown ball. I jumped for it just as I realized it was the soft lump of his chewing tobacco. The slimy wad hit my palm before I could pull my hand away. It broke apart on the concrete. He guffawed and went inside.

The younger neighbor boy ran over and asked, "Aren't you going to play?"

I gave him a shove, and his legs wobbled like those of a newborn goat as he grabbed for a carport pillar. Instantly, his brother had left the kickball game and was there, fist lifted, eyes shining. "Leave him alone," he told me.

It reminded me of a *G.I. Joe* episode that ended with a heroic younger version of a character giving a lesson about not bullying. I just looked away, into the forest, as if this were the most boring thing in the world.

I took my backpack and sat on the front porch that nobody used, since everyone went in and out the carport door. I opened *Taran Wanderer*. I'd read Lloyd Alexander's books at my old school and had liked this one, young Taran questing to learn who his parents were so he could marry Princess Eilonwy. Journey, discovery, the fear of violence—all had kept me riveted. But now I couldn't focus. I read each page twice. Why had I just been so mean? Maybe I was like my father, and I'd grow up to scare everyone. I didn't feel very scary. My head felt like the pinball in the machine my father had once taught me to play in a restaurant lobby.

Now it was my mother who pulled in, the tires of her van grinding the gravel. She worked at the stables where she boarded her horses, and she got out wearing a button-down shirt with rolled sleeves, and jeans, dirt rubbed into the denim on the fronts of her thighs.

"What's wrong?" she asked.

"I don't know."

"Come on. I'm going to look at some places to rent. I just have to change fast."

I climbed into the van, the hot interior smelling of oats and hay, of dog hair and dust. She came back, wearing a brown skirt and a blouse. We raced along the road, my window down, gusts slapping me in the face as I held my eyes closed. When I opened them, pastures rolled on toward the low, sloping line of distant mountains. A small farmhouse waited at the end of a winding driveway, and I sat up. This was the place. I was certain.

The sun seemed to be setting earlier here, shadows like capes on the backs of hills, and the wind felt particularly cool. I could see myself walking a path that threaded over the pastures. There would be shallow streams, and if I wanted, I could go all the way to the foot of the mountains, where the haze of distance resembled a faint line of mist.

But my mother had already finished talking to the owner. She walked back to the van, her chin lowered, her taut expression indicating she wanted to leave in a hurry.

She cranked the engine, and we jostled over the driveway's potholes to the paved road. I decided that if I explained how much I liked the place, she'd be happy, but instead she told me that the owner had flat out said he didn't rent to single mothers.

"Are you a single mother?"

"Yes. I am."

"What's wrong with that?"

"People think we can't pay the rent."

"Oh," I said. "Can you?"

"Yes, I can. But this place is a bit expensive. It's not right for us."

She was driving fast, and I felt nauseous from the van's soaring motion over the hilly road. I went back to letting the air from the window buffet my face.

This time we turned into a trailer park off a four-lane highway, a honeycomb of staggered mobile homes. I was getting that pinball feeling again. I knew from school that the mean kids lived here, and we passed a pack of them, slouching in jean jackets as they looked about with narrowed eyes, trying to find something to destroy. They saw me and stared as if I were a fish in an aquarium. Then they all laughed, showing their teeth like barking dogs. I glanced at my mother, and she said, "Your hair."

I touched my head and realized that the wind had made my hair stand up straight, as if I'd spiked it with gel like a rock star. I was going to pay for this tomorrow.

At the very back of the trailer park, where a forest began, she pulled up to a drab, white mobile home with gray trim, some of it missing.

A tubby man in a dress shirt and a Redskins cap came out, his eyes wedged up in the shadow of his visor. His mouth opened and stayed that way.

"I thought y'all'r Colombian," he said with the same ruminating motion as my uncle. He adjusted his visor with a meaty hand like a big, hairy pancake.

"British Columbia," my mother told him.

"Where's that?"

"Canada."

"Well, I was expecting dark little fellers like Mexicans. Come on in."

Water-stained fleurs-de-lis papered the walls, and in the back bedroom, a yellow cricket perched near a hole in the linoleum, twitching antennae as long as spider legs. I stomped, but not before it dove into its foxhole. My mother had been discussing the price, and they paused when my shoe banged down. I heard her say she'd take it. My head ached, the nausea stronger than ever.

As we were returning to my aunt's, I blurted, "I wish he'd die."

"What?" she asked. "Who?"

"André. Everything would be easier if he were dead. We could have stayed."

She swerved off the road and grabbed my arm.

"Don't ever say that again." She shook me, but I pulled free. The words had just bubbled up out of me. I had no idea where they'd come from.

"Why are you so afraid of him?" I asked. It was the only question that made sense.

She shut the van off and looked away, then back. She'd had her hair cut so that it framed her face, and her eyes seemed bigger, their

blue crystalline. Though she met my gaze, I didn't believe she'd tell me
why we needed to go so far away, or what about my father kept her up
at night or caused her and my aunt to shut the bedroom door and talk
in hushed voices.

"There are things I can't explain until you're older," she told me. "I
promise I will someday."

I glared off as if still angry, but in truth, she'd said enough. Her
words, few as they were, created a sense of expectation better than in
any book. They were the proof I'd been right all along to have suspicions
about my father. There was a reason for everything that had happened.

While my mother worked on the horse farm and as a secretary at IBM,
my brother, sister, and I lived off ramen. We tried every sort, discussing whether beef, chicken, or seafood, with its packets of salty shrimp
powder, was better. If we discovered a new flavor at the supermarket, we
gathered like rock 'n' roll groupies around an album.

"Pork! This one's pork!" or "Hot and Spicy! There're only three!
They're mine!"

School lunches consisted of flavorless rectangular pizzas marked
with what looked like tire tread, as well as chocolate milk, fries, and the
indispensable ketchup that, in Virginia, was considered a vegetable so
as to complete our nutritional requirements.

Meals like this sent a pang of disappointment through my gut. Hunger stalked me like a school bully. Hunger slept on my belly like a hot
cat. Hunger barked me into a panic like a vicious neighbor's dog when
I walked the road. I craved our meals in the valley, heaped spaghetti or
large bowls of meaty soup.

Good books were increasingly scarce. At the school library, I scoured
the shelves. I'd reread Tolkien, C. S. Lewis, Lloyd Alexander, and Madeleine
L'Engle, so I started in on mythology, hoping for relief. The Greeks evoked
the beginning of civilization so clearly I pictured the first, brilliant dawn
above the glimmering new earth and wished I'd been there to see how
it was before things got bad, which didn't take long. The Norse liked

the end, Ragnarok, doomsday, the sun swallowed by a wolf, the darkness of winter.

The square of bisected morning sunlight made its way across the wall as I lay with the only mythology book I had yet to finish. The metal roof of the trailer popped and ticked as if the sun were tapping fingers on it, and the room was getting muggy. My mother had gone to see her horses, my sister had spent the night at a friend's house, and my brother sat cross-legged before the TV, his Commodore VIC-20 plugged into it while he learned to program BASIC 2.0 from a dog-eared manual.

I went out the side door and stood in the sun, stretching my arms above my head.

A classmate's older brother, a stooped young man named Earl Darwin, walked down the street with a metal detector.

"Hey!" I called, and he turned, moving as if carved from wood. He spoke with strained vocal cords, invisible hands strangling him.

"What?" he squawked.

"What are you doing?"

"I'm prospecting for Civil War artifacts."

I asked what he meant, and he explained that he explored pastures with the metal detector. He showed me a green army shovel with a folding blade.

"If I dig for you, can I come?" I asked, thinking that finding ancient things was kind of like reading myths. He just nodded and said, "Sounds good to me."

As we walked down the long incline of mobile homes, their metal roofs throwing sunlight into our eyes, he asked about my family and how long I'd been here. He couldn't believe I had no religion, and, like Darwin, he set forth the order of the world: white churches and black churches, bad people and good ones, heaven and hell, a neighbor who shook in his lawn chair because he'd smoked oregano soaked in transmission fluid, a six-toed window washer who slept with all the single mothers, a teenage girl who'd gotten pregnant because the guy skimped on condoms and used Saran Wrap.

He clued me in on trailer-park characters: the fat black boy whose father brought him a G.I. Joe every week though the boy always tied them to a stake, doused them in gasoline, and torched them next to the windmills and flamingos on his tiny lawn; the pale muscular boy with sunken eyes who we saw surrounded by girls as he lifted his bicycle with one arm, a feat for which, Earl explained, he got laid—what I imagined might be like getting tucked in. He added that the boy's father had been killed in the field below the trailer park, his head staved in by a two-by-four. It occurred to me that something wasn't right with the fathers around here.

"He deserved it," Earl told me as we crossed the four lanes of highway into the horse pastures. "He was a faggot and kept grabbing people."

Americans loved cussing so much I wondered if it was genetic, like eye color. Maybe my mother had passed this on to me, though she didn't swear much. She did get angry easily, quick to say everyone was wrong and how things should really be done. This was definitely an American quality I had. Thinking about it made me feel like a character in a novel, proud and unashamed. If you didn't have an obsession and weren't willing to risk your life for what you believed, you probably belonged somewhere else.

Over the next hour, each time Earl's detector bleated, I dug up Civil War treasures: buckles from belts, boots, and harnesses, as well as lead bullets—dozens of them, a few mashed from impact. The thrill of discovery had me panting, hunched, scouring the red clay with my fingers until the object came into sight. This, I suddenly knew, was my purpose. Archaeology! Why hadn't I realized sooner? I loved mystery, and what could be more mysterious? I felt that we'd soon discover something amazing, a golden statue of Zeus or a Roman helmet.

An old farmer came out to see what we were up to.

"I dug up a safe one time," he said, his eyes eerily blue in his sunbronzed face.

"What kind of safe?" Earl tugged at his checkered shirt as if the afternoon heat were unbearable. I leaned close.

"An old safe," the farmer said—"a very old safe. It must have been thirty years ago. I was digging a septic field. I found that safe down in the ground, and I'll be durned if I didn't spend four years trying to git it open. Maybe five. I used everything. Sledgehammer. Welding kit. But that door wouldn't budge. So I put it back in the ground."

"You did what?" Earl exclaimed. I was practically bent double, as if to gnaw my way through the earth to find that safe.

"I got annoyed," the old man said.

"But there are stories of buried safes with Civil War gold," Earl told him. "Did it have any markings on it? Do you remember where you buried it?"

The old man looked off, his lips drawing down as if with thought, or to smirk. He shrugged. "I done forgot. It's been some time now."

Then he walked away, shuffling and bent forward, the baggy brown seat of his jeans hanging off his ass as if beneath he were nothing but bones—a malicious skeleton, one of the Confederate dead risen from the stale earth to torment us.

The idea of the safe made me crazy. I couldn't stand it. I lay awake at night and pictured myself digging. I heard the precise moment when the shovel's blade hit the rusted iron. I felt the jolt in my arm and sat up. I got out of bed as if to go pee and stood in the bathroom, turned on the light, and looked in the mirror.

"I found a safe," I told my reflection. "It's full of gold."

Then I shut off the light and went back to bed and pictured myself digging again, waiting to hear the clank of the shovel blade, shivering with anticipation.

But I still couldn't sleep, so I took my notebook and went into the bathroom. I sat on the toilet and wrote about a field where Civil War phantoms appeared under the full moon, living out hopeless battles. Buried beneath them was an old safe that the story's hero, a boy archaeologist, heard about from a spooky old man who vanished into the shadow of the forest. The boy had to find someone to help him dig it up and release the spirits of the dead so that he could claim the gold, but the only person he could ask was his father. I hesitated, pencil poised, trying to decide what kind of father this should be, if he could be trusted with the secret and what he'd do if allowed into the story. Frustrated, I went back to bed.

Each afternoon, returning from school, I paused at a rise on the trailer-park road. I looked out over the flat roofs—some narrow, some double-wide—beyond the patchwork of cramped yards with rusted hibachis and cannibalized cars—to the field where we'd been prospecting. I hated the farmer for forgetting where the safe was. Only my father would understand. He might be sitting at home sharpening a knife, or lying in wait for my mother in the shadows next to the post office, but he would definitely understand about the safe.

I couldn't bear it. His number was in one of the cards he sent, and I went to a pay phone and called collect. We'd talked only a few times since I'd left, briefly, with my mother passing the receiver around, and this was the first time I'd called him on my own. How bad could he really be? My mother and aunt whispered together at night about him, and several times my mother had told me he was dangerous and that we had to keep our lives secret from him. As the phone rang, my heart kicked like a car-struck jackrabbit in its frantic final seconds.

"Hey . . . Deni . . . ," he said after he'd accepted the charges. "Are you alone?"

"Yeah," I told him, thinking how strange he sounded, raspy and far away. He almost croaked when he talked, as if he'd gotten old.

"Are you okay?" he asked.

"Well, yeah, but there's something I wanted to ask you about."

"Oh," he said, his voice suddenly clear. "What is it? What's going on?"

"There's this safe," I told him. Instantly, I felt on the verge of tears.

"A safe?"

"Yeah, a safe." I repeated the farmer's story, the iron box in the red Virginia clay, pulsing like a heart just beneath the tawny grass, waiting to be dug up and split open.

"That farmer—that old guy," my father asked, "he really doesn't remember?"

"No, he doesn't remember! He doesn't!"

My father was silent.

"That fucker's lying," he shouted. "No one just puts a safe back in the ground."

"He said he did."

"I don't believe it."

"He said he was frustrated. He tried to open it."

"Goddamn it! I would have gotten it open. It's not that hard."

"It isn't?"

"No. It's easy. Son of a bitch, I wonder what was in it. What a fucking idiot!"

"Yeah," I said. "He's an idiot."

"That's right," he told me. "He's a goddamn fucking idiot."

I laughed. Then he asked how things were going. I talked a bit about school and stupid teachers and fishing and what I was eating these days. There was a long silence, and I realized that this was the moment when he would ask the questions that made my mother angry—what our phone number was or where we lived. But he just cleared his throat and told me he loved me. I said that I loved him, and we hung up.

I put my forehead against the hot plastic of the phone.

Had I betrayed her? I hadn't told him our number or home address. He hadn't asked. He'd seemed genuinely interested in the safe—and with good reason! But then I grit my teeth. If he hadn't been so crazy, we could have stayed. We wouldn't be here, in a trailer park. Did I hate him? She was terrified of him. There had been the night by the ferry. He'd knocked out the man and broken the woman's jaw, and I'd seen the bleeding scratches on his face, the blood on his hands.

This newness—the thrill of this new world—had worn off. Like one of those fat football halfbacks in remedial ed, the blazing sun pushed me to the ground and pulled my pockets inside out and gave me a kick. I dragged myself home, but that night I couldn't sleep, wondering if I hated him, wondering what was in the safe, or how he knew that safes were easy to open. He and I could dig it up and open it. Inside, there'd be something amazing.

Behind our trailer was dense, tufted, vine-hung undergrowth, the sort of weedy, stunted forest where, in movies, dead bodies were found. I crouched on the red clay bank of a river whose current moved with the slowness of a seeping wound. Pinwheels of oil and bits of trash and leaves decorated the surface. It looked like wet asphalt after a storm.

I could feel it in my bones—something terrible was going to happen any day now.

A hundred snakes were going to bite me. I'd stumble home, bloated blue with poison, my tongue as big as a wet hand towel, my eyes chunks of melting violet Jell-O. I would die and my mother would weep, and my father would say sorry.

I already had poison ivy blisters around my ankles and wrists and neck. I'd known I was going to get it. Soon I would cut my hand by accident.

The red pocketknife he'd sent in his latest box of gifts had *Vancouver* printed on the side. I chose a stick from the shore and began paring away its branches to make a spear so that I could kill a poisonous snake and inspect its fangs. I'd keep the skull next to my bed as a reminder, and this would make me mean. No one would fuck with me anymore. I sawed at the wood, the blade close to my hand as I waited for the moment it would slip.

"Fuck," I growled. I'd finished and hadn't cut myself.

I grabbed the crotch of my pants and pulled them up and squatted, heels in the mud as I waited for a son-of-a-bitch snake to come and fuck with me.

"Deni!" My mother was calling my name. I dropped the spear. I snapped the knife shut and ran back toward the trailer.

My brother and sister were inside, wrangling over toys that had just arrived. My father mailed them to a PO box my mother kept so that he wouldn't know where we lived—"Not that it would matter," she'd told me. "He could just wait for me there if he wanted. That worries me sometimes." He'd been sending packages crammed, with toys often, and she raged that he was giving us hundreds of dollars' worth of junk but no money for food or winter clothes.

"Wait for me!" I shouted and slid like a baseball player into the mess of torn packaging. My name had been written on a box with the photo of a Formula 1 racer.

"Mine, fuckers!" I hollered as I grabbed it.

"Deni, stop swearing," my mother said.

I didn't look at her. With a few strokes, I shredded the box. The remote-controlled car was bright red, and I slapped it to prove to myself that it was the real thing. When I put it on the floor and pressed the handset, it zoomed across the carpet and slammed into the wall.

"Whoa!" I shouted. "Check out its power!"

"Guys," my mother called. "I want you to meet someone."

A short, gray-haired man had appeared in the trailer suddenly, like a ghost.

"This is Dickie," she said.

He had the coarse face of a drinker, the wire glasses of a smart kid, and cramped biceps like G.I. Joe. His black Camaro was outside, and to my amazement, he sat at the table, lit up a Winston, and held it loosely in his lips, squinting through the smoke like a withered Marlon Brando.

"What's the goodies you got there?" he asked.

"Presents from my father," I said.

He blinked and glanced at my mother.

"Wait a sec. I forgot I brought something myself."

He went to the Camaro and came back carrying a Styrofoam package of chicken. I'd read a book in which a country boy took a pullet to a brothel, and from Dickie's expression, I half expected my mother to dance around in her bra.

But we were suckers. We gathered around the stove as she performed her alchemy—the flabby, translucent chicken breasts becoming prime white pieces the likes of which we rarely saw. The cramped kitchen smoked up with the fleshy reek of a truck stop, the sizzling as loud as rain on the trailer's metal roof.

I would have felt grateful, but Dickie ate quickly, and I was just emptying my plate when he speared the last morsel from the pan. I wanted to jab my fork in his face.

"Are you a window washer?" I asked, curious to see how many toes he had.

"What?" my mother said and explained that he worked for a phone company and she'd met him on a blind date. Afterward, she told us to go to our rooms.

"Okay," I said and took my book bag. But I left the red racer on, parked under the table.

I slouched to my room and sat on my bed and waited, holding the handset. My brother began his homework but glanced at me. I grinned. He raised an eyebrow.

Though the walls were thin as milk carton, the eavesdropping wasn't great. Dickie made small talk. He told my mother he'd had eight coffees while hanging out at the watercooler. She said, "Oh." I wished she'd tell him something shocking about my father—why she was so afraid and why we lived in Virginia. But she didn't. Then it got real quiet.

When the silence lasted almost a minute, I hit the accelerator on the remote control.

The engine made a zinging sound, the car banged into a wall, and my mother screamed.

I stuck my head out the door and looked at them and said, "Heh, heh." "Outside! Go outside!" she shouted.

Dickie was smiling his yellow teeth at me, but his eyes were as still and unentertained as nailheads.

"Boys," he said, and cleared his throat and swallowed.

Evicted, I took my remote-controlled car into the early evening. I revved it along the street, making it do swift 180s and 360s.

Normally, I didn't think much of the toys. They arrived, and I played with them until I got bored. But the car impressed me, its engine powerful, and I knew that my father had gone out of his way. This bugged me. If he really was bad, then why should I accept these presents?

More than six months had gone by since we'd left, and I'd never imagined that my mother would find another man. Whenever I thought of my father, I got angry, then remembered that I loved him. What was he doing now? Living in the same house, watching TV by himself, eyes cold and unfriendly? An image came to mind of him in a field, standing expressionless like a statue I'd seen in a book on archaeology, a figure alone in a vast desert, the face almost worn away. Nothing about him had ever made sense. He was too hard to think about, and I wanted to forget him. But the red car zoomed along the street, hopping when it struck cracks. It was a pretty amazing present. Why couldn't he be all good or all evil, like in a fantasy novel, not this mishmash of confused feelings?

A hunched, slightly bowlegged boy approached, head swiveling as he looked for the source of the car's shrill rev. His hair was buzzed close in the front and at the sides, long in the back. His squat face, blemished and sprouting a patchy beard, made his bug-eyes seem all the more prominent. Dickie must have looked like this when he was a boy.

He stopped, his gaze following the zigzags and straightaways of the red racer, his head moving like that of a cat watching a bird.

"You're gonna give me that car," he blurted.

"What?"

"I'm gonna take it."

I pushed the antenna down in the handset and went to stand next to the car.

"My dad gave it to me," I said. "You're going to have to fight me if you want it."

He appeared to consider this, his little whiskery face chewing at the thought.

"Well then," he said, "I'm gonna go get my daddy's gun and shoot you."

I picked up the car and ran. I entered the trailer as Dickie and my mother were kissing, one of his hands reaching into her blouse.

"They're going to shoot me!" I shouted.

I raced for my room, leaped into bed, and closed my eyes, clutching the car, its hot engine against my chest.

CROSSING WIDE SPACES

Not long after my mother met Dickie, we all got hepatitis A from devouring a dip that had soured for days on my aunt's table. While my mother was at work, Dickie showed up and took us to his house, jauntily saying that we'd be better off under his care. That evening, she picked us up in a fury, hair disheveled, the first pallor of illness in her face.

"How dare you take my children without my permission!"

"Hey, hey, I'm sorry—"

"No, don't you think for a second you know what's best for them. If you want to help, you ask me. You call me. I'll tell you where they belong."

He kept saying *please* and *sorry*, something my father never would have done. I expected her to throw him out, but he stayed, taking care of us, doing what she asked. Not long after, we moved in with him, into a brick rambler near Bealeton, a town that was little more than the intersection of two highways, a 7-Eleven, and a makeshift flea market with booths of pirated heavy-metal cassettes, secondhand tools, and Elvis memorabilia. Thirty feet of lawn separated our house from Route 28, and the fields beyond our backyard were overgrown, strewn with trash, and slated to be razed for a shopping center.

My mother, who'd never married, because my father had refused, tied the knot with Dickie in a courthouse pit stop, their only expenditures a ring and a new dress. Over the next three years, she accompanied him to annual sales conferences in New Orleans and Ocean City. He had two weeks a year for vacation, and we visited his family farm near Canton, Ohio, where his nephew had his uniform number shaved into his crew cut and I learned to make a muffler out of beer cans. The men fished at night, drinking as they jacklighted carp, shooting them with a bow and arrow. Whenever I expressed boredom, Dickie handed me an ancient bolt-action rifle and sent me to eliminate groundhogs, whose holes could break a horse's leg, though the pastures had long been unused, given over to a few rusted oil jacks that wearily raised and lowered their prehistoric birds' heads.

The only constant those years was the van. We didn't eat meals together, so we never seemed a family more than when we were on the road. If Dickie drove, we became prisoners, the van suddenly a box, a fight brewing, electricity in the air as before a summer storm. But like my father, he couldn't handle it, complaining that the wheel had too much play and felt like driving a boat. My mother sailed it between homes and school and work, used it as a bus for a day care where she worked, and refused offers by a local mechanic who wanted its massive engine for his race car. Her obese coworker at IBM broke the back of the passenger seat, and from then on we drove with my mother sitting up and the passenger reclined, our conversations looking like therapy sessions.

Sometimes, from the back, I stared down on cars piddling along behind. One was a state trooper's on Interstate 66. Remembering my father's stories, I gave him the finger, and he pulled us over, inspected the van, and questioned my mother about its origins and registration.

Often, though, I waited for the feeling I loved: not just the motion of the highway, but a luxurious sense of loss. Sitting in the back—always in summer, with a window open, air whipping through and stirring up dust—I smelled the places we'd lived, the hay and grain for the farm, the stacks of fresh pine for building stalls. As we traveled, it seemed as if, for as long as I could recall, I'd wanted to set out and never return.

When I was thirteen, I walked to school, relishing this time alone. After rainy nights, passing cars fanned moisture against my face. Or warm afternoons, I took a shortcut home through farmland, breaking dry stalks in my fingers, staring out over yellow fields gone to seed, the tall, rangy trees on windbreaks like images from the African savannah.

But wandering the halls, I cautiously eyed the clusters: rednecks and metalheads, preps and nerds, army brats with "Nuke Kaddafi" pins on their jean jackets. Sometimes I hung out with white kids, sometimes with black kids. Eventually, they all told me I was weird and to go away. My mother's talk about purpose made me surly. She'd forced me to take French 1, and even though it was ridiculously easy, whenever the teacher asked me a question, I'd say, "I don't know," then shrug and look off. I had no idea why I'd even learned this language that my father hated or what it had to do with his life in the first place. Nights, I dreamed that long black hair covered my body and I played football, though in reality I couldn't. My mother had banned me from violent sports not only because it was for brutes but because we had no insurance.

Only when I read or wrote did I feel calm. Was it like this for my siblings? My brother played video games as soon as he came home from school, his blinds drawn, his room a dim cavern. My sister sang behind her closed door, listening to the radio.

It seemed as if none of us had stopped changing since we'd crossed the border. My mother was different each time I blinked: cutoff jean shorts, a yellow halter top, a tight perm, then, before a dinner with Dickie, a narrow blue dress with heart-shaped mesh that showed a hint of cleavage, her hair wavy. The next morning she'd have on pleated trousers and a tight-waisted blouse, a steel barrette at the back of her head. Sometimes she talked differently, laughed differently, as if trying out a new voice.

"You all have a purpose in life," she reminded us when she convoked an evening talk—a recent idea of hers, since communication was important.

As she had for years, she spoke not to middling students but seminal thinkers. My sister had music in her blood. She could pick up an instrument she'd never seen and play a song as if there'd been cellos and pianos in the womb and she'd been waiting all these years to find them again. My brother was a computer genius. He'd befriended a few rural pioneers of the Commodore 64 and scored among the best in the state math exam. Myself, I'd be an archaeologist and learn as many languages as Heinrich Schliemann, who discovered Troy.

Later that night, Dickie disagreed.

"I had lots of dreams, too," he confided, "but that stuff just doesn't happen to everybody. I wanted to be a pilot. Look where I am now. Besides, you're lazy."

I shrugged. Normally I argued with him, but maybe he was right.

"I saw you rebuild that radio the other day," he said. "You'd be a good mechanic. You should talk to the guy at the junkyard and see if he'd hire you."

Life was so pathetic that I couldn't formulate a counterargument. In the new age, everything would be better, but I was getting tired of waiting for Armageddon.

"I have something important to say," my mother told us at our next evening talk. "There's a custody battle between your father and me. He's trying to get the right to see you, and I've offered reasonable terms. But he's refused, so I'm asking for full custody and no rights for him. I don't trust him. He might take you away and run off."

She paused and very slowly looked at each of us in turn. "How do you feel about this?"

None of us spoke. Whenever she mentioned my father, a sense of danger hung about us. He seemed unreal now, like something from long ago, the memory of a summer storm with its hail and hot rain and thunder. When I thought of him, I had the same disorientation that comes after a dream—not sure what day it was, what time, the uneasy sense that there was something I was trying to understand. At the borders of my life—in the highway fading to the gray smudge of distance, in the junior high rules that could be broken with a curse or a fight—I sensed him, as if he stood just out of sight, waiting.

The next morning, in English class, we had a substitute teacher, a goateed young prep from DC. I was reading a book about the discovery of ancient cities, and after class, I loitered and told him that I planned on being an archaeologist and a writer.

"No way, man," he said, "don't do that. Archaeology is boring. A friend of mine's at the Smithsonian now, but he used to be in the desert. He said it was the most boring thing ever. He was out there four years, living off warm martinis and antidepressants."

Though I guessed antidepressants might be like antifreeze, I was pretty sure that martinis were a sort of rodent—maybe small ones. I'd read about early North American fur trappers shipping martini pelts back to Europe, and I had no intention of eating such things just so I could be an archaeologist. Besides, I liked writing better.

In the clamor of the cafeteria, I sat with my notebook. I didn't know how a custody battle worked, so I couldn't write about it. I'd tried a story about running away and daydreamed constantly about fleeing school or home, but I realized I had no idea what was out there, what would really happen when I left.

My mother and brother often exchanged fantasy novels or knocked at my door, offering me tomes with half-naked elfin princesses on the cover. Like drug pushers, they kept at it until I got addicted and had to finish each epic series with them. There was always an impending confrontation between good and evil, a world that would be made barren and empty or that would be born again, and this appealed to me, that something definite would happen. But above all, in fantasy, you could just set out, and life was a little like my father's adventures: strangers and random fights and new landscapes. Briefly, my mind wandered to what else he might have done, to what could possibly make my mother feel that he was so dangerous.

Mandy, a pretty brunette with feathered hair and a short roller-skating skirt, sat nearby, and I told her I was writing a fantasy story about a wanderer with no identity. She just forced a smile, lifting her cheeks as if squinting into the sun, then turned away.

Maybe my mother was wrong and I didn't have a gift or purpose. I wanted to do something, anything. But even if I wrote my story now, nothing would change.

At the next table, two boys were talking about sex, one saying that the girl, a cheerleader, had put her feet behind her head. In my notebook, I began to sketch a tiny naked woman even though I'd probably never see one in the flesh. Ever.

After school, while other boys were busy destroying their uninsured knees playing football, I sat outside, penciling more naked women, dark little graphite V's between spread legs, tits like U's with a dot in them.

The women were pretty realistic, I thought. I was getting excited looking at them. Maybe this was my gift.

On my way home, I passed through the makeshift flea market. When I stopped to look at Quiet Riot and Metallica bootlegs, the man there noticed my notebook. He grabbed it and called the guys manning the booths of tools and Elvis statues. They laughed and snorted, pausing to wipe their mouths with the backs of their hands.

"I'll give you ten cents for each page you bring me," the bearded, overall-wearing proprietor of the tool booth said. "But I like variety, so keep them good."

Each day after school, I brought him a few pages, but soon thereafter the booths were shut down to make way for the shopping center, and the porn market dried up.

Dickie was baking cookies for an office party. It was the only thing he could cook, and he had a pair of red socks, like ceremonial trappings, that he wore for this activity. They had rubber grips so he didn't slip on the linoleum, as if baking were a high-risk procedure.

I was hanging around because I'd heard him and my mother whispering about the custody battle. Given that I'd unsuccessfully eavesdropped on the details, I thought maybe I could pry something from him.

"What do you think of the court case?" I asked while the cookies were puffing up in the oven. But he was opening a box he'd received in the mail.

"Check these out." He showed me dozens of ziplock bags containing white powder. His father had sent them.

"Cool," I said. "You're dealing drugs."

"Hey, watch your mouth."

"Okay. What're they for?"

"Peeing."

"What?"

"Peeing while I'm in the car."

I knew that he carried coffee cans for the DC rush hour. He also kept a life-size doll that my mother had made for my sister, but he put it in the passenger seat so he could drive in the HOV lane. His job seemed to have robbed him of dignity. I'd always felt that adults had the freedom that I longed for, but now I was seeing how wrong I'd been.

He returned from the bathroom. The powder had turned to gel. Therefore, I deduced, the piss couldn't spill. He held the bag to the window, the sunset making his congealed urine blaze like million-year-old amber.

"Jeez," he said, "this is great stuff."

I wasn't sure why I was so determined to find out about the custody battle, but I sensed that there had to be more to it than what they'd told me. I almost never talked to my father, maybe once every six months, and when I did, he'd try to tell a few stories: about one of his dogs that ran away and how he spent a day wandering the woods until he found it dead next to some poisoned meat left out to kill wild animals; or about how he bought a van with an engine problem, smoke pouring from the muffler, and a stupid police officer stopped him and said he didn't want a van like that on his highway. My father told him, "It's not your highway. I'm not breaking the law, and you're keeping me from taking my van to get it fixed." The stupid cop left, and my father kept driving the van like that, the engine using almost as much oil as gas. I always got interested if he was telling stories, but when he stopped, we didn't have much to say. He sounded tired and far away, though memories of wildness lingered, our adventures so unlike my boring existence now. No one else had seemed so full of life.

"Do you think the court case is necessary?" I asked Dickie.

"I don't know," he said. He jiggled the bag of urine. "The military must have invented these for pilots. The military makes all the best stuff."

Since he wasn't answering questions about the custody case, I asked what it was like to be in the military.

"You're too much of a pussy for the army," he said.

"Yeah? Thanks. Did you ever kill anyone?"

"Just once," he said. "I was putting up telephone poles in Vietnam, and some guys came out of the woods and shot my partner. I shot them."

"Really?" I sat down, ready to be enthralled.

He put on his white mitts—the ones no one else was allowed to use — and took out the pan. When he made cookies for work, he didn't share. There was no point asking, though he paraded them around. He did this, I knew, because he was itching for a fight. Someone shat on him at the office, and he came home hankering to shit on us. My mother had warned me that he had a bad temper but a good heart, as if this were a complicated medical condition.

"That's it?" I said.

"Huh?"

"You just shot them?"

"Yeah." Then he told a story about the friend who'd been shot, how one time they were drunk and goofing off. The friend had accidentally stabbed Dickie through the hand with a pair of needle-nose pliers.

"Why were you putting up telephone poles in Vietnam?" I interrupted.

"Because they needed them."

"Is that how you got into the phone business?"

"No. That's just a coincidence."

I sighed. The story sucked. There was no hope of getting details — about the custody battle or my father or even what must have been a grisly war scene.

The Pledge of Allegiance and pickup basketball, pep rallies, fights and cigarettes, cheap beer snuck into football games, a black cheerleader who disappeared and haunted us from the backs of milk cartons. Life had taken a reliable shape.

The summer before ninth grade, I worked any job I could find: mucking stalls on a horse farm, checking fence lines for breaks and repairing them, bucking hay. Back among the tribal rivalries of the junior high, my improved girth won me some respect.

"Farm work will turn you into a man," Dickie told me when I visited him in his basement redoubt, and he confided what a badass he'd been at my age. "I stole cigarettes from my dad. If I had a date, I stole flowers from the graveyard. If someone messed with me, I hit him when he wasn't looking."

I nodded. I supposed that a sucker punch was kind of like stealing a punch.

"I have to go take care of my poor man's Corvette," he said in an at once self-deprecating and proud fashion, and he went outside to change the oil on his Datsun, which he'd bought after selling his Camaro.

Alone in the basement, I took a pack of his cigarettes from the carton on the shelf and went up to my room, where I put it in my book bag.

After school, to undo my reputation as a bookworm, I hung out under the overpass and shared the cigarettes. I befriended Travis and Brad, both metalheads, though Travis was a redneck and Brad an army brat who bragged about unverifiable sexual exploits from his years in Germany and liked to speculate about what had really happened to Hitler's bones. I asked about their fathers. Brad's was always at a military base. Travis's was on welfare and spent his days in a room with a single upholstered chair and walls of narrow shelves that he'd built himself. He'd filled them with cassettes in plastic cases, each one containing a sermon. He sat in the chair for hours, listening to the word of God.

Sometimes, I told them my father's stories about fighting over a woman or driving a Model T on railways, then mixed and matched, taking away the Model T's brakes or having my father bite his enemy's nose. Speaking, I felt that weightlessness, the way words made everything possible. Brad and Travis saw my eyes get feverish and laughed. We got into pushing contests with our puffed-out chests, heads cocked back, about six inches between our eyes as we reeled back and forth, looking like roosters.

Weekends, we roamed the county, drinking what we could shoplift, getting into fights. We went to carnivals where the scene was so country that the babies crying sounded like part of the music. Hayseeds stumbled past with the swagger and eye-bulge squint of cartoon hound dogs as we drank ourselves sober from the spigot near the refreshment booth, splashing our faces. We stood in the shadows comparing knives.

Walking home late, I let the wind off passing trucks buffet me. When a solitary rig drew close, I timed its approach and stepped into the highway, just far enough that I was inches from it and could see the shaking, rushing metal blur past my face. My heart hammered, a thin acrid sweat breaking on my skin and drying just as quickly in the night air.

I'd been thinking of my father more and more. In his stories, he hitchhiked or drove cross-country, took dangerous jobs in the wilderness, or fought strangers to protect himself. No one else I'd met had a life like that. If he was living here instead of me, bored of school and tired of being at home, would he just stick his thumb out and catch the first ride and see where it took him, then figure out how to survive?

Eventually, even the highway quieted but for the occasional car sweeping down from the overpass, its headlights dwindling filaments against the empty dark.

I crossed through the unlit field behind my house, having forgotten it had been bulldozed, deep trenches cut into the earth for the cement footers of the shopping center, so that I had to move cautiously, as if infiltrating a war zone.

Daily, Dickie watched me when he thought I wasn't looking. I could see him contemplating the potential excesses of my badass behavior.

"This guy started a fight," I told him and described some pushing and how I'd held the kid's arms until he backed off.

Dickie nodded. He was clearly undecided.

"I've been there before," he said.

He'd told me about getting in trouble at school. Detention. Drinking and fights. Soon, my exploits would match his, and he'd see me as a badass in my own right. Maybe then he'd tell me what my mother wouldn't about the custody battle. It seemed unfair that he of all people knew more about my father than I did.

Walking the halls of the junior high, I held my shoulders stiffly, an electric tension in my spine. I felt that if I looked right or left, I'd go crazy, swinging and kicking.

So that I'd be late to class, I waited in the hall, hoping the intentional tardiness might draw the girls. But everyone saw me as a bookworm acting out. The rednecks shook their heads. There was a rural caste, and I confounded them. Still, I was diligent.

I slouched in my chair, wearing two-dollar shoplifted sunglasses with the tag still on the reflective lens. I took out a mechanical pencil and leaned over to the girl next to me.

"I need my fix," I whispered.

I clicked the shaft of lead out until it looked like a syringe. Then I slapped the inside of my arm. I had an audience now. I held the button and pressed the tip against a fat vein. The lead slid back into the canister, appearing to stab my flesh. I rolled my eyes and kicked my legs and whispered, "Oh yeah, baby, oh yeah," before I died in a blissful OD.

"Guess what?" I told Dickie that evening, leaning against his tool shelf.

He stood at his workbench, spraying WD-40 lubricant into the receiver of the telephone. It had been staticky, and he thought this might help. "Yeah?"

"I got detention. I got paddled in school."

"What?" He turned toward me.

I explained how the vice-principal had hit me three times across the backs of the thighs with a large wooden paddle drilled with holes for aerodynamics. School rumor had it he'd been in the big leagues.

I was about to describe my indifference after the punishment, how I'd said, "Whatever," and slouched out, but Dickie's lips drew back from nicotine-stained teeth.

He shoved me, and the back of my head hit the wall. He lunged and gripped my throat, pinning me there. My face pulsed, the room darkening and his furious grin expanding, caught as if in a bubble. He squeezed, digging his fingers, his palm crushing down on my windpipe. My eyes strained as if they would pop.

"You little shit," he said. "You need to learn a thing or two. If you ever act out again, I'll kick your ass."

The skin of my face felt like it would split.

"And I know you're taking cigarettes. If I ever catch you, I'll beat you senseless."

But he still wasn't done. I was sputtering, my tongue between my teeth.

"Not so tough, huh? When you're ready, you come get me. We'll see who wins."

The instant he let me go, I ran up the stairs. I was coughing, holding my throat. I slammed my door behind me, then stood there, panting.

My father sent cards often, and in each he wrote his number, as if afraid we hadn't received the previous one, or maybe because it often changed. I found one in the mess on my floor.

I opened the window and let myself down, then ducked across the yard and ran to the 7-Eleven.

But even as he was answering, I realized that I couldn't ask him for help, because he was crazy. And yet how much worse than everyone else could he really be?

"Hey, Deni," he said, sounding confused and sleepy.

"Hey," I said. He asked how I was doing, and I said, "Okay. Everything's going pretty good. I don't like school, but things are okay."

I spoke as if nothing had happened. If I told him what Dickie had done, he'd come here and kill Dickie. I knew that with more certainty than anything I'd ever known.

Since I had no idea what to say, I told him that I'd pierced my ear. I said this as if it were the most natural choice, and he said, "Yeah, that's popular now, isn't it?"

The truth was that a month before, I'd been at the 7-Eleven with Dickie, and the pimply cashier had a pierced ear. Dickie had told me that if I ever did this, he'd kick me out. The next week, at the mall, I had it done, and when I returned home, he stared but said nothing. In homeroom, my teacher made me wear a Band-Aid on my earlobe, and I told my father this last detail. He coughed and said, "That's stupid. What an idiot. Why do people do such stupid stuff?" Then he was quiet. He was just listening, waiting.

Pressure was building in my chest. I had so much to ask. The breathless desperation was like the desire for motion that made me walk the highway just to watch semis pass in the dark.

"Wouldn't you like to come see me?" he said.

I didn't answer. This was the question he used to ask when my mother drove my brother, my sister, and me to a phone so that we could talk to him. He'd say this, and one of us would start crying, and she'd take the phone from our hand and hang it up.

When he spoke again, he sounded drunk. He sounded like he might cry.

"I held you in my hands."

"What?"

"When you were born," he said. "I delivered you." He'd told this story often years before. We'd be night fishing for catfish, and he'd glance over, his look a mix of fondness and concern, and he'd tell me about the umbilical cord around my neck and how angry he'd been at my mother for not wanting to go to the hospital. He'd held me and massaged my chest and blown into my mouth over and over until I began to breathe. That he was telling this now made me feel that he knew everything about me.

"I wanted you to be born in the hospital," he said, "but your mother had those goddamn ideas of hers. She was afraid of doctors. She hated everything that was modern."

He hesitated and said that on the day of my birth, she'd left the kitchen a mess and he'd had to wash a pot to boil the scissors. He used to tell me this detail when I was little, and that she hadn't washed the dishes in time for my birth always seemed grievous. But I smiled now. It was strange that he told the story the same way, that he hadn't changed.

"She never was much good in the house," he said. "But I'm the one who brought you back to life, goddamn it. I held you in my hands."

That night, in a dream, I was alone in the valley. A bear came toward me across the fields, and I ran, calling out to my father. But there was only our distant farmhouse and sheds, dark against the land that unfurled below the mountains.

In detention, I hunched over *The Grapes of Wrath*.

My history teacher had told me to read it for extra credit. Forget archaeology's scurrying martinis and engine-fluid beverages. The bliss of desert solitude, of crossing wide spaces, could be had with no profession at all. I could be a drifter! The more I wanted to set out, the more I thought about my father. As Steinbeck's characters broke laws and wandered the continent, I tried to understand what drove them. What had driven him? What drove me? This mystery gripped my brain.

"Everyone pay attention!" It was Mrs. Henley, our Irish detention monitor. Boys claimed she smoked pot. She was a poet and had delinquents give what she called poetry slams.

"Get out a sheet of notebook paper. If you say one word crosswise, I'll send you to the office for a paddling so quick your head will spin. Now write whatever you're angry about. Write what's making you crazy. Don't worry about grammar and that stuff."

After we finished, she stood in the back of the room in her baggy housedress, her cheeks puffy as if from sleep, loose strands of hair hanging about them.

Large boys with faces smudged from shop class read poems like "Runaway," "Juvie," or "Foster Home." I wanted to write about how, reading Steinbeck, I'd realized all I didn't know about my father and his past, his family, and his reasons for everything he'd done. But I'd be embarrassed to tell the other kids these things, so I scrawled a short poem called "After the End of the World."

We walked to the lectern with lowered heads, appearing angry, and we listened to each other without looking.

I clutched my poem in my fist so that I had to uncrumple the sheet to read.

> desolation
> a vast space
> crossing through
> alone

I went and sat down. No one looked at me.

A big farm boy with shoulders like a beam got up and read: "We pass like grain through a sieve, a few held back and thrown away."

I clenched my fists and had to think about my foot in its sweaty sock to keep from tears.

After detention, I caught up with him outside and socked him in the arm.

"What the fuck?" he hollered.

"Fucking poet," I said.

He shoved me and drove me into the grass, the inside of his arm squeezing my neck. I jabbed my elbow repeatedly at his gut and threw a few punches over my shoulder, with the same awkward motion as scratching my back, but kept missing his face.

Then I stopped swinging, and we both lay there, gasping for air.

The custody battle was over.

"I won," she told us. "The judge denied him even visiting rights." Legally, my brother, my sister, and I had to wait until we were eighteen to see him, but she thought fifteen more reasonable. She said we could then decide for ourselves.

That evening, I sprayed WD-40 in my door hinges. She was calling her friends, and I crept out, lingering at the top of the stairs, then slinking down to her room like a predator.

"It's because of his past," she said. "He's not even allowed across the border."

I was so excited that it took all of my self-control to make it back to my room quietly. Not allowed across the border? Nothing could possibly sound more menacing or mysterious. Was I dreaming? I had the impression that my life was suddenly as exciting as I'd wanted.

And on my next outing, she said, ". . . he lost because of his record . . ."

Record? I hovered on the steps, trying to make out other words, my heart beating faster and faster. Did she mean like something with the police? Was he that bad? Or was it just because of the fight he'd been in at the ferry crossing? I crept back to my room and shut the door.

Never had I more desperately wished that the powers of the mind were real—that I could read her thoughts and know the truth about my father. But humans were so hateful that the very fabric of society depended on not knowing what went on in other people's heads.

I sat at my desk. Why did I even need to write? Behind everything I wanted, I sensed an impulse, deep inside me, like light filling the emptiness, a longing so rooted, so absolute in my certainty of it, that I pictured holy men in fantasy novels lighting fires to sacred powers. I knew that the messiness of life could be made perfect in a poem. All the lost places and people could be saved in a story. And just as stories reached into the past, they opened out into my future, as if I wrote to show myself who I could be. I got up and put on my shoes. I lifted the window screen and swung myself to the ground too quickly, my hand catching on the aluminum frame. Blood ran along my palm as I crouched in the dark, holding it, willing the pain away. An image came to me, startlingly vivid.

When I was six, my father had cut his hand working on a mower. I went into the bathroom to see him cleaning the wound. I climbed onto the toilet seat to look into the sink. There was the surprise, the pleasure at the sight of his cut, the way his fingers worked around it as blood fell in ribbons, darkening the water. Neither of us spoke, both absorbed in the slow, serious work.

Then he opened the gash with his fingers and showed it to me, letting the blood rush up to clean it before he closed it with his thumb.

It was a summer day, the fragrance of cut grass and mower exhaust through the window screens, and the brilliance of his blood and how I loved him.

There was something else I had to understand.

Tractor-trailer rigs idled on the side of the highway not far from the 7-Eleven. Diesel exhaust misted and blew past the cab lights.

"Hey," I said to a man waddling back to his rig. He was clutching four bags of chips, several large bottles of Dr Pepper, and a grease-stained paper bag.

"Yeah?"

"You going to Memphis?" I asked.

"Sorry, kid, I'm just heading to Roanoke."

To each trucker, I asked the same question, keeping my bandaged left hand in my pocket. I was almost fourteen, but I claimed to be sixteen and homeless. I was going to Memphis to stay with a cousin. I'd seen the city on the map, not so far away and yet in the heart of the country, flush with the Mississippi, which cut the continent in half.

Most of the truckers said they were heading elsewhere, but a husband and wife team heard me out. As I spoke, they gave each other dubious looks. Then he shrugged.

"What the hell," he said. He had sparse red hair and a scar like a divot in his cheek, another above his eyebrow. He'd done worse himself, I knew. He understood.

The tractor trailer had Oklahoma plates. The man said we'd be passing through Memphis in eleven or twelve hours. My mother had long ago ceded my independence, letting me be away entire weekends so long as I showed up on Sunday night. She might be angry that I hadn't told her where I was going, but that wasn't unusual anymore.

I kept track of signs as we gusted down Route 17 past Warrenton, then caught the ramp west onto Interstate 66 for a short jaunt before heading south on I-81.

Past the dark Appalachian ranges and vales of scattered house lights, through Virginia into Tennessee, I sensed the continent spreading before us. The man's wife slept in the cab's bunk as he shared his sandwiches with me and I invented stories about my cousin in Memphis. I told him how my stepfather had kicked me out, which seemed inevitable, written in my destiny.

Dawn breathed pale light over the countryside, as if we were gazing through misted glass. But no matter how I thrilled at all I saw, fear rumbled in my gut. I ate chicken-salad sandwiches until the cab smelled like mayonnaise and the man said, "Well, let's save some for later." I told stories of every near fight I'd had, every teacher and kid who'd done me wrong. Then I hesitated, certain that I had other stories, better ones, but not sure what they were, which ones were important enough or would sound true.

The sun flared at the horizon, not quite behind us, the light warm against my cheek, and as we drove, the landscape outside my window flickered beyond the tall roadside trees like the frames of an old film, clipped moments of stillness stitched together.

A few hours later, the woman joined us in the cab, the pouches under her eyes so swollen it looked as if her eyeballs were riding in boats.

"Where do we drop you off, kid?" she asked and drank coffee, horked and swallowed. It crossed my mind that my jawing could have made it hard for her to sleep.

"Soon," I said, squinting at the next roadside sign. Inside my skull, anxiety began to wail like feedback at the end of a heavy-metal song, when the guy in torn jeans shoved the electric guitar in front of the speakers. I pretended to recognize the names on signs.

"Not much further . . ." I wet my lips, wondering how I'd get back. It seemed as if there had been only three major turns, aside from some merging and interconnecting interstates near Knoxville. I could manage all that. I was sure I could.

The couple glanced at each other. A look of worry flitted between them, and the feedback behind my eyes ramped up.

"Here. This one," I said.

The engine chugged slow, and the man ground a gear, pulling the rig to a stop just beyond the exit.

Terrified, gut cramping, I thanked them and got down quickly to hide my fear. The truck jerked forward, mud flaps swaying, embossed with silver reclining nudes. The square end of the trailer diminished and melted into the heat lines over the interstate.

Where in the hell was the river? I was expecting a canyon, a rift between two worlds that I'd pictured on the map, like the long zipper on the front of a woman's jeans.

Heat poured off the concrete. It was everywhere, entrance and exit ramps, pickup trucks and cars drifting onto it with weekend laxity. I craned my neck as if the river might be beyond a guardrail. No luck. I had to hurry back.

I could feel the pressure of my feet against the ground as my heart beat vertigo into my bloodstream. My chest ached and I wanted to cry. I thought of my father's stories, journeys across the continent, winters logging in the north or mining in Alaska. Had I finally done something almost as incredible? My limited life, this body waiting on strength, it all seemed a sort of detention, a prison, and I was sick of waiting to be like him.

The heavy-metal reverb tore up my head as I ran along the ramp and crossed the overpass to the other side. I jumped a concrete barrier and began thumbing.

It took an hour to get a ride, again in a rig, and little by little, I calmed. I'd made it to Memphis, or close at least. I was heading home. Just three simple turns. That's all it would take. As the havoc in my skull drew to a close, I started to talk again. I described the father I hadn't seen in almost four years. At first, I said just a few things: that I was wandering the country like him, making my way. But hour after hour, as I had years before on the playground, telling tall tales, finding the past in snapshots, I discovered what I wanted to say. I put the pieces together as I spoke them. He'd traveled. We were the same. We'd been the same in so many ways, and now I was drinking and fighting. I couldn't help but break rules. He'd broken them, too. The words my mother had spoken over the phone fit together. He wasn't allowed across the border. He had his past. His record. After we'd left, the nights that he'd called and made threats, I'd overheard my mother's whispers and understood the gravity of her fear. I knew that whatever he'd done was serious. It had to be. He'd beaten a man up. He must have been to prison and done terrible, amazing things, and I would, too. That was being a man. That was freedom. Just hearing myself, I felt wounded, older, and stronger.

"What did he do?" the trucker asked.

"I don't know. I only know it was bad. He isn't even allowed in the United States."

My lack of knowledge seemed to satisfy him. It had the ring of truth, and he nodded solemnly.

Eventually, he let me off, and I caught another ride and continued telling stories, finding the same truths, becoming more certain. I described that early memory of the fight on the Indian reservation, seeing him with blood on his face.

The sun was falling like a burning cataclysm, the immolation of a fantasy realm, the horizon as red as sacrifice. I got off at the ramp to I-66. I was almost there. I caught a ride and was dropped off at Route 17. Three hours in the dark, I walked until someone slowed, lighting me up with their brights, no doubt studying me, making sure I was safe.

I'd done it, something worth bragging about. It was hard to believe. I arrived home a few hours before dawn on Sunday. I couldn't go inside yet. I had to pretend I was coming back from a friend's house.

The lock on the van's passenger door had been broken for over a year. I went into the back, opened the couch into a bed, and lay on it. The fabric smelled of dirt and hay and sawdust, of dogs and horses and sweet oats, of the far-off valley and the homes in between. I put my face to it and cried.

DISCOVERING FIRE

I had been nursing the question for days, waiting to be alone with my mother, and now we were, driving home.

"Was André ever in prison?" I asked, trying to sound nonchalant.

She didn't speak for a moment.

"Why are you asking about him? Have you seen him?"

"No," I said quickly, not wanting to scare her. "I was just thinking about him. It made sense to me. He's been to prison, right?"

She appeared to consider this. Then she exhaled, a tired, controlled sigh, though she still didn't look at me.

"Yes," she said, "but just for small things."

"What small things?" I didn't believe her. Her words hardly matched her fear. I craved details, to be trusted with this knowledge.

She didn't answer, sitting primly at the wheel as we cruised Route 28. We passed overgrown fields, their slated destruction announced by billboards with the names of subdivisions.

She pulled into our driveway and killed the engine and stared ahead, the backyard's dusty yellow broken by a swath of green near the clothesline, where the septic system ran.

"I don't want to talk about this."

"I have a right to know."

She sighed, not moving, still staring straight ahead.

"Okay," she said. "Okay."

I didn't speak, afraid to interrupt her.

"Your father . . . he spent a lot of time in prison."

Her expression wasn't easily read, and I studied it, conscious that in some way I might be hurting her with my questions.

"What for?"

"I was going to tell you when you were older. He got in trouble before you or your brother were born. He robbed banks."

She turned in her seat. I was used to the way she gazed openly, searching my expression, trying to see what I'd been up to at school or if I was lying, but I showed nothing. My father was a bank robber. The truth was better than I'd expected. I felt as if I were reading the stories of gods and their progenitors. This was what I'd wanted, something that would set me apart forever.

That same day, she sat down with my brother and me. He listened intently, his masked expression no different than when he played computer games for hours, but I knew what she was saying must be affecting him. I'd snuck into his room to read his notebooks and had been startled by the emotions in his stories. Men paced the smooth floors of control towers or faced the inky darkness above futuristic cities, gazing out with rage and loneliness.

"What your father did is wrong," she told us, "but he's still your father."

I nodded, and when the discussion was finished, I got up and went to my room. I shut the door and stood with my back to it.

Bank robbery.

Never again would I care about chores and homework. No one could tell me what to do.

I closed my eyes and took a breath, my heart speeding, my body bracing for the rush of adrenaline as I pulled the mask over my face. He and I burst through the doors, sweeping pistols before us and sending everyone diving to the floor. As if in a cartoon, he glided across the lobby to the vault and, pulling on a handle like that of a microwave oven, swung it open. A very serious manager stepped out, holding before him a single white bag marked with a golden dollar sign.

"Fuck yeah!" my father shouted once we were in the car, the engine revving.

We escaped over dusty roads and desolate ranges, laughing, the wind in our hair.

This is how it worked, I knew. In fantasy or gritty American fiction, the best characters refused the laws of a weak, conformist society. They craved intensity and the unknown.

I opened my eyes. Starving, I hurried to the kitchen to see what was in the fridge. As I ate, I considered my new existence as if reading it in a book. I wanted to fight, to test myself and write about it. I would be a novelist and an outlaw.

Another card had arrived. It bore glittery words, "Thinking About You." Inside was his number, nothing else. As if in a movie about prison, I felt like an inmate who receives a gift in which the means of escape are hidden. I left the house and went down the highway to the 7-Eleven.

A storm was blowing in, the sky dark and the power lines swaying. Trucks slowed and chugged into turns where the highways intersected, and after I dialed collect, his voice came thinly onto the line.

We hadn't spoken in months. He sounded different, reserved and unsure of himself, nothing like what I'd imagined since my mother had confessed his crimes to us.

He asked how I was, and I told him, "I'm okay. I'm just sick of school."

"Oh," he said. He asked how my brother and sister were, and I said, "Okay." I talked a bit about rebuilding an old motorcycle I'd found in the barn where my mother kept her horses and a leather jacket I wanted. But then I ran out of things to say and we were silent for so long that I knew I had to tell him, that I had to share the only thing I could think about.

"Bonnie told me."

"She told you what?"

"About"—I said—"about your crimes."

He didn't speak.

Clouds were moving in, drawing evening with them.

"What did she tell you?"

"She didn't say much. I was the one who asked. I guess I already knew."

"You already knew what?"

"That you'd been to jail. I was proud of you. She said you robbed banks."

Again the long silence. Wind blew through the dust of the parking lot, knocking a crushed Styrofoam cup against the brick wall.

"She said that?" he asked, softly.

"I want to know about what you did."

"What I did?"

"I want to know everything. It's amazing. No one else has a father like you."

He was breathing into the receiver.

"What do you want to know?"

"About the banks. Did you only rob banks?"

"No."

"What else did you rob?"

"I . . ." He sighed. "Lots of things."

"Like what?"

"You want to know about this? You're proud?"

"It's amazing. I think it's amazing."

I'd been almost panting, my heartbeat too fast. I sensed how much of a stranger he was. Four years had gone by, and I'd imagined him as he was before, living in the same house, driving the same car. But from the way he spoke, the care with which he chose his words, I knew he'd changed.

"I robbed banks," he said. "It's true. I robbed a lot of banks. And jewelry stores."

"How many?"

"Maybe . . . I don't know . . . maybe fifty banks. Armed robbery wasn't a big deal. It was easy. I only did one bank burglary. That's different."

"What do you mean?"

"Burglary is when you go in at night and take everything. You go into the vault. Robbery is with a gun. Anyone can do that. But burglary takes brains."

The image of him with a gun, robbing a bank as if it were nothing, impressed me, but burglary didn't interest me at all.

"What about the jewelry stores?"

"Lots of them," he said as if to please me. "I unloaded what I got with the mob."

"The mob?"

"It's not that big of a deal. It's pretty common. I probably robbed—I don't know—fifty jewelry stores, too. It was like a job."

His voice became hoarse, and he coughed. I asked how bank robbery worked, and he told me about surveillance, knowing what time the armored truck came on payday. That's when the tellers had more money. He hesitated, clearing his throat, and said, "Anyway."

I could hardly breathe, hardly think of what to ask next. I had so many questions. I wanted him to speak, but he grew silent. Then the words came out of my mouth.

"Have you ever killed anyone?"

Rain had begun to fall, striking up the parking lot dust, the sky flat and low and gray, the wind strong.

"No," he said finally, his voice so hoarse he was almost whispering. "Listen, Deni, I got out of crime because of you guys. I wanted a family. I didn't want to go back to jail and not see my children. That's why I stopped."

"But it's amazing. I think it's amazing. No one else has a father like you."

The downpour began in force, gusting under the overhang, soaking me where I huddled at the phone. Lightning flared beyond the highway, illuminating the cluttered rooftops of a subdivision. Thunder shook the ground, and the line went dead.

I hung up and pulled my jean jacket over my head and ran home.

"Watch this," Brad said, hoisting a Coke bottle plugged with a burning rag. We'd filled it with the proportions of gasoline and dish soap necessary to make a good Molotov cocktail, according to what he claimed he'd learned during riots in Germany. Standing in a field, he hurled it against the weathered husk of a junked car, and fire spread along the door.

"See that?" he said to Travis and me. "The dish soap makes the gasoline stick. You get that stuff on your skin and you're going to burn to death."

Since my house was close to the junior high, we often walked there. Dickie commuted from DC and my mother had to pick up my brother and sister from their schools, so no one was around until six. We smoked Dickie's cigarettes and went through the materials that he compulsively bought for his crowded shop. We made flamethrowers out of spray cans of engine lubricant or paint. We put Styrofoam peanuts in jars of gasoline, concocting what we called homemade napalm. In overgrown fields, well out of sight of the highway, we set things ablaze. Bottles of rubbing alcohol and cans of spray paint wrapped with burning rags burst as we shot them with the .22 rifle I'd gotten for my fourteenth birthday. We filled an old TV tube with gasoline and ran into the trees as it exploded. We competed to see who could hold a lighter's flame under his palm the longest. It seemed there could be no love for life without a love for fire.

When I was alone, restlessness drove me from books to my notepads, then into the fields and along the sides of the highway, and back to my books again. A few times I hounded my mother for details of my father's crimes, insisting that she must know more, but she claimed she didn't. I was desperate to hear these stories, yet I didn't call him again. I was less than a year from fifteen, and I sensed that calling would open our life to him and put my mother in danger. I knew that if I talked more, all my frustration and anger would come spilling out. It was better to wait, to call him just before I turned fifteen, and then to leave once and for all.

To calm myself, I made a list of everything I'd do:

Steal a car

Break into a house

Get shot (revised to, Get shot and survive)

Rob a bank

But what was the point of breaking and entering if I hadn't even lost my virginity? I had tried, to be sure, but I was too frank, too honest. With men, I showed nothing. But to girls I wanted to reveal everything, all that I'd read and dreamed. I gazed at the letter sewn to the chest of their cheerleading outfits: *T* for the school mascot, the Trojan. We all carried one in our wallets. The older boys sold them, ancient, wallet worn, meeting us in the bathrooms and slipping them into our palms for a few dollars, so that we could hurry back into the adolescent throng like illegal immigrants carrying fake passports.

But what was the point of condoms if I couldn't show the rough indifference of the older boys, the meanness that drew girls like crows to roadkill.

"My father was a bank robber," I told Travis and Brad. They looked me over, seeing the kid who'd always been obsessed with books.

"Yeah right," they said.

Furious, I was determined to impress them.

For as long as I'd lived on Route 28, my neighbors had had a dirt bike in their carport, and I'd never seen it moved or used. I came up with a plan, then went over and knocked.

The woman next door had messy, dark hair and a slack, somewhat harried expression. I'd often seen her rushing two small children out to her claptrap Buick. I told her some friends and I were looking to buy a motorbike and wanted to know if theirs was for sale. Her eyes lit up at the mention of money, and she went into the kitchen and made a phone call. She was speaking to her stepson, she told me. It was his bike, and he wanted nine hundred dollars.

"I don't know why he's asking so much. He hasn't touched that thing in years."

I put on a disappointed face. I told her that my friends and I would have to save up more. She seemed to want to negotiate, but I left.

Back in my room, I moved my desk to the window facing her carport, and each day after school, while reading *East of Eden* or *Tortilla Flat*, I kept a log of my neighbors' comings and goings. This must have been how it was done for banks. The husband returned each evening around seven thirty. The mother was never back before five o'clock. The only wild card was a lanky young man with long hair who showed up once a week. He wore acid-washed jeans and made himself a sandwich in the kitchen, took a beer, and devoured both in the carport. Then he left. His arrivals had no clear pattern but were rare enough and usually took place around four o'clock, an hour before the woman—his step-mother, I assumed—returned.

The next week, I knocked again, and she answered.

"I'm doing a fund-raiser for a field trip," I told her. "We're cleaning up carports. It only costs fifty cents."

"That's all?" Her mouth hung open, showing small crooked teeth.

She got the change out of her wallet and gave it to me, and while I was sweeping, she took her children to the Buick, telling me that she was off to get groceries.

I pointed to where a faded yellow raft lay deflated in the corner.

"This is getting mildewed," I said. "I'll hang it out to dry, okay?"

"Sounds great," she called. "Thank you. This garage has been a mess forever."

Since Dickie obsessively used sprays for mildew in the basement, I knew about it, but the raft didn't appear to have any. I'd simply noticed it while keeping track of the family. The cluttered carport was no more than a concrete slab built off the house, with a roof supported by metal posts and no walls, so I'd itemized everything in it while trying to come up with a plan. I hung the raft over the motorcycle. It covered it perfectly, barely revealing the front tire. I cleaned, making sure that the job was impeccable. I went home just before my mother arrived at six o'clock.

I watched the house for another week. Then I told Brad and Travis my plan.

"If we leave school right away, we can be at my house by three thirty. That gives us one hour to strip the motorcycle." I didn't mention the stepson who occasionally returned.

Brad gave his cigarette a flick, trying to look tough and accustomed, though he resembled a fidgety society lady in a movie.

"We can do that," he said in a nasal voice.

"Fuck yeah," Travis agreed. "That's easy." He was smaller but gruffer than Brad, with long mousy hair from which his pointy nose and chin emerged.

After school, carrying empty gym bags and backpacks, we half-jogged to my house.

No one was at my place or the neighbor's. With socket-wrench kits and a bucket of Dickie's tools, we ran to the carport, threw back the rubber raft, and got on our knees. We removed the carriage bolts, then quickly detached the engine, the gas tank, the seat, the chain, the brakes, even the gauges and wires, leaving only the naked frame.

I hung the raft back over the bike as Brad and Travis ran the pieces to the concrete room built off the outdoor stairs to my basement. That was where I kept the old motorcycle I'd found in the barn. With so many parts scattered about, no one would notice new ones.

Brad and Travis put the engine, the gas tank, and the seat into gym bags. Then they walked back to school to call Brad's mother for a ride.

The night of the dance, a hurricane dispersed into a tropical storm, wind and rain pressing up the coast. Gusts shook power lines and lampposts along the road to school.

"But you only got the engine," Elizabeth said. I knew her from pre-algebra, and in the loud cafeteria, she stood close to hear my story, tilting her head back to see from beneath bangs as stiff as a blond garden rake.

"It's cool," I said. "I'll get the rest. I have a plan."

I could hardly believe it—how quickly crime won respect. I was no longer the same kid, and others saw this, that I wasn't afraid of the police, of anyone.

Brad and Travis joined us and told Elizabeth and me to follow them. Two sisters were also there, one bleach blond, the other quite dark, and both referred to as the Watermelon Sisters.

We crossed the field behind the junior high and made our way, with a six-pack of Busch, to a new subdivision. We went into an unfinished home with plywood floors and empty doorways hung with plastic. The wind was so strong that the walls shook.

"I don't know if this is safe," Elizabeth said, gripping my wrist.

We each held a lukewarm beer. Travis grabbed the arm of the dark Watermelon Sister and led her to another room, beyond several plastic sheets. We could hear him tearing insulation from the wall and spreading it on the floor, then the two of them lying down and struggling with their clothes.

Brad was telling his Watermelon Sister about living in Germany, about what really happened to Hitler's body and how a friend's dad had his jawbone.

"You see, they know it was his because there are so many gold fillings in the teeth. My friend's dad keeps it locked in his filing cabinet. It's worth millions."

As he spoke, he leaned close to his Watermelon Sister, but she put her palm against his chest and pushed him back. He stopped talking, and she changed the subject to a girl who'd talked shit about her and how that wasn't cool and there was going to be a reckoning.

The wind kept slamming the walls and thrashing at the plastic, blowing up dust that stung our eyes. Elizabeth stood close. She sipped her beer and told me how, each morning when she did her hair, she looked for spiders on the walls and gave them a shot of hair spray, then watched as they walked slower and slower and finally froze. She said she wanted four more piercings in each ear and an eagle tattoo on her back with wings that went down her arms.

I told her how my father was an ex-con and that someday I'd rob a bank, and about my list—steal a car, break into a house, get shot. Wind knocked against the walls as some forgotten Steinbeck character, invoked as if in a séance, spoke through me.

"If you get shot, you're close to death. Imagine how badly you want to live."

She stepped close and pushed her lips to mine. I kissed back, careful not to spread saliva, following the rules I'd heard from Brad: not to slobber, to stay close to the lips, to let her put her tongue in my mouth first, and, above all—the cardinal rule—never to exhale into her mouth while kissing, or else the air would make a sound like a duck.

As I imagined divers did, I controlled my breathing. We kissed, and she rubbed my jeans. The world sparkled and anguished, and then she pulled away.

Travis and the Watermelon Sister had come back and were saying that we had to go. They were scratching their arms and legs as if fleas were devouring them.

As we returned to the dance, he kept clawing at his limbs, rubbing and patting, sighing and groaning, as if having sex with himself now.

"Goddamn," he hollered and clutched his balls. "I can't stop itching."

"Maybe you got crabs," Brad told him.

"Ew," Elizabeth and the other Watermelon Sister said.

"No, you dipshit," Travis told him. "It's the insulation. Fiberglass itches like hell."

The girl who'd been with Travis stayed quiet, her shoulders pulled in as she walked ahead, one hand reaching up under her skirt to rub at her ass and thighs.

Brad was staring for each glimpse of pale skin.

"Was it worth it?" he asked Travis.

"Hell yeah. It's always worth it."

The Watermelon Sister walked faster, leaving us behind, dark hair whipping about in the hurricane's final push.

The next day we arrived at school to see that, on the hill with the new subdivision, the house where we'd been had collapsed, pummeled by the wind. Though I wanted to claim this disaster, to say I'd started a fire or kicked the walls like a martial artist, I didn't think I could get away with the lie. Besides, it was enough to say I'd been inside, drinking just before it fell.

Brad and Travis and Elizabeth liked the story and took it up, saying it collapsed just after we left, while we were crossing the field.

We all heard it, we agreed.

"I heard something, anyway," Elizabeth said. "I was scared just being in there."

Despite our stories, something about it seemed grim, an omen, a bad beginning for love.

The narrow lane, shaded by high trees, followed the sunlit train tracks, then veered over them and wound down through the dense forest that, with each turn, became increasingly crowded with battered cars.

Dickie came here often to look for the parts he claimed he'd been seeking forever, even though he just cleaned them and never used them. I liked the wrecked vehicles, trucks torn nearly in half, cars like accordions, motorcycles squashed as small as suitcases. I pictured the swarming lights of police cars and ambulances, arms and legs sticking out from crushed metal, a bereaved wife falling to her knees as she tore at her hair.

"Hey," Dickie called. He was holding his bucket of tools and stood hunched in the shadow of a massive oak. "Why don't you go ask the old man for a job?"

"I don't want to," I said, making myself appear stern and uninterested. Dickie and his ideas were beneath me. I'd accompanied him just to get out of the house for a while.

"What the hell? Come on. You'd be a good mechanic."

"I don't want to be a mechanic."

He curved his back like an angry dog. "Get your ass down there!"

My dirty sneakers scuffed dark red lines in the sunburned clay. I knocked at the trailer.

The old man pulled the door open with one hand while checking his fly with the other.

"Yeah, what do you want?" Head tilted back, mouth open, he studied me from beneath his glasses.

"I was wondering if you need to hire someone."

"Hire someone?" He glanced around the fields and forest that looked like a crowded parking lot decades after Armageddon. "To do what?"

"I don't know."

"Hell, boy." He shook his head as if I were the nuttiest damn kid on earth and he had nothing but sympathy. "I don't make no money, can't pay no money."

Later, when Dickie and I got home, I saw the oily metal stashed under the front seats. He'd used me as a distraction so he could take things without paying. He'd also stolen the old man's portable welding kit. Pathetic, I thought—robbing a junkyard.

He carried it all into the basement to clean, and I worked out on the back porch. How much longer would I have to live like this? With my feet propped on the steps, I did push-ups until sweat ran into my eyes and dripped from the tip of my nose. I did sit-ups with a thirty-pound dumbbell behind my head, counting *eight goddamn it, nine goddamn it, ten motherfucker*. I wanted a new life, a new body, money, and respect—to get laid. I did biceps curls until the veins in my arms bulged and my hands shook and I couldn't flex my fingers to hold the weights.

Dickie slunk up from the basement and stood, wiping his greasy hands on his work jeans as he blinked in the sunlight.

"Check it out," I told him and came down from the porch. I flexed my arm.

His eyes popped open. Then he lifted his right hand as if to make a muscle too, but he grabbed the meat of my arm. My knees almost gave out.

"Have you been using my stuff to make bombs?"

"No!"

"Bullshit. I'm missing a lot of stuff."

"I don't know what you're talking about." My jaw clenched as he dug his fingers, but I forced myself to show nothing. That was how you won with men, by not caring, by making them feel stupid.

"Don't let me catch you in my shop. I'll tear your fucking arm off."

He let go and went back downstairs.

The next day, each finger was imprinted in black on my skin. After school, when my mother came home, I showed her. Her eyes lingered.

"What did you do?" she asked, her face drawn. "You must have done something."

"Don't blame me," I shouted, though I knew she'd yell at Dickie in private. "I don't want to stay here anymore. I want to go back and live with André."

I stormed outside, onto the back porch and down the stairs, intending to sulk in the fields, where I could find things to smash.

She caught hold of my sleeve in the yard. Her hair had gone entirely gray, though she called it frosted, and the curls of her perm had relaxed so that a few strands hung about her face.

"You know what? Your father was just a kid. He had to be the center of attention. But he was worse than a kid because you couldn't question a damn thing he did. If he came home late, he had to wake you guys up. He'd play games so you knew he was the good guy. I was the bad one. I made you go to bed. I made you eat good food. He'd let you do anything as long as it didn't threaten him. And he'd take you places with those people of his, let them drink around you or whatever. If you want that, fine, you can go back when you're fifteen. But if you do, your life won't be what you want. It will be what he wants. You'll be there for him. Maybe that doesn't make sense now, but it will someday."

I refused to look at her. Stars were appearing behind the filmy light of the nearby subdivisions. A firefly blinked above the trash bins.

"Why did you stay with him so long?" I asked.

She looked away. "I was afraid. I didn't believe in myself, and he kept me from believing in myself."

Dickie opened the screen door onto the porch. He leaned on the banister, the sleeves of his T-shirt lifting above his faded army tattoo, an eagle just beneath his shoulder.

"I'm getting tired of this. Why don't y'all come inside?"

"Go back in the house," she told him with a coldness that made me proud. "We're talking."

"Christ," he said. The screen door clacked behind him, and the stove light flickered as he passed in front of it.

"All I ask," she went on, "is that you trust me. I'm doing what's best for you. That's why I took you away. I wish I could tell you more and someday I will."

"Why someday and not now?"

"I can't."

I clenched my fists. "I'm sick of everything here. I hate it. I want to go."

"You're not fifteen. I told you you can go when you are."

"He can't be that bad."

"You don't know how bad he can be. He told everyone that I left because he was going bankrupt, but I left because he was crazy. I always told myself I'd know when it was time. Then one morning he was reading an article about a man who went bankrupt and killed his wife and children and himself. He said it made sense to him. That's why I took you so far away. I told him that a psychic said I should leave, about the earthquake and that stuff. If I'd said he was crazy, he might have hurt me. But I gave him another reason."

It made sense. Nobody wanted to hear that something was his fault.

But I didn't believe he'd have hurt us. People talked all sorts of shit when they were angry. He hadn't meant it. My fondest memories were of times with him, his wildness, our adventures.

She put her cheek against my shoulder. Cars passed on Route 28. Pods from the maple helicoptered down with each gust of wind and disappeared in the dusk, on the shingles of the roof.

A leather jacket came in the mail, but it was the wrong kind, glossy and thin, the seams making a V in the back. It was something a European rock star would wear. I'd wanted the heavy, armored look of a biker, but this would have to do.

At school, Elizabeth told me that we weren't girlfriend and boyfriend. Though she was thirteen, she said, "Sorry. You're just a kid. I like men."

Every day, Travis and Brad wanted to know how we'd get the motorbike frame. I said we had to wait—that it would be soon. But I could hardly wait myself. This seemed the longest year of my life, and to take the edge off my impatience, we broke into a storage unit one night, disappointed that it held only boxes of old Christmas decorations and one of smoke detectors, which we stole, thinking they might be worth something. We prowled farmland, smashing the windows of old cars on blocks, taking rusty pipes and knocking out headlights and reflectors, gouging the few still-inflated tires with our pocketknives. We broke into a house and took tools and cassettes, spare change and more knives.

I saw crime everywhere. My brother kept to his room, curtains drawn, the only light his computer screen. He was pale, with etiolated hair, but surely a hacker breaking into government databases, taking over the world like the computer in *The Terminator*. I still snuck into the vaultlike silence of his room to read his stories: men who stared women in the eye, longing, or who looked out windows. Longing was in the inky darkness, in the canyons between the towers of the future, in the galactic space between alien nations. But the men never did anything. They watched. They calculated. The women paced before them in black skirts and high boots.

Did he feel what I did? Did he burn with the same obsessions?

From time to time, he went into the kitchen and took a jar of hot peppers from the fridge. He slouched at the table, eating them until tears gathered in his eyes.

Two dozen people sat on a basement carpet before a medium, a woman who communicated the wisdom of a celestial being.

I was next to my mother and Dickie, who had his knees pulled to his chest, his eyes wary. Over the years, my mother had tried to convert him to her vision of the unpolluted palate, but he still smoked and now he was drinking again, watching shoot-'em-up action flicks and eating dinner before a TV loud enough to drown the steady and unconscious smack of his chewing. The séance was a victory for her, and for me, a return to childhood magic.

The medium sat, spine straight, palms on her knees. Her facial muscles slowly relaxed, becoming lugubrious, like those of a drunken man. With half-lidded eyes, she surveyed the audience. Her assistant announced that she was ready.

Someone asked about a recurrent nightmare, and the medium cleared her throat.

"This dream," she said, sounding like a man, "it is an expression of fear, but there is no real fear, only the unknown. There is no danger . . ."

Her words on life and death and the currents of pain and the fractured, dissatisfied selves that haunt our sleep—the unknown both within and outside us—seemed obvious. But I, too, had a recurrent dream. In the valley, I went to the shed where my father had built the pen for his German shepherds. A man stood inside, covered in matted hair, his hands on the two-by-four slats. I could hardly see him or decipher his rough, muddled language, but I understood that he was asking to be let out. I fled, knowing that sooner or later he'd break free and find me.

All that night, after returning home, I read a bulky fantasy novel. Dawn reached my window as I began the last chapter. The hero accepted his destiny and trekked to a tower in desolate mountains to face a being so evil that its origins were a mystery. This was his purpose, to destroy the source of evil itself. But the confrontation was inconclusive.

The being vanished. There was an unforeseen glitch in the prophecy, some mystical red tape that the hero would have to sort out in the sequel. My mother was already reading it.

I tossed the novel on the floor and stood. Blood buzzed in my ears. I shuffled to the bathroom and peed. Then I stared in the mirror: a pimply boy with a bad haircut and not nearly enough muscle. I went out the front door. The highway swayed like a rope bridge, and I stumbled alongside it. Before I'd left British Columbia, my father had told me that if I stayed, he'd give me direction. He'd teach me how to fight.

Dawn lit the rural dregs of a landscape bought up and hewn into subdivisions, the bashed fenders and bald tires and rusted appliances of forgotten lives appearing through the October leaves after a dry summer. On the gravel shoulder, I saw myself from the sky, as if my father might be looking down, ashamed of my worn-out jeans and dirty sneakers, the scraps and flattened cans, the cigarette butts and bottle caps that littered my path.

We were moving again, to a mobile home in the woods, beneath a leviathan electrical tower whose lines cut a swath through the boondocks. My mother and Dickie would build a house there, and the cramped trailer would be temporary quarters. But I didn't care. I was almost fifteen.

I walked to the neighbor's carport and knocked. The last of the evening commute shuttled along Route 28. The woman answered, looking tired, the TV loud inside.

"My friends and I put some money together," I told her. "It's almost enough. I thought maybe I could try the motorbike out first."

"Sure," she said, again perking up at the mention of money.

I felt as I had standing next to the highway at night, inching nearer to each passing rig, wind against my skin and in my hair, metal blurring just before my eyes.

The yellow raft slid from the bike frame. The woman just stared.

"My stepson must have taken all the parts."

I made myself look disappointed, even a little angry.

"I wanted to buy it. I was trying to get the money together."

She went into the kitchen and took the phone. An argument ensued between the father watching TV and drinking beer and his son, as she repeated what they said.

"I didn't touch your piece-of-crap bike," the father yelled over his shoulder.

"He said he didn't touch your bike," she called into the receiver.

"Your loser friends probably did it," the father hollered. "They know you don't use that thing."

When they'd finished and she'd hung up, I chewed my lip and shrugged.

"Hey, look, I guess I could use the frame if you're just going to throw it away."

"I don't know," she said.

I took a twenty-dollar bill from my pocket.

"I could give you twenty dollars for it."

She stared at the money.

"Oh, heck," she said and reached for the bill. "I'm just going to say we threw it away."

That weekend, I packed: childhood books on fish, those of myths; the many fantasy series, Civil War accounts, and tomes about ancient cities; and of course Steinbeck's novels. They all traced a line into mystery: primal shapes beneath dark water, the world's creation, the excesses of violence and the ceaseless vanishing of empires, and at last, the solitary longing of a drifter.

Back at school, minutes stretched into years. What would the medium say about my future, and would I want to hear? My body felt caught in a current, pulled by floodwaters.

There was a home football game that night, and after it started, I walked out and sat in the parking lot, on the curb between two cars. The tidal roar of cheering reached me. Floodlights gave the suburban sky a cadaverous hue. I was so frustrated, so impatient, I could hardly breathe, as if the air refused to fill my lungs. The emptiness in me joined me to the world, everything I saw made to satisfy me, to fit into the story I could hear myself writing.

I closed my eyes, the click of cooling engines soft behind the syllables of my speech, as if the racing machine of time had faded back into the song of creation.

That Saturday, when no one was home, I took the phone into the trailer's back bedroom, pushing down the extra-long cord so I could close the door. My father's number had changed again, and I dialed it from yet another card he'd sent.

As soon as he answered, I told him I wanted to go back and live with him. A woman chatted in the background, dishes clinking, and he fumbled with the receiver.

"Come back?" The noises became muffled, as if he were holding his hand over the mouthpiece.

"I want to live with you. I'm almost fifteen. I'm allowed to now."

He didn't speak, and I added, "I need to get away from here. I hate it."

"Okay," he said.

"Will you send me a ticket?" Asking this, I had never felt braver.

"Does your mother know?"

"I haven't told her yet."

"Tell her you want to get to know me. I'll send you the ticket, but tell her you want to leave with her blessings."

Later, when I repeated his words, saying, "I want to leave with your blessings," she gritted her teeth. "Don't you ever use his words with me. He told you to say that."

"No, he didn't," I lied.

She looked tired and distant. I knew that she'd been inspired to build the new house, that she still had energy and hope, but she must have realized that everything was falling apart, that it was time for me to leave. It was better for all of us.

"If you don't let me go," I said, "I'll run away."

"No." She shook her head. "You don't have to do that. You can go.

I guess it's what you need to do. When you get the ticket, I'll drive you to the airport."

Later, I told my brother and sister, but they just nodded and said nothing. Over the years, we'd become increasingly distant, and now I closed myself off to everyone.

That night, I tried to picture my father's face but couldn't. Unable to sleep, I lit a candle as my mother had done for me when I was child wanting to meditate on levitation. I put it on a wooden chair in the middle of my room, then sat and stared, the flame's faint shifts like those of a feather held between fingertips. Something was being asked of me, and I would face it.

I must have fallen asleep. When I opened my eyes, the candle was gone and the chair was on fire. In that moment, before I panicked, I knew that this was one of the most beautiful things I'd ever seen.

part III

THE BIG JOB

The last half of my flight was a slow sunset that ended shortly after I landed. Just before Vancouver, the plane dropped into clouds, racing blindly toward the city and mountains I wished to see.

As we taxied on the runway, I tore up a letter my mother had given me. . . . *He could charm anyone. He knew what to tell me to make me do and think what he wanted. But you are more adult than I was. You will see through him and decide what is best. You are your own man, and no matter what he wants, you will make the right decisions. . . .*

This was a technique of hers, to praise me for being what she wanted, and after reading her letter, I wondered if she'd learned it from him. I tore the paper into strips and shoved them in the pocket of the seat in front of me, then stood to get my backpack.

I had on torn jeans and a black T-shirt, and in the forward shuffle of the immigration line, I considered my appearance—my posture, my stride, the way I held my head, whether I should gesticulate when I spoke or hook my thumbs in my belt loops. Was frequent eye contact childish, an aloof gaze more masculine?

The crowded customs hall opened on a lobby, cavernous and silent but for echoing footsteps.

It took me a while to notice the man at the window, gazing out as a plane touched down on the distant runway with a semblance of gentleness. He turned and stared, hands in the pockets of his leather jacket. He had on white running shoes and crisp jeans, the denim creased from the shelves. It was the first time I'd seen him without a beard.

"Hey," he said and came forward. Awkwardly, he shook my hand and gave me a sort of half hug that neither of us put much energy into.

I stood a good bit taller, and he looked me over, then glanced around the room and back. I'd recalled a towering man, shadowed eyes that seemed angry even when he smiled. He was darker than I remembered, his features chiseled and, when he spoke, his accent thicker than over the phone. He looked like someone I might pass on the street.

He stepped back and reached out to pat my arm. The cuffs of his blue shirt showed an inch past those of his jacket.

"I'm happy you're here," he told me. "Are you hungry?"

"Sure," I said and had to cough to bring moisture to my throat.

We paced a bit as if making a serious decision, as if he might tell me something. A map of the airport was set into the wall, and we stopped before it. He lowered his head, looking at his shoes, then glanced quickly at my torn jeans. He drew in his cheeks as if to spit, but swallowed.

I felt dizzy. This wasn't what I'd imagined. I forced myself to stand straighter. He had to realize I was no longer a child.

His expression became impassive, his eyes collecting information in their steady, nondisclosing fashion. It was a look of strength that I knew I could quickly master.

Outside, a misting rain was falling.

"That's my truck," he told me. He motioned with his jaw to a red and gray GMC.

"I like having a new one." His lips hinted at a smile. "Having a nice car is like wearing a good suit. If you want a loan or you want to be trusted in a deal, people see your car and they know you're making money."

The inside smelled of cologne and vaguely of fish. As he drove, he talked about music. He said he liked what was new, what was popular, and had the same tastes as young people.

Going a little too fast, he steered the truck through scattered traffic, then jerked the wheel and took us onto a spur and into a sluggish procession of wet cars.

"I need to check on the market," he said. "Then we can go eat."

The barn-shaped building's parking lot was mostly empty, a line of broken flowerpots against the wall, an old woman in a mustard trench coat shuffling in circles, searching for change.

As we walked through the doors into the airy space of glass displays and food stalls, I thought to mention Granville Island, where he'd once had a shop. The babble of scents—bagels and flowers, seafood and hot dogs and bread—recalled my brother, my sister, and me running between booths.

"Deni," he said, "meet Sara."

A young woman stepped away from the stainless-steel counter, blond, thin-boned, and petite, round sapphire earrings a shade darker than her eyes. He put his hand on the small of her back, and his quiet demeanor, the vague sense of a hidden fragility, vanished. He stood, chest lifted, eyes no longer veiled but like a flash of light on dark water.

With a snap, she pulled off a yellow glove and shook my hand, her fingers clammy.

"How was your trip?" she asked.

"We'll need to get Deni settled," he interrupted, and she smiled thinly, as if humoring him.

"Bill is at the delivery door," she said, and he hurried to the back of the shop and went just outside. She and I stood awkwardly, not looking at each other as we listened.

"Where do you want this?" a man asked, his voice unfriendly.

"Leave it here. I'll get my son to help me bring it in."

"Huh?" A pause. "This on credit again?"

"I'll have money for you at the end of the month."

"Fine, fine . . . How's the shop?"

"Business picks up closer to Christmas."

"Always does."

At the display, a woman with a purple head scarf scrutinized a tray of raw squid, squinting as if reading fine print in the mess of tentacles. Sara glanced at her, then looked at me. She held my gaze a little too long.

"We'll get you settled," she said and winked, then turned her slight hips to the counter.

I wasn't used to being flirted with so openly. Her smile had told me that with her, everything would be easy.

"What do you think?" my father asked, walking back from the door.

"What?" The pulse in my jaw resonated with another one behind my knee.

"What's funny?" He frowned, glancing about. "This shop took a long time to put together."

A few salespeople at nearby stalls were looking over. Suddenly, there was that pent-up energy I remembered from childhood, the sense that he'd do something wild. He approached and in a quiet, tense voice explained how long it took to get a business going again, after the separation, the bankruptcy.

"Your mother left me with nothing," he said. I considered telling him that she'd left with nothing, too, but my head hurt, a buzz in my ears like the static of a rapidly turned radio knob. He was proud of his shop and thought I was laughing at it.

I glanced at the display coolers, the white ice with salmon, green crabs, orange-mesh bags of mussels. Maybe the store wasn't as fancy as those he used to run. I wasn't sure and I didn't care. I simply commanded my face to show nothing.

He was studying me, searching. He dropped his gaze. He stood like that, lips pursed, eyes on the floor. He picked up a quarter.

"Anyway," he said and let out a sigh. "Come on. Help me bring in the delivery."

The rain had churned into fog, inseparable from the sky. The light was fading, and the damp chilled my lungs. Beneath the ice in the crate shone the dark eyes of small metallic fish.

The restaurant had a neon sign—Knight and Day. A mermaid coughed irregular spouts into a fountain, her breasts mossy, the water brown. Drizzle gusted. The mist had disappeared into night.

As my father crossed the parking lot, he checked his pockets for his keys. The image jarred a memory, a younger him doing the same. But the man I remembered was large and strong. My father seemed to hover between two selves, like a TV screen caught between channels.

We sat at a window facing the street. The emptiness of the dining room gave it a tawdry look, a few hunched men eating late dinners alone. The air of tension around my father returned, vanished, and returned again, like the flickering of a fluorescent bulb. Despite my age, he ordered me a beer. This was where he went after work, he told me. He knew the waitress by name and commented on her legs. She had bleached hair and blue, bruised shadows under her eyes from running makeup.

"You don't like talking about women?" he asked when I glanced away.

"I just don't think she's pretty."

He laughed. "Of course she's pretty. Look at her. Either a girl's pretty or not pretty. She's pretty. Maybe you're too young to know."

He didn't speak for a moment, and I said, "I want to hear about the banks."

My voice ended in a croak, as if these were my dying words.

"What?" he asked.

"The robberies. You know, Bonnie tried to make it sound bad—"

He slid his place mat back and forth, staring at it, breathing through his mouth, lips slightly parted and jaw pushed forward. He did this because his nose had been broken so many times. As a boy I'd occasionally imitated the look, hoping for the sculpted chin, the furrow below the bottom lip like the mark of a finger pressed into clay.

And as I had when I was a child, I studied him. Whatever had taken place earlier, the confusion and discomfort could be wiped away like mist on glass.

"I'm proud," I told him with a confidence that surprised me. "I'm proud to have a father who's done incredible things. I've always dreamed of being like that."

"I don't know why in the fuck she ever told you," he said. With his fingertips, he continued to slide the place mat back and forth.

"What was it like?"

"What?"

"Robbing banks."

His gaze was briefly sad, but he said nothing, just sighed and shook his head.

"I don't care about all this other stuff," I told him. "I want to hear about that."

"What other stuff?"

"The market. It's boring. I want to hear about your crimes."

I moved my hand dismissively, and he stopped fidgeting. He thrust his jaw forward, narrowing his eyes. Then something changed, the way the mood around an actor might shift after he's asked to get into character.

"You want to hear those stories?"

"Yes," I said. "More than anything. They're what matter."

His jaw had gone a bit crooked, and he was squinting one eye, working something out.

"I don't talk about it anymore."

"But it's amazing."

"That's what you think."

"Who wouldn't?"

"A lot of people." He scrutinized me. "I know why you want to hear about it. You're like me. You have that in you. Some people are just like that."

"What do you mean?"

"You'd be good at it. Not everyone is. It takes something. You have to be a little crazy. You have to want that kind of life and the way it feels. It's scary, but it's a rush, too. You have to like that. I think you probably would."

"I want to hear about it," I told him, more softly than intended, as if coaxing.

Very faintly, he nodded. "What do you want to hear?"

"Just a story. A good one."

"A good one?" He considered. "There was this one bank job in particular. In the pen, that's all the guys talked about. The big job. The last crime. Once you did it, you'd never have to work again. Everyone had ideas. Everyone was a fucking genius of crime. I didn't know anything until I went to prison. I was just a kid. It was like going to school, and there were all these men talking about the big job. I didn't go in with plans, but once

I was there I learned fast. The big job was all that mattered to me. I imagined one perfect crime. It's like I'd have been famous if I did it. It's stupid."

"It's not stupid," I said, thrilled that he was talking to me like this, like a man. "Did you do it?"

"Yeah. I did a perfect one, but someone else fucked it up. It was the biggest one. It was the craziest. The best aren't always the craziest. But this one was. I planned it for a long time."

"Could it still be done?" I asked.

He shrugged, then stared off, as if composing himself or remembering or simply accepting that he was going to tell something he hadn't spoken of in years.

"There were three of us—me, my partner, and his girlfriend. I set the whole thing up. I knew more than they did. It was in 1967, in Hollywood. I rented a surveillance apartment across the street from the bank. I planned the job for the night LBJ was in town. He was giving a speech, and I knew that all the police would be looking after him."

His words confused me. I'd seen him as wild and careless in his risks. This calculation was new, and it felt dangerous.

"For a week before I broke in, I parked a box truck in an alley by the bank. I parked it right next to a window with bars in it. The night LBJ was giving his speech, I backed the truck up to the window and went into the box and cut the bars. No one could see me because I was inside and the window was hidden by the back of the truck. And if anyone did come by, they didn't think anything because the truck had been parked there all week."

As he spoke, he reminded me of someone doing math, first considering an equation, staring off blankly, trying to work it out in his head, then seeing how it could be done, certainty and confidence returning to his gaze. Telling the story, he seemed stronger than he ever had, as if this were who he really was and his words were bringing him back.

"I used a gas-powered jackhammer to blow a hole through the vault. My friend was with me, and his girlfriend watched from the apartment across the street. They had walkie-talkies, and whenever she saw someone, I stopped jackhammering.

"The hole I made wasn't very big because the concrete had bars running through it. I could blow out only what was between them. Then I pulled myself in. I threw all of the money out. But when I went to leave, I couldn't. It's hard to explain, but the jackhammering made a grain in the concrete that pointed inward. When I tried to crawl out, it hooked on my clothes. I didn't want to tell my friend, because with half a million in the truck, I was worried. I took off my clothes and put them through the hole. Then I pulled myself out. I had scrapes everywhere. I was covered in blood . . ."

He paused, swallowed, and looked down, his expression confused, as if he were struggling to connect his life now to his past.

"Right before we left, we smashed open all the safe-deposit boxes. That was probably the only dumb thing we did. We already had a lot of money.

"But the police found out it was me. It wasn't my fault. It was my partner's job to make sure the surveillance apartment was clean. His girlfriend and me took the money into the country. She had a gun so she could feel safe, and he should've been ten minutes behind. Only thing is, he got nervous about the apartment and was afraid we'd left prints, so he decided to set fire to it. I don't know what the fuck he was thinking, because the police would see right away it was connected. We'd already cleaned it once, and he just had to wipe the knobs down one last time if he thought there were fingerprints. He could have splashed soapy water. Instead, he poured gasoline on everything.

"In the kitchen the gasoline dripped down to the pilot light. The whole place went up. I don't know how he didn't get killed. His eyes got burned. That's the only serious thing that happened to him, other than getting arrested.

"I guess the police made him a deal, because he told them everything. I already had a criminal record. All the police had to do was get my files and fingerprints. They sent pictures all over the country. It was about a year before they found me in Miami . . ."

He looked up and studied me, his eyes moving in slow, barely discernable increments. All this was bigger, more complex than I'd expected, more businesslike. He spoke of his partner as a disappointed employer might of an employee. And yet I was relieved that my earlier impressions were false. He was more than he'd seemed to be.

"Never repeat any of this," he told me, his voice stark, his eyes on my face—"not to anyone. Nobody ever needs to know what I've done."

His house stood off a wooded lane on the edge of Surrey, a sprawling suburb. Trees and overgrown hedges and a high fence closed it in, and his six dogs ran free. He'd bred German shepherds since before I was born, calling them simply "shepherds," and now, oddly, he sold new litters to the police. He also had three cats, and hair of various colors crosshatched the carpets and linoleum. A sweaty crust of flea powder edged the rugs.

He'd built the back patio into a high enclosure where he kept a hulking breeding stud. When he'd run across the ad for the hundred-and-fifty-pound shepherd and gone to see it, the people at the kennel had directed him to the cage but kept their distance. True to what he'd read—and to what I saw through the chain links—the dog had bullish shoulders and a handsome snout brimming with teeth. My father walked up, opened the gate, and went inside. Everyone stopped what they were doing and watched. He petted the dog, inspected its paws and mouth, and decided he liked it. Only later did the owner tell him that he was the first person the dog had allowed near it in almost a year.

Unfortunately, the same was true of the years to follow. The patio door had two crossbars like those on a barn, and when I passed it the dog's heavy, padded steps approached and it snuffled about the cracks at the bottom and sides, then began to growl. It stood and put its paws against the door, and the wood creaked and popped softly within its frame.

I slept on a dusty couch in the basement. Cobwebs strung the ceiling, and the floor's peeling linoleum was like leather. The furnace came on with a loud whirring, the air smelling of exhaust.

"What's there to eat for breakfast?" I asked in the morning, opening the fridge.

Aside from Pepsi and cream-filled chocolate rolls, it held only a plate and cup.

"Why do you have dirty dishes in here?"

"So they don't get moldy and I can reuse them without washing," he told me.

Though he'd gone bankrupt five years earlier, he now had three stores. There was the one in the public market as well as the same snack bar at the ferry landing where he'd had his fight years ago. He seemed to be retracing his steps. He'd owned even his main store before the bankruptcy, a rundown building, the rotting floors reinforced by loosely placed plywood, so that crossing the room felt like walking on ice.

His acquaintances reminded me of when I was a boy. He'd taken me along to meetings with Native American men in gravel parking lots near highways, during which I chewed strips of smoked salmon as he spoke in a hushed voice. I grew accustomed to the presence of men whose strength I sensed in their stillness, in the way they watched.

His employees had fallen on hard times, evicted or newly paroled. They cleaned fish behind the store, glaring at the knife and bloody cutting board. Everyone he knew worked for him in some capacity. They borrowed money or wanted to sell him things, and he had a list of men who'd tried to take him for a ride and who could no longer be trusted. Oddly, even these men came by and spoke with him, shaking his hand before leaving.

That first week, we made deliveries often. He was reticent when I asked for stories. He said his life had changed, that he wasn't the same person. Sometimes he told me how happy he was to have me back. He smiled, but then pursed his lips, studying me intently. Often, when we passed stores, he asked if I liked anything and insisted on buying whatever I showed interest in. He got me the leather jacket I wanted, bulky and thick. And then, as soon as I put it on, his gaze went dead.

I couldn't stand his work: the odor of fish, the scales that stuck to everything like dull sequins. I was waiting for crime stories, my thoughts following the paths of novels. But before long these novels became a problem. Whenever I was bored, waiting in the car or while he talked to employees, I read.

"It's rude," he told me.

"I'm just waiting."

"You don't need to read."

"But I'm just sitting in the truck," I said.

"Didn't she teach you to do anything other than read those goddamn books?"

"What?"

"You read those books too much." He pulled into the street, acting engrossed by the traffic. The way he said *books* made them sound childish, as if he wanted me to behave like a man.

It had never occurred to me that I could rebel only against those who refused to accept what I was. Since my criminal interests didn't anger him, they seemed innocent, whereas the literature my mother had encouraged was questionable. I realized he'd probably never read a novel. What was it like to be someone who'd never finished a last page, never experienced that amalgam of fullness and loss, satisfaction and longing?

We drove along the highway through tepid, quickly vanishing sunlight. He had another meeting, he told me, this time in the offices of a packinghouse, and he parked and hunched off through the drizzle. Soon, the windows were opaque with rain and condensation. I put down my book. Why had I come back? What had I imagined? A fantasy of my father and me crossing the bright tiles of a bank, dark figures set against the light?

I dug around in the trash on the floorboards for a pen and a scrap of paper. I drew his face, the dark curl on his forehead making him resemble a cartoonish Elvis. He appeared somewhat Mexican, distinctly foreign, and I couldn't understand how he was my father.

Footsteps padded over the concrete, and his shadow moved across the driver's window as the door handle clicked. I crumpled the paper.

Our next stop was a late lunch at an A&W. He didn't appear talkative, so I told him about the motorcycle theft, then, when he showed no interest, about a summer day when Brad and Travis and I had walked the train tracks and decided to derail a train. We'd found a heavy, rusted plate of indeterminable origin and hefted it onto a rail. We'd waited on the embankment, but after an hour the train hadn't come and we went home.

He barely looked at me, busy dipping fries in ketchup, three or four at a time, and pushing them into his mouth. It seemed as if he was finished with crime stories for good.

"Why do you do this?" I asked.

"What?"

"This work. Fish. It sucks."

He flinched, then drew himself up, straightening his back as if to command respect.

"You used to love helping in my stores when you were a kid."

I shrugged, not sure why he cared so much. "What about school?"

"What about it?"

"When am I going back?"

"It'd be better for you to work a bit," he said. "You were never good at school. Why don't you take some time off so we can get to know each other?"

"But I am going back, right?" I hated his stores, and school was the only escape I could think of.

Derision tweaked his upper lip, making him look a little like Elvis after all.

"You don't know how hard it was to get the business going again after the recession," he said. "Your mother just left. She didn't care that I was struggling. I lost everything and ended up living out of an old van. You really don't understand."

It was my turn to focus on the food. He was blaming my mother for his bankruptcy, but I remembered how he'd spent money before we'd left. Even now he lavished it on employees, tossing crisp hundreds on fast-food counters or giving Sara a fifty and telling her to get herself a coffee, then not accepting the change. Maybe my mother was right to leave.

We drove back through the city, the tops of skyscrapers hidden in the mist. He asked me to help with the next few errands, and this was a relief, though we hardly spoke.

By dinner, he appeared pensive. We were in another of his drab restaurants, and I worried that my aloofness might bring out his temper.

I remembered how angry he could get, how frightening. But now he looked uncertain.

"When I learned to crack safes, I wasn't much older than you." He glanced at my face to see if I was interested. "It wasn't easy. You had to be really focused to do it, but I liked the challenge. That's when I started crime. Everything else happened because of that . . ."

He described his departure from his village in Quebec, how he worked as a logger when he was sixteen, away from home all winter— and then in mines and construction. "But one day a friend died on a high-rise. He fell headfirst, and I realized I had to do something different."

He spoke softly, sounding tired, as if he had little interest in sharing his past but knew it was the only way to reach me. Someone in Montreal taught him safecracking, he said, his voice becoming angry—and this same person, his first partner, later set him up. In prison, my father learned how to burglarize banks and launder money.

"I did a lot after that. I tried to get out of crime a few times, but it was hard to go back to shit work. I ended up in California and Nevada, pulling armed robberies. We'd head to Vegas and blow our earnings in a weekend, then rob another store or bank, and drive to a resort in Tahoe. I'd grown up with snow, but I had no idea how to ski. We'd buy the most expensive ski clothes and hang out in the bar and pick up models. I'd tell them I was a businessman but that I couldn't say what I did. They loved it. Then I went to prison again and was deported. That's around the time I met your mother."

He hesitated. "But crime," he said, "crime was a good life. I've seen some crazy things." He leaned forward, smiling, and described what it was like to blow fifty thousand dollars in a night at a Vegas casino. "Diana Ross was next to me for about forty thousand of it. If I hadn't been trying to get back what I'd lost, I'd have taken her home . . ."

He no longer spoke as if his words were for me. His gaze opened out as if just to the left of me spread the vista of his past. Staring into it, he grew silent.

"What's the scariest thing you've done?" I asked, afraid that he'd stop talking. He looked at me as if remembering I was there.

Deni Y. Béchard

He sighed and smiled slowly. "The time I got the front page. I forget which paper it was. I should have made the front page for the burglary, but LBJ got it then. I got the second. He was the president, and that seemed pretty fair to me.

"But the thing is, it wasn't really me who made the front page. It was the guy I robbed. He owned a jewelry store that'd been held up five times, and he'd just been interviewed for an article on crime in LA. I guess he said something about how he'd never let it happen again. He said he had a gun and would rather shoot or get shot. If I'd known that, I'd have done some other place. You don't want to rob people like that. Common sense doesn't work with them . . ."

Our food had arrived, but he didn't pause to eat, just kept staring off, serious now. I struggled to make sense of the way he changed as he spoke. With each word, he seemed more dangerous, more real, more certain, as if there was nothing he couldn't face.

"We used to dress up nice when we did a job, that way no one would suspect us. People think the poor are criminals. We'd just go in and ask to look at the jewelry, then hold them up. I sold it all to some guys I knew in the mob. They didn't give us much, but jewelry stores were easier than banks. There was almost never security.

"Anyway, when I pulled my gun on this guy, he grabbed his. I almost shot him. There was at least a second—and that's a long time—when we stood with our guns pointed at each other. I saw he wasn't going to shoot. I don't know how I knew. I told him I would kill him. He had his gun aimed at my chest, but I had mine to his head and that's scarier. I asked if he was ready to die, and he put the gun down."

He studied me now, maybe wondering why he was telling this, what it meant. I wished he was still the person he'd been, the one he seemed to be when he spoke. My heart had sped up just hearing the story.

"I don't talk about this anymore," he said. "I barely think about it. But that was a crazy moment. I thought I'd shoot him. If you kill someone, the police don't give up on you the way they do when you pull a robbery. Insurance can't do anything for dead people."

Suddenly, I wasn't sure what I was looking for. I saw my mother's face so clearly she might have been there. She'd said she trusted me. She'd written that my father charmed people, but there was nothing he wanted from me, and she'd been wrong about so much.

"You want me to tell you these stories?" he asked.

"Yes," I said. "I love them. I want to hear them all."

He nodded. "I remember getting the paper the next day. The guy described me as over six feet tall and dark. I thought that was funny. It's amazing what fear will make you see."

"Do you miss it?" I asked.

"Sometimes." His expression softened. "You'd be good at crime. It takes people with nerves. But you have to want that feeling. I don't know why I did. I just did. I was so angry. When I was growing up, we were so fucking poor. I didn't want to have a miserable life."

All this made sense. It was how I'd felt in Virginia, why I'd come here.

Then he referred to the story I'd told him earlier, the one I thought he'd ignored, about trying to derail the train.

"I did things like that," he said. "When I was a kid, some friends and I went into a work site and pushed a big roll of metal fencing over a hill. It could have killed someone. We didn't care. We just wanted something to happen. I remember, when I left Quebec, after I got out of prison, I was so angry. I was driving to Calgary, and I couldn't stop thinking how I'd never had a chance, just a shitty life. The angrier I got, the faster I drove. A police car came after me, and I couldn't stop. I knew that the longer I waited, the worse it'd be, that I was ruining my life, but I didn't care. I hated everyone. By the time I got to the city, there were three cop cars behind me. I drove over medians and through parking lots and yards, down sidewalks and alleys. People were jumping out of the way. I knew I couldn't escape. More police joined in, and we just kept going until I ran out of gas. By then I wasn't angry anymore. I was laughing. I couldn't stop laughing.

"That's probably the angriest I've ever seen police," he told me, though he said nothing else about the arrest. "I started robbing banks not long after that. It felt good, you know. Each time I got away with it, it was like winning the lottery. I loved that life."

For a moment after he stopped speaking, he kept his eyes lowered. Then he looked up. His expression reminded me of when I was a boy and he would read the paper in his chair. Sometimes I went to the living room door and watched. He was serious and concentrated and sat a long time without moving. Then he lifted his eyes, and there was a moment when he was just seeing me, staring, before warmth entered his expression. He had the intensity of a guard dog fixing its gaze, trying to recognize the person approaching.

That evening, when we got home, he sat and turned on the TV as he always did, the channel muted and set to hockey.

"Have you ever thought about being a criminal?" he asked.

I tried to swallow but couldn't. Years with Dickie had taught me to be cautious. I mixed a shrug and a nod, letting my head tip to the side thoughtfully, the entire gesture slow and considered so I could insist he'd misunderstood if he was angry.

"You're like me," he said. "You'd be good at it."

Up to this point, my fantasies had been of easy heists and open horizons, the distant blue jewel of a roadblock on a desert highway. Again, I thought of my mother.

"It's a good life. You have the best of everything," he added. He set his elbows against his knees and studied his watch, tracing the dial with a flat fingertip. He was cleaning it, I realized, picking away fish scales. "It's better than what I do now. A lot better."

"Isn't it different than how it used to be?" I asked, hoping he'd say it was still possible.

"You have to find the right bank. I still know people out there."

He hunched in his chair but didn't speak.

The phone rang, and he looked at it as if unsure of where he was. He answered. He listened for a long time, the receiver cradled against his shoulder as he moved his fingers through his arm hair. He wrote down some prices and replied "Yes" several times.

I stared at the muted TV. I'd never considered actually stopping school or not writing. All my futures had coexisted in my imagination.

He murmured prices as silent hockey players slipped across the hazy screen.

After he was off the phone, I waited for him to say something else about crime, but he didn't, and I was afraid to ask.

It was dark, raining again as we arrived at the market with two plastic crates of fish, each about five hundred gallons. They'd been loaded by forklift, and normally we emptied them by hand. I hated this work.

"Can't we just put the truck in reverse and hit the brakes?" I asked. It was the sort of comment I'd made often over the years, adults rolling their eyes, but he turned in his seat to judge the distance to the delivery door.

Sara stood, lit red in our taillights, and he yelled out the window, telling her to get out of the way. He jammed the accelerator, and the truck shot forward and stopped sharply at the edge of the lot. The crates slid to the back window.

"This should work," he said.

Then he threw the truck into reverse and hit the gas. I twisted in my seat. The market wall was approaching fast. He slammed the brakes.

The tires screeched, and the crates hopped from the bed of the truck and seemed to hang briefly, suspended. They landed upright and skidded to the wide delivery door.

We got out, shocked into silence, and inspected the crates.

Heads lifted, everyone in the market stared at us, like deer in a field.

He smiled at me, his grin easy, not followed by scrutiny or anger. I laughed as if we'd done something like this every day of our lives, as if we'd just lurched from the railroad before the train passed.

We did it again three days later, though one of the crates spilled, hundreds of small salmon flashing across the market floor, under counters. For the next hour, we gathered them, customers and nearby vendors occasionally bringing us a fish, offering it to us as if it were a wallet forgotten in a restaurant.

"Are you getting along with him?" my mother asked the next morning when I called. I'd told him I wanted to stay home and write. He'd agreed, though he'd left with a scowl.

"Of course," I said in an annoyed voice. I talked a little about his life, that he was alone and didn't appear to have anyone close, even that he liked a girl who worked for him.

"Be careful," she said. "He might be recording his calls."

"I doubt it," I replied, glancing at the gray, loosely kinked phone cord on the dirty rug.

"What school are you going to go to?"

"We've looked at a few . . ."

"A few . . . ," she repeated. "You should enroll soon."

"I know. I will. Don't worry. I'll be fine."

After our conversation, I wandered through the house. There were details I found strange: a sign on the kitchen wall that read God Bless This Mess, or doilies on the couch's end tables, a vase of withered flowers in the dining room. It was as if a woman had been living there.

His room had the musty smell of a lair. Heaps of stiff clothes covered the floors of his closets, loosely folded jeans and button-down shirts on top of his dressers, price tags still on them. I counted a dozen pairs of running shoes, the laces and suede white, the soles unscuffed. Each had an orange sale sticker. In the closet, between two casual leather jackets, a Kmart bag on a hanger held seven red shotgun shells.

They felt heavy and cold in my palm. The printing on the casings read Slugs.

I went to the dresser and opened a drawer. It held photographs. A blond infant standing among dandelions. Two boys playing at the edge of a mud puddle. There were no images of children past the age of ten, as if their lives had ended.

In a field, my mother held me, my brother standing next to her. My father must have taken the photo. What had drawn her to him? That he was free and a rebel? I knew from living in the US—the trailer park had taught me this almost overnight—that Americans admired those who weren't afraid of the law. Maybe she'd had that wildness in her, too— the way she'd run away, rejecting the Vietnam War and her family. She'd wanted a free-spirited life and had probably thought she could find that with him. But she must have seen something other than a criminal. I knew her. If she hadn't, she wouldn't have stayed.

I kept searching. A rubber band held a dozen social insurance cards, each with a different name, one of them my brother's. My father must have named him after one of his aliases. This made sense. He wouldn't want to live under a name he didn't like—and naming oneself, starting a new life, might be like naming a child.

I pulled a box from under the bed: every sort of card, Christmas, birthday, get well, all unused, all for children. Another box was filled with fishing equipment, tangled lines and lures, faded cork floaters, three-pronged hooks, a hand scale, a fly-fishing kit, a bag of old back-lashed reels.

I found a Valentine's card I'd made for him in school, concentric multicolored hearts on construction paper, like the echo of affection. I sat in his chair. On the wall were three portraits of us our mother had given him for his birthday, simple charcoal sketches by a mall artist that made us look chubby. I hadn't found the shotgun in any of the obvious places.

Nothing, not even the trees outside, seemed to move, and then a German shepherd barked behind the house.

Sara sat on the freezer next to me, thigh to thigh, and took my hand and held it in her lap in a childish way. "Does André talk about me?" she asked.

I hesitated. He'd just gone to get something from his truck. I couldn't figure out their relationship, because she never came by his house and she mostly spoke of her high school friends, though she'd recently dropped out.

"Well, yeah," I told her, "I guess. I mean, he likes you."

"Really!" she said, as if she had no idea.

He came back into the market, walking quickly, then slowed, see-ing us sitting close.

"You ready?" he called and looked away as if distracted. I got off the freezer.

Soon we were back at Knight and Day, beneath the same dim, green metal lamps. He hadn't said much other than to order, and sat, rolling the edge of his paper place mat.

"You know," he told me, "I'm thinking about starting a new family."

"You'd want that?" I asked. Nothing seemed more miserable to me.

"Why wouldn't I? There's Sara. She needs to calm down."

"But are you two even together?"

"She drives my car. That Cavalier, the maroon one, it's mine. I shouldn't have been able to get it, not after the bankruptcy." He spoke as if having the car were strange, but it was his interest in Sara that bothered me. She was only eighteen.

His eyes stilled, looking into mine. What did he see? I had no idea if I was giving anything away, and I tried to make my face show nothing.

"Listen. I have a job for you. Some Indians are making a delivery tonight, and I want you to take care of it."

"What do you mean?"

"Business has been hard. It wasn't easy to start up again. So I buy from the Indians. They can fish as much as they want. And they always have good quality."

I just nodded, trying to mask my thoughts. I didn't say that what he was doing was illegal. That would be ridiculous. But this wasn't the crime I wanted.

"They're bringing a load of salmon to the place near the ferry. You can stay there for a few days. A girl who works for me lives there. She'll explain things to you if you need help. There's a road behind the house and some old freezers in the woods. The Indians have been there before. There's also a scale. Make sure you use it. Don't let them use theirs. And make sure you clean the ice off the plate if there's any. You have to watch that they don't weigh the salmon with ice in them. Check the cut where they were gutted."

After a pause, he said, "There should be about two thousand pounds. You can do this?"

"Of course," I said, not sure that I wanted to. But at least he trusted me and thought I could handle it.

"Just make sure nobody can see from the road. And I want you to do the weighing. You should be the one to read from the scale and write it down. You've seen me do it. It's easy."

The road descended through rocky pine forest. The green numbers on the dash read 10:17, and the truck's tires vibrated against the ridged surface of a bridge. I watched a lamppost pass, catching my reflection in the window.

"She's eighteen," he said of the girl who worked at the ferry. "You guys should get along."

The green trailer with a hand-lettered Fish 'n' Chips sign looked the same as I remembered, next to the misted river, just off the road where cars lined up. A few drivers stretched their legs as the ferry's lights moved across the dark expanse.

Gravel crunched loosely beneath the tires, and my father parked, though the driveway continued, rutted and muddy, into the forest. Yellow paint peeled from the house like birch bark, and a strand of green and red bulbs hung between a post and the snack bar awning, their color flaking, showing bright specks of light. A girl came to the door. Dark, curly hair framed her face, her skin faintly olive. She wore jeans, and a thin white shirt hung against her breasts.

Little was said beyond introductions, my father the only one speaking, the girl's eyes darting back to him after each time she glanced at me. Her name was Jasmine, and he told her I'd be sleeping on the couch. She forced a smile, her front teeth separated by a gap like a coin slot.

He and I then walked back along the looping driveway. It was dark beneath the pines but for the pale rectangles of two ancient freezers. He told me to put the salmon in them and handed me a wad of twenties.

"A thousand dollars," he said. "Don't give it to them until the end."

After he'd left, Jasmine and I hardly spoke. She lingered in the kitchen.

"I put some blankets on the couch," she told me.

"Thanks."

"Are you okay? Is there anything you need?"

"No, I'm fine."

"Okay, well, good night," she said and went upstairs.

The room with the couch had a scantily decorated Christmas tree that leaned in its stand, anchored to the outlet by a string of lights. I lay and stared at the ceiling, trying to feel that this was important, that I was doing something serious and impressive.

After weeks dreaming of the addictive terror of risk and the hard-earned win like a lottery jackpot, here I was. Maybe even when the crime was serious, you were alone in a dingy room, waiting on something you didn't care about, just for money. I'd wanted the thrill, that and to be with my father. I hadn't imagined ex-cons like his surly employees, warily meeting my gaze as if waiting for an accusation. People my age seemed hopeful, and I hadn't really considered life without school. My mother had been obsessed with education when I was little. She and my teachers had encouraged writing and yet did I love novels because I'd loved my father's stories? He'd never even read one.

I gazed past the threadbare curtains. Drivers sat behind damp windows, exhaust rising in the glow of taillights. Cars and trucks left the landing, tires banging over corrugated metal. Motors started up. Mist lay thick and low, variously tinged and glittering like rain beneath the streetlamp. The light changed at the entrance, the mist now green. The cars crept forward until the line was empty. The mist shone red again, eddying, settling against the dark asphalt.

I had no idea when I should expect the delivery. From the couch, I watched the line build up and load. A cop parked next to the restrooms, to sleep or lie in wait for those who sped along the lonely straightaway that extinguished itself at the river.

The police car was gone by midnight, when a green truck approached the streetlamp, body filler at the wheel wells and door edges. As it turned, its headlights plunged through the front window, into my eyes. It drove past the house, into the woods above the river. A moment later, a small blue pickup followed.

My heart was speeding. With a notepad and pen, I followed the tracks over the brittle ice.

The rain had stopped, and with the cold, the mist had almost lifted.

The moon, emerging from scattered clouds, hung over the river. Everything seemed amplified, vivid, washed in adrenaline—the late ferry run, the sound of the heavy engine across the water, the vessel's square bulk folding back the current, the river dragging its stiff belly against the night.

Four barrel-chested men stood behind the truck, the lid of a wooden crate against its side, a scale on the tailgate. They wore baseball caps, dark hair to their shoulders. Without introducing myself, I told them about the scale near the house, surprised to find myself breathless.

"We have our own. It's better," one of them said. He was shorter and burlier than the others, his face lost beneath his visor.

"I'm supposed to use my father's scale," I repeated.

They had begun setting up, and as one, they paused and turned and looked at me, four faceless men bulked against the dark.

"We're using our scale," the shortest one repeated.

"Okay," I conceded, then reconsidered. "But he wants me to weigh it."

"We're weighing it. You write it down."

He asked for the money, and I hesitated. My cold fingers had a hard time taking the wad of bills from the front pocket of my jeans. He counted it and put it in his jacket.

The men began loading a small plastic crate. The weights on the scale were set at a hundred, and each time the bar balanced, they dumped the crate into a garbage bag and carried it to the battered, iced-over freezers in the woods. I stood by the scale, making a tick on the paper for each bag. The short man told me which number it was, and I confirmed it.

The truck's shocks creaked, and my fingers ached as I tried to keep my records legible. The moon melted to a pale splotch low in the clouds, occasional flurries pushed by the wind. When I'd insisted on using the scale, I must have sounded like a boy, repeating my father's orders. But there was no threat in their responses, simply firmness, as if they were commanding a child. Though I resented this, they spoke to me kindly, telling me what to do, asking me to hand them another garbage bag.

The last of the fish had been weighed out. The short man patted me on the arm and thanked me. The gesture seemed deliberate, as if to reassure. They climbed into their trucks and drove to the road, slowing at the edge of the asphalt before accelerating.

Flurries tumbled down. The ferry's red and yellow lights moved above the water, slowing at the far shore, the clang of metal reaching me as if from a great distance.

THE CROSSING

I woke early, the skin of my face hot from the night in the cold air. I pulled on my shoes and walked out to the road. Five cars waited, windows pale with condensation. The ferry landing reached into the current like a broken bridge, the far shore appearing briefly beneath mist.

Dead grass and weeds grew from the house's gutters and shingles. I tried to recall that night years ago. It was late when he came inside, his shirt torn, hands bleeding, the skin around his eyes gouged. The fight was later ruled self-defense, all charges dropped. Had my mother, witnessing his violence, his ability to leave two people unconscious in a matter of seconds, felt trapped or protected?

I heard the steady acceleration of the truck's engine before I saw him. He braked and turned, his tires digging into the frozen gravel, and drove back into the forest. He was already standing at one of the rust-pitted freezers, the top lifted, when I got there.

"Help me load this," he said without looking at me. "Then we'll get something to eat."

Afterward, at a restaurant on a busy street in Fort Langley, he told me I'd done a good job. "You did what I asked you to, right?"

"Yeah, of course."

He nodded, silent, as he scrutinized my face.

"Listen, I want you to stay at the ferry for a while."

"Why? How long?"

"For the holidays. I'm too busy right now, and Jasmine needs help. She's lonely. You can stick around until after Christmas."

"What about school?"

He shrugged and smiled unconvincingly. "Why do you need it? I didn't."

I'd been friends with dropouts over the years, but I'd never seen myself that way, even when I hated school. Besides, if I stopped going, my mother might do something crazy.

"I have to go back to school," I said.

He dropped his gaze and sighed. "Listen, a year off wouldn't hurt. We'd have time to get to know each other. You might not even need to go back. I never had an education."

I looked away to hide my anger. Cars flashed past on the street. An old man shuffled along in a raincoat, and two girls ran woodenly in high heels to the bus stop.

"Besides," he told me, "it will feel good for you to be a man. Make some money and get out in the world."

I still didn't say anything. He sounded wise and honest, concerned with my best interest without mentioning his own goals. I realized how easy it would be to like what he said, but I didn't want his life. Though I'd resented having to go to school, it now seemed the only escape. He indulged his fidget, moving the paper place mat back and forth with his fingertips.

"You know," he said, "after I pulled the big job, I thought I'd never have to work again. I never thought I'd be here . . ."

I looked at him but didn't speak, knowing he'd tell stories now, trying to charm me.

"It was a year after the burglary in Hollywood . . ." He furrowed his brow as if remembering. "I was in a bar in Miami, talking to a girl, and a man came up and slapped her. I didn't even think about it. I broke his nose with a punch. There was blood everywhere, all over his shirt. The girl started swearing at me, and someone told me she was a whore getting it from her pimp."

He shook his head, appearing disappointed, as if he might have liked her.

"I left, and as I was starting my car, the pimp ran out. He had a bruiser with him carrying a metal bar. I fired up the engine just as the bruiser put the bar through the ragtop."

He motioned to the back of his head, behind his ear. "It passed right there and almost hit me. I kicked the door open as he was pulling it out, and the edge of the door hit him. Then I kneed him in the face, threw him down, and kicked him in the neck. The pimp had a knife, and I took the bar from the ragtop and hit him across the knees. That's when the police arrived.

"The three of us, me and the pimp and the bruiser, we were taken to the station. The cops had come for the pimp, not for me. They asked me to give a statement saying I'd fought in self-defense. They were pretty happy about getting him. This one cop joked with me about boxing and asked how I'd taken down the bruiser.

"I just had to give that statement. I was almost out of there. Me and that cop, we were walking out, talking about the fight, when another cop called from inside. He asked if my green card had been checked. The guy who was with me didn't seem too worried, but the cop who'd asked said I had an accent. The other guy told me there was no problem. They just needed to see my papers. He was smiling with all his talk about knockouts. I told him my wallet had been stolen."

He sighed, maybe seeing this from the perspective of all that followed. He didn't sound sad, just contemplative, as if this were no longer about him. The other cop wanted to check his fingerprints. The fingerprints found a match, and my father fit the description given by the man with the burned eyes.

"The cop who'd talked with me about boxing couldn't look at me," he said. "He was embarrassed to have spoken to a criminal the way you talk to a normal man."

He cleared his throat as if embarrassed himself, as if he'd meant to tell me something amazing that would make me forget about school. I had the impression he was only now discovering his past, trying to see where it fit in his life, as if the stories were surprising him, too, changing him, his eyes different, a hint of rage in them.

"But after the arrest," he said and forced a smile, "after that—that was funny. The police wanted me to fly to California. My trial was going to be there, but you can't force a convict to fly. It's not legal.

"They offered me a big meal, wine even, if I'd take the plane. I said I would, and I stuffed myself. It was a great meal. Steak, lobster, wine. But when I got to the airport the next day, I said I wouldn't fly. I shook my head and told them, 'I'm not getting on. I just remembered I'm afraid of planes.'" He laughed, repeating the line, and he let himself look at me, smiling. "After that big meal they bribed me with, they were furious. They had to drive me across the country, from Florida to California. I didn't like the drive either, but I figured I stood a better chance of jumping out of a moving car than out of a plane."

Seeing his face, I knew that I was right, that this was new for him. He smiled like someone hearing a story for the first time, losing himself in it.

"During that trip, I spent every night in a different jail. Whenever I got to a new one, a local cop had to fill out a form with my personal information. Each time, when he asked my occupation, I said, 'Unemployed bank robber.' Most of those guys laughed, but there were some real hard-asses who asked over and over. I guess they finally just wrote down unemployed, because I didn't change what I was saying."

Outside the snack bar window, the fog broke beneath occasional rain, but the sun remained caught in mist, like a dull, fat fly in a web.

"How long will you be staying?" Jasmine asked.

"I don't know," I said and sank deeper into my jacket, breathing against its collar to warm my throat. I closed my dog-eared novel. "How long have you been living here?"

"A few months, I guess."

"Where do you know André from?"

"He was friends with my parents. He offered me a job." She explained that her stepfather was a drunk and my father had helped her leave home. I couldn't see the appeal in living at a ferry landing on a lonely stretch of river. She didn't even have a car.

I told her my own stories, about life in Virginia, stealing the motor-cycle, but she didn't smile. She squinched up her face. "That's stupid."

Drivers had shut off their engines, customers braving the rain, hurrying toward us.

"What? I—"

"It's dumb. Does your father know?"

She got up, went to the orange counter, and took an order for coffee.

I stared off along the line. The rain fell harder, rushing from the overhang onto the shoulders of the man reaching for the sugar. An old couple turned back to their camper.

I couldn't imagine my life after Christmas. Was this being a man? He was using me, but I didn't know what for. If I didn't return to school, I'd have to repeat the year. With a rage that surprised me, I hated him.

"I'm going inside," I told Jasmine and ran through the rain and sat on the couch.

From the window, I could see the orange counter and, just inside, in the angle of unmoving light, the curve of her breasts beneath her sweater. Shadows hid her face. She appeared too still. At the docks, the green light lit up, and the traffic crept forward.

After dark, as rain fell past the strand of colored bulbs, the red and gray GMC pulled into the driveway. I hid my book. Jasmine had just closed the snack bar, and my father came inside with a grease-stained bag of Chinese food. But once we were at the table together, we hardly spoke. He asked a few questions about sales, then looked at the cassettes next to the radio.

"One time," he said, "when I was traveling in the States, I pulled into a gas station right after Elvis had been there. I even saw his Cadillac leaving, and the attendant told me it was Elvis. It's too bad I didn't get there earlier. I'd have liked to see the King."

I considered this other brand of story, innocuous, innocent, a groupie's celebrity sighting. He couldn't tell his real stories with Jasmine there. Who had he been before I'd come back? How much had he changed for me? She glanced between us, and not wanting to seem like a boy, I gazed at him evenly, without interest or emotion.

His hand rested on the table, half curled into a fist, and he rubbed the muscle on the back of his forearm absently. Slowly, he flattened his hand against the wood and studied it. He put it in his lap, rolled his shoulders, and swallowed. He met my gaze and stared.

"I can't believe I have to stay here," I told Jasmine after he'd left.

"Why? What's wrong with being here?"

"He wants to start a new family. That's why he's making me live here." I repeated some of what he'd told me and explained his interest in Sara. She listened intently.

"Is she his girlfriend?" she asked.

"I don't think so. He just likes her, but she's too young."

She pulled her knee to her chest and wrapped her arms around it. Her brow was furrowed, her bottom lip slightly loose, as if in a pout. She traced the leg seam of her jeans with a fingertip.

After a moment, she got up and went into the bathroom. I could hear her brushing her teeth. Then the door clicked shut, and there was only the sound of water whining in the cold pipes. I sat at the table and opened the notebook in which I'd started a fantasy novel. When she came back, she'd changed into her nightgown. It had flimsy straps, and as she got a glass of water, the spreading lines of her collarbone shone beneath the kitchen's naked bulb. The olive skin of her legs moved against the pale, ruffled fringe. She stood next to me and looked at my cramped scrawl. Her hip touched my shoulder as she leaned forward, her nightgown loose at the front, my eyeballs twisting painfully in their sockets, trying for a glimpse even as I held my face to the page.

"Why do you write this stupid stuff?" she asked. With the glass of water in her fingers, she went upstairs, crouching to avoid the low ceiling, the curve of her ass lifted.

The rain slackened to a drizzle, and I left the house, fumbling with my jacket, hurrying past the snack bar, panting. Anxiety, the feeling of being trapped, had come quickly. The water on the ground had frozen, and I almost slipped. I stopped near the landing. The ferry's horn called from over the river, red and yellow lights in the mist. A pickup appeared on the dark road, slowing to enter the docks.

A week had gone by. My father had called a few times to ask how we were doing, but he was too busy to visit. I slept or read or hung out in the snack bar. Jasmine kept her distance, arms crossed, shoulders drawn in. Nights, I sat at the table, creating a fantasy world, drawing maps, while upstairs she lay in her attic bedroom, reading a romance novel.

Now would be the time to hitchhike, but where? I realized how safe my adventures had been before. Could I cross the country again? Cross the border? The problem was the same as in the realistic stories I'd tried to write, the ones in which I escaped but only got so far before the options ran out. If I went back to my mother, she and Dickie would win. My father was a liar. He had nothing but stories.

The string of flaking colored bulbs swayed faintly with the wind. I went inside and took the phone. Who could I call?

Under the sink, a mildewed, six-year-old phone book left its cover glued to the bottom of the cabinet when I lifted it. It had been there since before my mother fled. I found the name of a classmate from elementary school, a girl I'd liked named Deborah. The address seemed right, and I tore out the page and threw the book back on its cover. It left sooty streaks on my hands, and I wiped them on my jeans. The ferry horn sounded, and a car door closed in the line.

I went to the couch and sat. Then I picked up the receiver and dialed.

After four or five rings, a groggy adult answered, and I asked for Deborah. The voice that finally said hello sounded awake, my age but not familiar. I told her who I was.

"Of course, I remember you. How are you?" She sounded somewhat pleased.

"I'm good."

There was a moment of silence as I thought of what to say.

"Where are you?" she asked. "You disappeared. Nobody knew what happened."

"I'm back."

"Nearby?"

"No. But maybe soon. I moved to the States. My parents separated, and we went to live there. How about you?"

"What?"

"I don't know. What school do you go to?"

She named one I'd never heard of, then said it was private and asked about mine.

"I just moved back," I told her. "I took a month off. I'll probably start again soon."

The silence held a little longer. Outside, beyond the window, the line had built up. A few passengers got out for air, pant legs flashing through headlights. I asked about other friends. A few had moved away, and two attended her school. This struck me as odd, but I recalled that their houses had been nicer than mine. She asked what I was doing, and I told her, "I work for my father. I hate his fucking fish business."

"Things were hard for you, weren't they?" she asked.

Her question shocked me, its innocent honesty.

"Actually, I'm going to be a writer. I'm working on a novel right now. Every night. I pretty much don't even sleep."

"Oh," she said. "That's interesting."

I told her about the book, the hero fleeing through an imaginary land. It sounded impossibly stupid.

"Well," she said after a pause, "if you're ever around, you should call again."

I put down the phone, the muscles of my jaw trembling. I pressed my palms to my face and promised myself I'd never cry over something so stupid. I made the emotions stop, as if crushing them with an act so tangible I could feel the pressure in my chest. Fear and sadness seemed weak and childlike. I could escape. How hard could it be? How smart was my father if this was his life? I'd just have to be patient. Still, I wished he would prove that he was more than what he seemed.

For the rest of the night, I filled my notebook. A young man of uncertain parentage appeared from a sky torn asunder, as if he too had arrived in a plane. But even as I wrote, I hated it. My hero became surly, defying prophecies and kings, leaving the places of his youth. I wanted to write something real, but I had just a feeling—no story, no characters. I knew only that when I wrote, I was who I truly wanted to be.

I turned off the light.

The clock's bony red numbers read 4:50. The moon had set, and there was a deep predawn darkness over the river. I rubbed my eyes, not wanting to sleep and wake to the misted lineup before the docks.

Steinbeck's characters had seemed like losers to me, men wandering and escaping. Why did people like to read about criminals? Because they were free? They survived, always chasing a dream.

My father had traveled cross-country. Dressed in a suit, he'd driven from Los Angeles to Las Vegas, he and his friends armed with guns, drinking, laughing over money they'd stolen. He'd described more innocent adventures in his youth working in the wind, running along the beams of skyscrapers, until the day his friend tripped and died.

As if in a fantasy novel, it seemed that only after some terrible thing happened, the journey would begin.

He arrived shortly before noon. Freezing rain was falling, and we drove to a diner, where we sat in a booth and ordered coffee, fries, bacon, and eggs. Outside, a few semis had been left running, faint vibrations rattling the windows.

"I want to go back to school," I said.

"Come on. You were never good at school. A year off won't hurt."

"I want to go back in January."

He looked me in the eye. "Listen, you can't just come into my life and expect me to do what you want. I'm too busy to support you through school. Besides, it isn't for you. That's clear to me. You and me, we're the same that way. You just have to grow up and see what the world's really like. You have no idea."

I was twisting my napkin. I forced myself to stop, to sit up straight. I tried to work through my rage, looking for a solution, my thoughts like water against a barrier, seeping into it, searching out fissures. When I'd left Virginia, I was a decent if indifferent student. Now school seemed the only freedom possible.

"You know," he went on, "I didn't pay for you to come out here so you could live like a king. I can't let you turn my life upside down."

"What? What am I doing wrong?"

He waved his hand. "You almost never called. Five years is a long time. You didn't even write. You want to be a writer, and you didn't write."

"I wanted to come back, but I wasn't allowed."

"You could've run away," he said, his lip drawing back from his teeth, one of his incisors faintly darker. "It's easy. You just take a bus. You stole a motorcycle but you couldn't figure out how to come back." He hesitated, then repeated, "Five years," as if these words contained all the wrong in the world.

Finally I understood. All this time he'd been torn between pride and anger. I'd come back, so in a way he'd won. But I'd also let him down, and now I had to prove myself.

"She said you were dangerous," I offered, wanting him to understand.

"What? She had no right. The day she left and took the three of you, I came back to the house while she was packing. She had some friends helping her. They were from one of those spiritualist groups, and they all got scared and left, even the men. A bunch of cowards. She told me you guys were in the States already. She said the police knew all about it."

He took a breath and shook his head.

"I'm not allowed across the border. She knew what the police could do to me."

He hesitated, searching for the point he was trying to make. He sounded as if he were continuing an argument he'd carried on in his head for years.

"I let her leave. I didn't have to do that."

I had nothing to say. I'd finished eating and now I listened, looking down, forced to wait this out just as I was waiting out my detention by the river.

"You can't understand what it was like," he said. "After she took you, I spent weeks in bed. I couldn't do anything. I could barely move."

He was staring through me, his eyes shining, wet with rage.

"I deserve another chance. I'm still young."

He looked down and picked at his cold fries. He pushed one around the plate, smearing the ketchup, then ate it.

A tall, stooped man came from the kitchen, pens in his shirt pocket, and my father smiled, instantly transformed. He shook his hand. It was the manager, asking what fish were available. My father introduced me as his son, but I didn't offer to shake the man's hand, barely nodded.

After he left, as soon as the kitchen door closed, my father leaned forward sharply.

"Let me tell you something. That guy—you don't know a thing about him. He could be anybody. He could kill you just like that. You understand? So don't be rude."

I shrugged.

"You know," he said, "I saw a guy get his head blown off. We were in a bar in Alaska, and a friend I worked with got into an argument with a pimp. The pimp walked away, but he sent his whore over to slap my friend. My friend didn't say anything. He just left. Then ten minutes later, he came back with a shotgun and emptied both barrels in the pimp's face.

"I saw that guy years later in the pen, and he told me he didn't regret a thing. He wasn't crazy. Even in the pen, he kept to himself. That's how easy it is. So don't go making people feel stupid. A man has to live with himself. Be polite."

Sleet was falling hard, obscuring the drab country beyond the highway, the roadside grass pale and distinct. Ice gathered on the windshield, the wipers pressing it away in layers. He held the steering wheel in both hands, and in the gloom, they seemed too large and dark, reminding me of how they'd looked to me when I was a boy. They gripped the plastic as if he had to keep them busy.

"You think you're tough," he said, and from his tone I knew he'd do something, the way as a child I'd sensed his recklessness moments before he swerved through traffic.

I didn't speak, and he continued. "That's good, because you're going to do a job for me."

I held my hands between my knees as he cut into a subdivision of identical unkempt houses, the postage-stamp yards tangles of frozen weeds. He coasted a ways and stopped. He looked past me, through the passenger window. An ancient Ford tow truck filled a driveway, all bare rusted metal and tied-up chains. It belonged to Brandon, a man who occasionally worked for him, a slacker who always wore a stained Canucks cap. I'd met him at the market.

"Brandon owes me fifty dollars. I want you to get it for me."

He groped beneath the seat, pushing at pop cans and candy-bar wrappers, and took out a wooden baseball bat with Slugger printed on the side. He put it in my hands.

"Fifty dollars is nothing," I said, digging my fingertips at the smooth, hard wood.

"It's a question of principles. I don't let anyone laugh at me."

As soon as the door closed, he pulled away. I was instantly wet. The bat felt too heavy, and I cradled it against my arm. The small print on the side said it had a lead core.

The address plaque read 64 Picadilly, printed with faded flowers that still stood out against the gray plastic siding. Very little of the tow truck was without rust. My father had once told me it dated to the fifties, like those he'd seen in Montreal. My footsteps moved far below my body as they carried me toward the door. I hesitated, then knocked.

A pregnant girl answered, hardly older than me, blond, her skin shiny as if she were sick. Her abdomen bulged below her breasts, her protruding navel clearly visible through a man's T-shirt that was stretched and threadbare and yellow with age.

"Is Brandon here?" I asked, holding the bat casually in back of my leg, as if I were inviting him out to play.

"He's gone," she said and looked at the bat, her eyes widening.

"I'm supposed to pick up some money he owes my father."

"He's not here." Her posture was rigid, movements stiff, both of us locked in the same automatic dream. She closed the door and snapped the lock.

I drifted to the sidewalk as rain made icicles in my hair. I couldn't manage this simple task, the amount of money insignificant, as if to make me feel unimportant. I considered the child growing inside the girl's belly, the life it would have.

I circled the house, through weeds and mud, peering at drawn blinds as water seeped into my shoes. I stopped at the tow truck, trying to look busy and serious since she might be watching. I squinted into the cab and under the crumbling chassis. My shoes squelched. What would he do? Smash a window? Kick in the door? I could beat on the tow truck, though it looked as if it had already endured the bats of numerous creditors. I told myself that I had to stop thinking, just force my way into the house and take the money.

"What?" she asked, the door open enough for her to look at me above the chain. With a kick, I could break it. Her skin gleamed, her face puffy, her hair limp against her shoulders. That she didn't threaten to call the police seemed a sign of her guilt. But as I was asking for the money, trying to explain, a feeling of disgust came over me, so strong I wanted to vomit. Fifty pathetic dollars, taken from this pitiful house, from a pregnant girl.

I walked back to the road.

My father's truck returned and stopped, and I got inside.

He asked me nothing.

A space heater sat on the freezer, and Jasmine and I held our hands before it, staring at the line as hazing rain iced up the road. I'd finished my last novel, yet another world saved from cataclysm. The sky here was as dark as in that land whose sun had been extinguished, but it wasn't my destiny to change it. I wished snow would fall and erase everything.

A radio sat on the shelf, and having nothing to read, I took it down. I cleaned dust from the dial, then searched the static until a voice came through with startling clarity.

The forecast was dismal. The weatherman mused that a white Christmas would be nice, not this slush and freezing rain. Then an announcer gave the time. He spoke of the year in review, the historic events the world wouldn't soon forget. In December alone, Czechoslovakia and Romania had overturned Communist dictatorships. The list included Tiananmen Square and the anti-apartheid movement, Soviet withdrawal from Afghanistan and the fall of the Berlin Wall. Democracy movements were taking over in Latin America, General Colin Powell was the first black chairman of the Joint Chiefs of Staff, New York had its first black mayor, and Virginia had elected the first black governor since Reconstruction. There was the three-million-dollar price on the head of Salman Rushdie by Ayatollah Khomeini, and later the ayatollah's death. The recap went on, a countdown not unlike Casey Kasem's *American Top 40*, but edged with violence and urgency. These events, the world itself, seemed in no way connected to my life, and I couldn't imagine writing something important enough for people to want to kill me.

"Why do you stay here?" I asked, standing as if to pace the tiny room. I said how angry I was, that I felt trapped.

A flush came into her cheeks, her dark eyes wide and bottomless.

"Stop complaining," she told me and looked away.

Footsteps on the porch woke me. Jasmine turned her body to fit the register drawer through the doorway. Outside, the string of colored lights swayed. The rain had stopped.

She set the drawer on the kitchen table and came into the room. I moved my feet so she could sit on the couch.

"Are you okay?" she asked.

"Yeah, I'm fine."

She put her hand on my leg and rubbed it, as if to reassure me. We just stared at each other, her fingers on my thigh.

"I want to tell you something," she said.

"What?" I asked, still half-asleep.

"Your father and me—we used to live together."

I didn't speak. Her hand rested on my jeans, slightly curved, appearing awkward now, and she took it away and put it in her lap.

"He made me stay here because you were coming," she said.

When I'd called from Virginia to ask if I could live with him, I'd heard a woman's voice and the sound of dishes being washed.

She described the last few years, the way he'd started his business again, her words reminding me of how he'd worked when I was a boy. She thought they'd have a family.

What had I failed to grasp? It was hard for me to understand, to make sense of who he really was or wanted to be. Was he just trying to have a normal life: a good car, a successful business, nice clothes, and an attractive girlfriend? Sara was much prettier, and maybe when I'd returned he'd wanted to impress me. Had he hidden the parts that looked wrong? I'd pushed him. I knew that. I'd wanted his wildness, but this wasn't what I expected to find.

She finished, and then just sat. The clang of the ferry docking filled the silence.

What had he been expecting when I came back? My fantasies seemed cold things, robberies and escapes. My fondest memories were of the days he and I had spent fishing, hours by rivers, scanning the water. I'd dreamed of a mythical fish that, when finally caught, granted wishes. But the fish came up, glittering desperately in the sunlight, and he gutted it, sweeping out the deflated organs with his knife.

She put her hand on my side, as if to comfort me.

Christmas Eve, a wind blew up. Frost patterned the dirty windows, the yard a sheet of ice. Tepid air blew in the vents, and I woke on the couch, wondering if I'd been remembering or dreaming the valley: clouds moved too quickly, turning in on themselves as our mother led us across a field of dead grass, pines the only green on the mountain. Her graying hair was pulled back, and it seemed that the warmth of my hand against my chest was the reassurance of hers. We'd gone for a walk after the snow had melted, springtime almost here. In the way she'd breathed and carried herself, I'd sensed her relief that winter was finally ending.

And then, in sleep, just images. A tree shrouded in mist. A child straggling below mountains. The valley echoing, hoots and laughter, then so silent that a German shepherd came to the slats of the pen and peered at the heavy sky.

I sat up, unsure of where I was. I rubbed my eyes. The curtains were drawn, a wand of streetlight through a hole. I lifted my fingers to it and they glistened. The furnace thrummed and wind rattled the panes. When I opened my eyes again, the room held a thin gray light.

No sounds came from the ferry landing, no idling engines in the line. I slid the curtains open. The asphalt glistened, its cracks and crumbling shoulder a sheen of ice.

I pulled my shoes on and went outside. The cold had thinned the mist that lingered, pushed about by the wind. Far above, sunlight flirted with the clouds. The cold felt good in my lungs. It made me want to clean out everything, to leave and forget. I stepped carefully up the driveway and onto the landing, the walk separated by a railing and scattered with salt. Melting ice dripped into the water from the planks beneath me.

The river stretched out, gray and faintly rippled, so wide that the opposite landing looked like a snag of driftwood. The ferry, a white barge parked among the lit poles, began to hum. It struck me as odd that I hadn't crossed, that a person could simply choose his freedom and leave.

Halfway along the docks, I stopped. As the sun penetrated the clouds, I glimpsed high white mountains in the distance. The ferry set out, its wake grooving the water. A tiny figure stood at the railing, one hand holding down a hat.

What had driven my father to leave his home, his family, to travel the continent and become someone else, to rob banks and risk his life over and over? What would drive me?

A wall of fog moved along the river. Briefly, I could hardly see my lifted hands before it passed. Then the sun broke in along the clouds, revealing a range of white mountains that shone against the sky.

BORROWING FACES

"So that's it? You've made up your mind?" he asked.

"Yes," I said and went back to my plate of greasy chicken caccia-
tore, one of our ceremonial dinners, consumed like a smoldering peace
pipe while our talk hinted at war.

"And you know you're on your own then? I'll give you some money
to get started, but that's all."

"Yeah. That's fine," I said, chewing between words.

We'd been wrangling over the future. He wanted me to work for
him and thought his threat carried some weight: *If you choose to go to
school, you'll have to move out and live on your own.* He didn't seem to
realize that I wasn't living with him. I insisted on school.

After New Year's, he drove me to the rundown house of a short
gray-haired woman who had a room for rent. Her easy smile softened the
heaviness in her face. Her daughter, petite and auburn, a year younger
than I was, had worked at my father's store over the summer.

My window faced the highway, one pane broken, masking tape
holding a cardboard patch. I looked through the dirty unbroken glass
that, with the passing of cars, shook in its crumbled glazing. As if I'd
come to rent the window, I said, "It's fine."

That night, as headlights fanned across the ceiling and the engines
of big trucks vibrated in the floorboards, I lay in bed. Though I didn't like
this room, I was closer to choosing my life, to being a man. Emotions fell
away—fear, anger, sadness. Cars revved up the incline or swished down
the opposite lane. The cold stung my nostrils, and I parted my lips. I

breathed, feeling a delicate sliver of cool air between my teeth. I sensed my path taking shape.

The next evening, over a dinner of boiled pork, my landlady told her own stories, of a principled father and a suicidal mother. She sipped warm scotch cut with tap water and had difficulty walking even when sober, something to do with years of drinking.

Afterward, I called my mother. As the phone rang, I cleared my throat, trying to relax my voice.

"It's me," I told her.

"Deni. Hey. How are you?" She sounded happy, though every time we'd spoken since I'd left I could detect fear in her words. "Where— where are you?"

"I'm living with André."

"Is everything okay?"

"Yeah. Of course. I just called to say hi. I'm fine."

"Oh." She hesitated. "That's good."

"You know, I'm writing a lot," I said. Since there was no way I was going back to her and Dickie, I couldn't tell her about my life. It made me feel strong to be able to reassure her, to keep my problems to myself. Still, I had to talk about something else.

"I've been writing stories and poetry. I even wrote a short novel, but I'm not sure it's any good."

"I bet it's great."

"I don't think so."

"Can you send me some stuff?"

"Maybe. I need to read everything again, but I wrote a poem that might be okay. Do you want me to read it to you?"

"I would love that."

I already had the page, and I tried to take my time with the words, but halfway through I realized how childish the poem was, about the world in the mind's eye, its freedom. I sped up, mumbling the last lines.

"Oh," she said. "That was great."

"Really? I don't like it anymore."

"You went a bit fast in the end, but I liked what I heard."

After we said good-bye, I lay staring at the ceiling. She loved art and studied it at university before running away with a draft dodger. Every now and then, when I was little, she drew a picture that amazed me—a lightly penciled, perfectly realistic tree and house for the cover of a story I'd written, or, when I struggled with my portrait of Frankenstein, unable to make his strangler's paws believable, she sketched a hand with dark creases and smudged, shadowed areas. It looked more real than my own, as if it had just finished changing a truck tire and might now reach from the paper to snatch my pencil.

The air brakes of semis thudded on the highway. Why had she given up art? To ignore such a gift confused me. When I was seven or eight, we were in a mall where artists set up stands and drew portraits. One exhibited caricatures: a vampiric, hooked-nosed Pierre Trudeau; Reagan with a massive jaw and a tuft of goofy black hair. Impressed, I wanted to know if she could draw like that, and she told me it was easy.

"Will you do one when we get home?" I asked over and over until she agreed.

That afternoon, while she was sitting on the back steps in the sunlight, I brought a pencil and pad for her, pushing them into her hands. My brother and sister edged close.

"Draw André," I requested.

She looked into the distance, toward the mountain beyond the fields, and a smile came onto her lips, a faint, mischievous narrowing to her eyes.

She sized up the blank page and began to sketch. My father's head took shape like a balloon about to pop, stamped with a ridiculous toothy smile and the big blank eyes of a happy idiot. Yet it was unquestionably him, with his dark beard and curly hair.

"What about his body?" I asked when she'd finished.

She moved her pencil down and drew a miniature torso, arms and legs sticking out like pins. It looked tiny in proportion to the head, as if I were seeing it from high above.

We all stared a long time, and then my sister threw her head back and burst into laughter. She couldn't stop, and after a few seconds, we joined her.

I found a job at an Italian restaurant, washed dishes and minced garlic and ate everything sent back: small pizzas that I folded and forced into my mouth, risotto that I spooned rapidly, my cheeks bulging as I went about my tasks. I rode there each evening on a rusted, rickety bike without brakes that I'd found leaning against the wall in my landlady's shed. I puffed through the cooling air, grinding uphill, and then rushed back, late at night, down that dark, thrilling, terrifying sweep of highway.

Daily, the mirror in my room confronted me. I showed it an indifferent face, a thuggish stance. I picked up gestures and expressions anywhere: the glowering brow of a burly redheaded man arguing over a beer bottle refund in a convenience store, or the squint of an Italian tough waiting for his girlfriend in a sports car. On the public bus the day I went to enroll in school, I wore my leather jacket. A gray-bearded man with reflective sunglasses and a Harley-Davidson vest sat next to me. He prodded my arm.

"Thick," he said. "Good choice. It's hard to stab a man through leather like that."

On my first day in class, when another student said, "What's up with the jacket?" I explained that I wore leather because it was hard to stab someone through it.

"I just want to play it safe," I said gruffly. "You never know. It's happened before."

My stories soon established me as the school's best fighter, its most unpredictable and volatile student. The one time I was confronted— three lanky bullies appearing from the hallway crowd, peach fuzz on their chins, oversize Raiders jackets slung back on their shoulders—I puffed my chest, bugged my eyes, and conjured the scariest face I knew—my father's, though I had no idea exactly when I'd seen him this way.

"You fuck with me," I hissed, "I'm going to kill you—all of you." Spit flecked my lips, and the boys edged back as I showed them all the white my eyes could muster.

"Yeah, you just be careful," the one in the middle said and glanced from side to side at his cohorts. They turned and strutted awkwardly until they reached the end of the hall and pushed out the double doors into the pale sunlight.

By lunch, I was back at the corner table, writing a poem about the highway at night, the chug of diesel engines and big trucks downshifting to low gears. The cold slip of air behind each passing car evoked everything I could ever want to tell another person.

Teachers saw that I liked to write and encouraged me, but I knew— lying in the dark bedroom as my poetic semis blundered past, winter air seeping through the cardboard—that in my old dream of levitation the monk who rises must first make peace with solitude.

Unable to sleep, I got up and wrote. I attempted novels about futuristic societies verging on collapse, or stories about wanderers, a boy who meets a girl on a roadside and can briefly reveal his tenderness before moving on with the hard-set face of the man he has yet to become. It seemed as if only when I was finding the words, writing them, could I understand what I really felt.

"You know," my father said over dinner, in what was to become our weekly routine. He intoned the two words in the voice he used when about to introduce an idea I might not like. "You know, I was thinking. There are these two men I buy from. They're crab fishermen, a father and son. They work together. They drink together. They're a real team. You used to love working with fish when you were a kid."

I kept my eyes half-lidded. I shrugged and forked ravioli into my mouth, drank some beer, chewed and swallowed.

"Yeah, well," I said out of the side of my mouth, "I'm not a kid anymore."

"What do you want to do? Just go to school?"

"What's wrong with that? I'm fifteen."

"And then what?"

"I want to be a writer."

"Why? What do you have to write? You're just a kid."

"No I'm not."

I hunched, affecting the glowering brow of the burly redheaded man in the convenience store. I shoveled some more ravioli into my mouth, drank and swallowed.

"I need rent money," I told him.

"Don't you have it? You said you're working."

He forced an incredulous smile, as if I had to be kidding after my show of certainty.

"Almost."

"How much do you need?"

"A hundred and fifty more."

"How about this? I give you the money, and you work it off for me this summer."

I sighed, squinting like the Italian tough waiting in the sports car, but this was exactly what I'd expected. I knew that he thought I couldn't survive on my own, that I'd come back to him and give up on school, but I wouldn't.

"Fine," I said.

He took a wad of cash from his pocket and peeled off three fifties and tossed them before me, his eyes attempting compassion.

That I'd work for him in June created constant apprehension, distracting me at school and keeping me up at night. He mentioned the job frequently over the next months, but I just nodded and refused to say anything on the subject.

The face that worked best against him, I had learned, was impassive: the outside the opposite of the inside, offering nothing. I studied it in teachers when students complained, in the principal when he dealt with misbehavior, in the bus drivers who refused those who couldn't pay the fare, in the police who directed traffic outside my school. This was how men dealt with the world. My father told stories, maybe to impress me or just to fill the silence, and though I enjoyed them, I did little more than nod. If I needed his money, I took it as if it meant nothing.

One night, entering a restaurant, we passed a man who was trying to ask for directions at the register, his English heavily accented. My father stopped abruptly and spoke in French, offering to help. The man, portly, with a ruff of gray hair, smiled and told him where he needed to go. As my father explained, his words seemed to come in spurts. He'd hesitate, then point outside, in the direction of the highway, and his mouth would hang open, and suddenly he'd give a list of instructions in a rush. Then he'd pause again, searching for words.

The man's eyes narrowed. "*Ça fait longtemps que t'es parti?*"

My father flushed and looked off.

"*Plusieurs années,*" he said, then asked, "*Tu viens d'où?*"

"*Chicoutimi,*" the man told him, but the friendliness had faded slightly from his expression. He thanked my father for the directions and hurried out.

My father pulled at his jacket as if it hadn't been sitting right on his shoulders. He sighed and glanced around the restaurant, blinking. Even after we were seated, he seemed uncomfortable and kept exhaling loudly, sounding annoyed. I wanted to ask him when he'd last spoken French, or any of the questions that came to mind when I thought about his past—who his parents were, where he'd grown up—but I didn't want to upset him further.

"I was seeing this girl," he finally told me, looking about as if unsure of what to say, and he rummaged in his jacket's inside pocket and took out a Polaroid. A young woman sat on his couch. She had short, spruced-up dark hair and looked a little older than Jasmine.

"She's pretty, huh?"

"Yeah," I told him. "Yeah, she is. Are you still dating her?"

He shrugged and put the photo away. "Not really."

"What happened?"

"It just wasn't working."

"And what about Sara?"

He scrunched up his cheeks as if with confusion, then went on to confess that he'd asked her to move in with him and start a family, but that she'd run away with the car he was lending her. Eventually the police brought it back, though he didn't press charges.

"It's strange," he said, "how people can disappear in the same town."

The thought occurred to me that for a criminal he relied on the police a little too much.

When I asked about Jasmine, he said only that she hadn't wanted to do her job. He'd driven her to the countryside where her mother lived and dropped her off. Telling me this, he appeared distracted, his expression haggard. His life seemed empty, and in that emptiness I saw a threat. I didn't want to be the person to fill it.

But complete freedom, I knew, would come only when I had wheels of my own. This seemed a biological truth: without a license and a car, nothing was possible.

After we'd finished eating, when one waitress was vacuuming and the other putting chairs upside down on tables, he looked around as if to leave, then hesitated and took the toothpick from his mouth.

"You know, I get it," he said. "I remember when I didn't want to listen to anyone. But I was a good kid. I logged or worked in mines, and I sent money to my family. Then, when I was eighteen, I guess, I realized what bullshit it was. I decided I'd had enough, and I left and hitchhiked across Canada, all the way to Vancouver. You wouldn't really understand, but the world was changing back then. When I was a kid, I didn't have many opportunities. Then I was a young man, and everything seemed possible. The music was different. People were dressing different. Quebec was changing, but I didn't have an education or any skills other than manual labor. I was angry at my family. I'd given them everything, and my younger brothers and sisters had gone to school, but my parents had done nothing for me.

"Anyway, I started hitchhiking. This was before crime. I just wanted to get away from everyone. I was in Ontario, and I'd been dropped off and was walking, looking for my next ride. There was a river next to the road, and I saw a man on a boulder right in the middle of the rapids. It must have been springtime because the water was high. My English wasn't very good back then, but I waved down a truck and stayed until some men with ropes and life vests got there."

He paused. He'd been holding the toothpick in his fingers, rolling it back and forth, and now he put it down and stared off.

"When we finally pulled the guy out, we saw that he was from the reservation. He had a long black braid, and he didn't say anything. We took him to a diner and gave him some dry clothes and a cup of coffee. That's when he told us his friend had been taken by the river. That's how he said it. 'The river took my friend.' The men who rescued him were pretty angry he'd waited so long to tell them. A police officer kept saying, 'It's just like one of them.'

"I joined the search party, and we spent all day walking the river, looking for the missing friend. I was just trying to be helpful, but I understood the Indian. When you know someone's dead, what's the point? I just cared about myself, about what I was going to do with my life, and I didn't want to waste my time on a dead guy. But I helped even if it was pointless, because that's what you're supposed to do. When we got back to the diner, the Indian was gone. He didn't even help us look. I thought a lot about that, and it made sense to me. I'd been worrying about making money for my family when I had nothing for myself. I was living just to work shit jobs. It really got me thinking about what I wanted. We're not alive for that long, and you might as well go for it and make yourself happy."

We were the only diners left, sitting in a forest of upturned chair legs, and I wasn't sure why he'd told the story, what had caused him to remember or try to make peace. But I was in total agreement. I didn't have sympathy for anyone. The only person who mattered was me, and I would do whatever was necessary to make my life the way I wanted it.

The rain and sleet that dogged the winter, the cold that froze the puddles left by the Northwest's constant drizzle, gave way to sunny, mild days. But while other students relished the sunlight and wore T-shirts and shorts, I brooded, thinking of how I could avoid working for my father. For three months, he'd helped pay the rent. At school, I'd done everything I could to be a good student. I wrote for the yearbook, the school newspaper, ran cross-country, and worked out every day afterward in hopes of returning home as late as possible. I refused drugs with a conviction that startled me, and I didn't drink but for the occasional beer with my father. Instead, I wrote, feeling as if I stood on the edge of a cliff—as if, were I to look away from the page, vertigo would overcome me.

Students were crowding into the cafeteria, laughing, and pushing into line. I stopped at the bulletin board. I knew every post for contests and clubs, but there was a new one, a green photocopy: a Mandarin summer camp on Vancouver Island had fifteen places for BC students. I pulled the sheet down and hurried to my English classroom, but it was empty. My history teacher, a lean Trinidadian man, sat at his desk next door, eating rice from Tupperware. I asked if we could talk. He had me pull up a chair, and ate as I explained. His eyes bugged out when I described my father's crimes. I knew I wasn't being fair, but I was desperate.

By that afternoon, my teachers had met with the principal, who then called me into his office. They had agreed to write recommendations, and though the program didn't offer scholarships, the principal had called its director and explained my situation. He'd proposed using school funds to pay for me.

When the time came to tell my father, I prepared my face.

"Mandarin—what do you mean?" he asked over dinner. "Like the oranges?"

"No. Chinese. I'm going to learn beginner's Chinese."

"Chinese!" he shouted and stood from his chair. Other diners turned.

"Fucking Chinese! You're fucking going to learn Chinese!"

"It's useful, you know," I told him—that and some stuff I'd heard at school about how the Chinese might dominate the world. I remained seated, managing to stay impassive.

"But you're supposed to work for me," he said, showing his palms and then extending them slowly, as if offering a sword. The gesture was so full of frustration and confusion and supplication that I actually felt bad for him.

"I want to study Chinese," I insisted, my expression empty, offering nothing he could fight. "It's a big scholarship. Not everyone gets it. It was made especially for me. I can't turn it down."

He sat in his chair as if shot, staring, mouth open, eyebrows lifted.

"They made it just for you?"

"Yes."

"Why?"

"Because I'm a good student."

He nodded once, then picked up his fork and stared down at the heap of twisted spaghetti, shaking his head as if his job were to untangle it.

A strip of yellow light gleamed beneath the drawn blinds. Across the small dorm room, my fat Taiwanese roommate snored. I inhaled the ethereal reek of his father's cologne, with which he doused himself in hopes, I assumed, of easing homesickness.

That summer had begun with a long sigh of relief, but shortly after I'd exhaled it, I started plotting my next escape. Other students studied Chinese diligently while I wrote stories in my room and daydreamed. Before I'd left for the camp, my father told me that I still owed him that money and had to work it off. He added that if I worked for him, he'd forgive what I owed and would pay me instead.

An angry, restless sweat seeped from my pores and made the sheets cling. He wasn't going to give up. Like the irregular idle of an old engine, my heart repeatedly grew loud, then faint, as if roaming my chest. A nervous current pulsed along my spine. I got up and left the room. I sat on the dorm steps. Beneath streetlamps, the trees on the University of Victoria campus appeared golden and motionless, peaceful and indifferent.

After a while organizing my thoughts, I went to the pay phone just inside the door. My mother answered on the second ring, her voice thick with sleep. I apologized.

"It's okay," she said quickly and cleared her throat. "I'm happy to hear from you."

I described the camp, then brought up my plans for September.

She said that if I came back, she'd help me buy a car. She'd bought my brother a used Honda two years before. I told her I didn't like my father's life, and I asked why she'd really left him.

"Well, lots of reasons," she said. "Our relationship might have survived if there'd been family around or even real friends. But there was no one else. He didn't want anyone to tell him how to live, or to say that he might be doing things wrong. And . . . and I guess I wanted to change and grow, and I couldn't do that with him. I had to leave."

What she described made sense: his strange, deracinated existence. His anger had raged in a vacuum, without check or equal. No one else had seemed so free, and yet she'd felt trapped. I realized how much courage leaving must have taken. She'd tried to create all she wanted with him, but in their isolation, she'd struggled to transform her life.

Once, at the Granville Island market, when I was five or six, he'd gone outside and crouched at the edge of the quay. He held his sunglasses a foot before his eyes, peering down through them, something he did to cut the glare on the water in order to see the fish. I came out and, loving his ritual of scanning below the surface, ran to him and tried to climb onto his shoulders, jumping and knocking him forward. Though surprised, he caught himself and shoved both of us back, practically throwing himself away from the edge.

"What in the hell do you think you're doing?" he yelled. "Get out of here!"

My mother came into the sunlight beyond the market building, and I ran to her. When I could talk through my tears, I asked what had made him so angry.

"He can't swim," she said, holding me.

"He can't swim?" I repeated.

"No, he never learned. People don't swim where he comes from. It's too dangerous. The water's too cold."

I hadn't realized there were things he couldn't do, and I struggled to understand his confidence, how he could steer a boat or stand in a river and fish when he couldn't do this one thing that all children learned. He'd rarely shown weakness, all of us seeming helpless next to him, and only now did I realize that he might have liked us that way. It didn't fully make sense to me why someone who'd craved freedom as much as he did couldn't see that we wanted the same thing.

Even though I knew that I would refuse to work for him, his face came to me, its disappointment and regret each time we'd met for dinner. There were so many aspects to him, so many contradictions. When I was a boy, he'd once sped his truck across a field, racing through tall, sunlit grass until he hit a hidden stump and broke not only his axle but his tooth against the steering wheel. When he came back to the house and told me what had happened, showing me the shard of tooth in his palm, I asked why he drove like that. He appeared confused, unable to explain, and he went on to tell the story again, making it sound less dramatic, as if he were just crossing a field. But I'd seen him be reckless often, and sensed how he breathed more easily in the thrill of that headlong rush. This had seemed normal, the dangers never real to me. Riding my bike on the narrow road, I swerved in front of oncoming trucks and tractors just to see them brake. I built jumps out of cinder blocks and slippery, half-decayed planks so that I could feel the joy of levitation at last.

But now, remembering this, I began to understand that the same impulse in him was part of what had ruined our family. Why were we so reckless and unsatisfied? It was simply a fact, a truth as clear as any physical need. And this longing still seemed to be my only distinct feeling—not sadness or fear or anger. When had I lost that core of emotion? At the ferry? When I held the baseball bat? All that remained was what I wanted, what I had to do. Beyond that, I felt empty.

After I said good-bye to my mother and she hung up, I punched in his number. I didn't give myself time to think. My hand dialed with an automatic motion.

"Deni," he said. "How's your Chinese?"

"Good. Listen. I was thinking about next year."

"Next year."

"For eleventh grade. I want to go back to Virginia."

"To Virginia," he repeated, his voice absent of all intonation.

"Yeah, I want to study there. I like that school better."

The plan I'd formulated involved turning sixteen in Virginia, getting a driver's license and a car, and moving out. It wasn't that this would be easier there, but by moving between Vancouver and Virginia, I could break his hold. Dickie had already lost his power, and it would be easy for me to find a job and earn money.

"You listen here," he said in a furious voice that no longer bothered me — "if you go back, you can't expect anything from me. I'm cutting you off."

"Okay," I said. "That's okay."

He didn't speak, and I just stood there holding the phone, waiting for the silence to drag on long enough that one of us would hang up.

part IV

THE HUNT

The house was largely finished, sitting on a hill of naked red clay, the wet bulldozed terrain deeply eroded and surrounded by forest.

"Welcome back," Dickie said, crossing the empty living room with a heavy-footed hunch. He hiked the corners of his mouth, the skin rucking up around his eyes.

My brother and sister came out of their rooms, his dark hair crushed on the side from his pillow, though it was evening, my sister's carefully brushed sheen reaching to her shoulders, their eyes glassy with solitude.

I hitched my thumbs in my jeans and nodded, sizing up Dickie, measuring myself, significantly taller and built from months of weight lifting.

"I'll get dinner on the table," my mother said and escaped to the kitchen.

As we ate, she told me she'd received her certification in massage therapy and started a practice. Her enthusiasm reminded me of when she'd left my father, as if she needed the gravity of new ideas, new passions and possibilities, to pull herself free.

After eating, everyone slunk off to a different room, Dickie to the basement.

I read and later tried to sleep, but couldn't. I got up and opened my door, the house silent, living and dining rooms without furniture, wires dangling from holes in the ceiling. I put on my shoes and went outside, then started down the driveway, into the forest.

The gravel offered a faint path, a ragged strip of sky above, palely lit by a shard of moon. I stopped. Not a single tree distinguished itself from the dark. If I stepped off the driveway, into the forest, would my eyes adjust and my senses recalibrate—touch, smell, hearing, the electric antennae of intuition? What was out there, and what did I want? I'd known before I arrived that I wouldn't stay long. As soon as I had a car, I'd move out. Even on the flight, telling myself this had calmed me. But back here, I felt demoted, a boy again, as if the conflict with my father— the steady facing off over dinners and beers in drab restaurants—had indicated a sort of respect, a station that, while not manhood, felt close.

When I was a child following him through fields of spruce and pine, he'd seemed attuned, his shoulders relaxed, his step fluid and ready for the spongy, uneven earth. He prowled, head shifting side to side in subtle motions as he scanned the rows. I'd imagined him a loup-garou, verging on the wild, so far from a normal life that the dark, animal transformation could no longer be resisted. And yet what did that creature want once the old self had been shed? What would satisfy it?

I walked for hours, following the network of long driveways, gravel roads freshly cut through forests for new homes. When I became afraid, I imagined myself wild, hunting, eager for a fight. When this didn't work, I pictured myself dead. All was lost, and nothing could hurt me. I'd let go of life. It worked. Fear dissolved. Was this how it was for him when my mother took us, when he couldn't get out of bed and gave up on everything? Did the hunter have to die as a man?

I came to moonlit gravel but kept to the dark. Prey, not hunters, stood in the light. I returned with silent steps, pausing to scan the forest, to study myself—the mechanisms of my body—so that each new step would be quieter.

I eased the front door open and crept inside. The fridge switched on, the buzz of its motor loud in the empty, unfinished rooms. I peeled off my shoes and crossed the floor, stepping slowly. I crouched at my mother's door. There was no sound inside. I slipped down the basement stairs, testing each step with the ball of my foot.

A weak yellow bulb lit a water-stained lampshade. The crowded shelves of Dickie's shop surrounded an unlit woodstove, and he lay facedown on a rug before it. A dozen beer cans stood in rank next to a rocking chair.

I moved silently, pausing often, examining everything—the spray paint that would color nothing, the lacquers and enamels that would never protect, whose cans would rust with the tools gathered here.

The marriage was fraying—I had no doubt now—the knickknacks of their affection abandoned, her presents to him become shop rags: the T-shirt drawn with lines like those on a butcher's diagram (love handles, beer belly, man boobs), the boxers that said It's Not the Size that Counts. Both hung from nails, blackened and greasy. The mug that read Small Men Do It Best held a stiff, dried-out paintbrush and a residue of turpentine. There wasn't enough love left to sustain the sort of self-effacing humor that I'd never trusted anyway.

Summer ended and I began eleventh grade. Soon the cooling leaves turned and dropped, revealing the deforested swath of power lines. Dickie came home from work and got out of his truck with his finger crooked in the plastic netting of a six-pack of Coors. He took his gun and threw his orange vest over his oxford. From my window, I could see his back as he drank, facing the open space beneath power lines. Occasionally, his shotgun pounded the silence as he clipped the squirrels that scurried past, preparing for winter.

When I'd turned fourteen, almost two years earlier, he'd taken me deer hunting. A classmate had told me about his first hunting trip, how he and his uncle drove all night and through the dawn to a remote mountain camp. After he shot a sixteen-point buck, his uncle cut out the beast's heart and put it in the boy's hands, then painted his cheeks with the blood of his first kill. The idea of primitive rite thrilled me, the sense of brotherhood and initiation by hunting down something elusive and possibly dangerous.

But Dickie just drove us in his Datsun past a new subdivision of identical houses with sunbaked dirt for yards, then pulled to the side of the highway.

"This is a secret place I know," he said and chuckled, shaking his head.

From the hatch, he took a rifle that looked huge in his arms. He gave me an old shotgun, its stock scuffed as if it had been dragged on asphalt. A trail cut into the forest, and next to it ran two fresh wheel ruts, at the end of which someone had dumped a stove.

A hundred feet into the woods, we came to a depressed clearing of beaten grass. He motioned for quiet and grinned conspiratorially, as if we were doing something sneaky.

We sat at the bottom of a large oak and loaded our guns and waited.

"Deer hunting is about patience," he said, but then a squirrel began to run along the branches above us, and he trained his shotgun on it, one eye pinched shut.

"Bang, bang, I got you," he said softly. "Heh heh. Bang bang. Got you again."

I leaned against the oak, my feet propped in its gnarled roots. The November air hadn't cooled much, yellow and red leaves still on trees and bushes, and I thought of the novels I loved, civilization on the verge of collapse, a warrior traveling into the unknown.

"Psst," Dickie said.

A scrawny deer emerged into the clearing, stepping gingerly. It paused and began to twitch its ears wildly. Moving slowly, I aimed my shotgun. Dickie had his own stock to his shoulder. "Is that a buck?" he whispered. "Wait . . . wait until you see the horns . . ."

Directly opposite me, on the other side of the clearing, a hunter stood from the bushes. He aimed his rifle at the deer and at me, and my bowels clenched. The deer bolted.

"Dang it," Dickie said. "That might have been a buck."

I followed him into the clearing, and three other hunters came out of the bushes, one of them zipping up his fly, two holding bonus-size cans of Coors. Each cradled a rifle with a scope. Dickie was talking to the man who'd aimed his gun at me.

"Was that a buck?" he asked.

"Couldn't be sure," the man replied. He towered over us, his short-cropped beard and eyebrows as red as his hunting vest, as if he'd dyed them for the season. He pulled an open beer from the netting on the front of his hunting vest.

"I thought I might have seen some little horns," Dickie said.

The man finished chugging. "Yeah, it could've had tiny antlers." He crunched the empty can and tossed it behind him.

"Looked like a doe to me," another hunter said, pushing plastic bifocals up his nose. He held a half-rolled *Playboy* magazine.

"I thought it might've been a little buck," Dickie pressed on, but everyone lost interest and wandered back to their bushes and trees.

We left soon after. Dickie told me it wasn't worth staying, that those fools had ruined everything. This had been my only experience deer hunting. Now he hunched before the power lines, hoping for a buck.

I'd be sixteen soon.

Leaves fell, ticking away the seconds.

I blared music — Metallica or the Rolling Stones — and read whatever I could find: *The Stranger, The Great Gatsby, The Sun Also Rises,* interplanetary sci-fi, a fantasy series with another elusive Dark Lord whose henchmen seemed more threatening than he did. As the characters traveled to East Egg or the mountains of Spain, or across monster-inhabited lands and eerily desolate solar systems, I relished their freedom.

Then, finally, my birthday came, and I had my driver's license.

I did a quick reckoning. Of the few things in my room, only the schoolbooks, some copied cassettes, and a few changes of clothes were mine. It would all fit in the blue three-hundred-dollar Honda my mother had found.

I twisted the stereo's knob. The plastic speakers rattled against the floor with Megadeth's bass line. Dickie had hardly spoken to me since I returned, barely looked at me if we passed each other. But when my mother told him that I had my license, I felt the atmosphere shift. He'd been my age once, and he knew his duty.

The guitar riff had risen to a wild pitch when he threw the door open. His eyes weren't furious, the drama scripted. It was a prophecy whose edicts we—youthful hero and dodgy lord of darkness—were destined to fulfill long before we met.

"Out!" he shouted with perfunctory rage. "Just get the hell out!"

He seemed afraid, yelling drunkenly before scurrying down the basement stairs.

The narrative of exile was mine. If I stayed, I'd be no different than everyone else, lacking courage. Sameness seemed like a disease, or a form of retardation, like not hitting puberty.

"So, yeah," I said that evening over dinner, to the parents of a classmate I'd called from a pay phone, "he kicked me out. He's a drunk. I doubt my mom will stay with him . . ."

But when I called my mother later, she tried to convince me I was wrong.

"He said he didn't kick you out!"

"Well, he did."

"He didn't mean it. I talked to him. You can come back."

"No, I can't. I'm not living in that house with him. You're not even happy . . ."

Her silence told me that I was right about one thing—she'd rather not be there either. It wasn't that Dickie wanted me gone. He wanted all of us to disappear, and she knew it.

From couch to guest bedroom I went, consuming food, books, and the sitcoms other families watched, laughing with them. I mowed their yards, chopped firewood, and washed dishes. I loved the car, the smell of sunlight on the cracked plastic dashboard, the taste of dust when I ripped down dirt roads.

Until this point, the weeks had been predictable, unlike this satisfying challenge of finding a place to sleep, of measuring the days when a friend said, "My parents agreed that you can stay over until Wednesday," and another offered me a basement couch for the weekend. The details of survival, of getting enough food, of telling stories to parents that won me further invitations, of being among strangers, talking, doing chores, finding odd jobs on farms—the sense of action, of achievement—nothing could have made me happier.

When I didn't have a couch, I lived out of my car. I got a job mucking stalls and another washing dishes at Pizza Hut, where I subsisted off mistaken orders. In January, I moved in with a friend who had an apartment, and changed schools to be nearby, but the apartment ended up crowded with cast-off youths jockeying for the bathroom, for the stale pizza in the fridge, for places to sleep. Three months later, after a dispute, I went back to my itinerant life.

Half-asleep, often late and disheveled, I rushed to school each day from a different direction. In science class, as we learned about the origins of life, I wondered where the shift had occurred, from one protozoan digesting another to an organism just longing, staring at the horizon, wanting to feel fully alive.

The highways to school or work or friends' houses seemed to pulse, to rumble with the arterial thrill of my blood. I wondered if this was how my father felt when he left Quebec. Sometimes he came to me, his wild joy when I raced through traffic, or his rage when someone confronted me. Why did he seem to hold the secret to what I was looking for?

My life was building to a crescendo, I told myself. With each curve of the highway, I felt that I was arriving, only to be disappointed when nothing changed.

One afternoon, I was driving down a hill on a country road that ended at a T where another beaten strip of gravel followed the wooded shore of a small, rocky river, when my brake pedal went soft. I slammed my foot two, three times, but there was only a hollow chopping sound, like a hatchet striking dry wood. I threw the gearshift into first and popped the clutch, and the car jerked, the gear whining as I slowed. I spun the steering wheel before I reached the T, and came onto the road sliding sideways. Then I slammed the gas, gravel rattling against the undercarriage, and the right tires bumped the raised grassy shoulder before their treads caught and shot me forward.

I eased up on the accelerator and coasted, then switched the ignition off and let the car putter and jerk to a stop. I got out and stood and caught my breath. Crickets whirred in the tall grass, and somewhere, behind the few faint sunlit clouds, a jet rumbled.

I went to the front and knelt. Brake fluid dripped from the burst caliper, and I sighed and sat against the bumper. The dust that I'd stirred up at the T was catching up like a slow shadow, drifting over the car, speckling the paint.

I didn't have enough money to repair this, and between work and school and the houses of friends where I commandeered the empty bedrooms of older siblings who'd left for college, I had to drive constantly. Briefly, I found it hard to swallow or breathe. I told myself I was fine. I could handle this, enjoy it, even. I'd driven a bike without brakes in BC, and my father had traveled from Calgary to Tijuana in a truck without brakes.

I walked along the road to clear my head, then turned. The paint along the front edge of the Honda's hood and roof had long ago worn away, as if from a sandstorm. At a glance, no one would know that it lacked brakes. The emergency didn't work either, but I could stop by downshifting hard or cutting the engine.

I got back in, started it, and practiced accelerating then stopping, seeing how long it took after I switched off the ignition. Putting the car in first gear also worked. So long as I didn't tailgate or come up fast on a stop sign or a red light, I should be fine.

By the end of the day, I felt exultant. I understood what my father must have experienced crossing the United States this way, testing himself.

Just before sunset, I pulled into the driveway of a girl who'd invited me to dinner. She was a senior, and in the carefree energy of that last week of school, the sun a growing presence in the blue, humid sky, she'd invited me over.

"Do you want to sleep here tonight?" she asked as we ate canned ravioli, only the two of us at the table. Her long brown hair lay against one shoulder, and she wore a blue summery dress with tiny white flowers on it.

"What about your parents?" I glanced around the empty house.

"Don't worry about them."

As she explained the plan, a state trooper pulled into the driveway, and I almost jumped out of my seat.

"That's my stepfather," she said. "He doesn't care about anything. He won't even notice you."

He came through the front door in uniform, didn't say hello or look at us, and prepared a sandwich in the kitchen with brisk, silent motions. His gray face had a metallic tinge, his chin protruding more than his small nose, as if to hold the strap of his round state trooper's hat.

I said good-bye to her and drove to a nearby church, where I parked as she'd instructed. When it was fully dark, I crept back through the woods, pausing just beyond her yard to survey the windows. Then I moved quickly to the basement door and let myself inside.

But the tryst lacked heart, her plan a little too smooth in its execution, and our passions muted so as not to betray my presence. Lawmen seemed far scarier than criminals. Still, I did my best. Later, as she snored softly, I stared at the ceiling, planning, thinking through the next steps. She tried to draw close in her sleep, but I pulled away. I'd had a few flings over the past year, but survival overshadowed romance, and if someone held on even a little tightly, I panicked and fled.

Now I had to decide what to do once school let out. I was running out of avenues, nearly penniless, my car without brakes, its engine knocking, the muffler coughing black smoke. I hadn't called my father since I left, but he might understand. I'd never managed to hold all the different versions of him in my head: the reckless, entertaining man I'd known as a boy; the criminal I'd imagined; or the fishmonger, racketeer, and thug.

Maybe I could go back for a few months, for a breather. Then I could escape again, stay moving. He'd realize that I was living as he had. His stories of travel still inspired me, and I saw myself in them just as I'd once imagined bank robberies, the raised pistol as motionless as a planetary body, or the sudden dusk of shot-out lights.

When I woke, dawn hung like sea scum in the glass. I dressed and crept into the empty basement, the house silent but for the gnawing of carpenter bees in a beam above the door. I eased it open. This part scared me, the thought of her stepfather dressed for work, gun on his hip as he had his coffee and looked out the upstairs window. My exposed back tingled as I high-stepped across the yard, into the woods.

When I made it to the church, my pant legs were wet with dew. I swung the car door open and sat inside and started my homework. Sunlight spilled over the forested horizon, making the nerves behind my eyes pulse, and a family of five large, ragged stray cats returned from a night of hunting to their home beneath the church's foundation. They sat just outside, nuzzling each other with scarred faces, their calico tufts brilliant in the early light.

My mother was waiting in the parking lot outside Pizza Hut, her van door open. My shift had finished, and I glanced around to make sure that my co-workers couldn't see me.

"How are you doing?" she asked.

"I'm fine. Why are you here?"

"I wanted to check on you. I didn't know how to get in touch. You should call more."

"Listen, I can't talk now."

"I just wanted to know if you're finishing school this year."

"Yeah, I am. I'll be fine. I have two days left. It's easy—too easy."

She stared at me, her gray hair pinned back. She had one hand on the door, her sleeve rolled to the elbow, her forearm finely muscled.

"I'm not moving back," I told her.

"I'm not asking you to. I don't know how much longer I'm going to be able to stay with him either."

"So what will you do?" I said, suddenly worried, and yet angry at her for making me think of anything but myself.

"I don't know yet. I'm figuring it out."

"I might go back to André."

"Have you been in touch with him?"

"No, but I think I could be." I didn't tell her that my car had no brakes, or that I was sleeping at a friend's house. I'd stopped seeing the girl. She'd told me she felt I didn't need anyone, that she couldn't get close. A mother of a friend was a guidance counselor. She'd read an article I'd written for the school paper, and when she'd found out I was living out of my car, insisted I stay with them.

"Well, I guess you're fine," my mother told me, and we spoke a bit longer, mostly about my classes, before she said good-bye. She gave me a hug, pulling me close.

When she let go, I glanced to make sure that my co-workers were still in the kitchen.

Her van lumbered into traffic and sailed off, and I drove slowly until I was past the stoplights for which I had to turn off the car and downshift. On a country road, coasting over hills, I tried to decide. She'd trusted me. She'd let me take chances and go back to my father. Having fought for her freedom against him, had she recognized my own need? Remembering this gave me confidence, made me feel that whatever happened, I'd be fine.

I parked at a pay phone. This wouldn't be a surrender. I'd tell my story, and he'd want me to come back. Moths fluttered about the lit panels of the booth as I dialed.

"You're doing what?" he said when I told him how I was getting around.

"That's what you did."

"That must've been in the early sixties. Things have changed. You don't drive without brakes now."

"Well, it's working for me."

"So," he said, "what are you doing? Where are you living?"

"With a friend."

"I'll give you work. Just get on a bus and come back. I'll send you the money. Is there a Western Union near you?"

"I can find one."

Four days later, as I boarded a Greyhound, my stomach knotted. Countryside scrolled in the windows, the landscape and motion I loved. I tried to make sense of my life, to find a trace of the purpose my mother had described so often.

I made up stories for other passengers, inventing a more interesting childhood. At one point, another adolescent ruffian chimed in about his own tough upbringing. The competition started, and eventually he tried to convince everyone that, because of a series of motorcycle accidents, all his tendons had been surgically replaced with metal cables. The adults yawned and went back to staring out the windows with the half-lidded eyes of the incapacitated: operated patients waking from anesthesia, boxers roused after knockouts, zoo carnivores in musty cages.

The sun was setting above the distant mountains, evening tilting in the sky.

To sleep, I unlaced my shoes and huddled against the window, the vibrating glass cool on my forehead. When I opened my eyes, the dark landscapes dropped away from the highway, mapped out by distant house lights like fallen constellations.

"How about that one?" my father asked, motioning with his chin to a small SUV, a red and white GMC. "You can pay it off."

"But I don't want to work for you."

"What do you expect? To get money for free? Come on. I'll help you buy it. You can do deliveries. It'll be like you're working for yourself."

We stared at the freshly washed SUV, its panels gleaming beneath the June sky. I sensed a trap, but I was desperate for cash.

"Let's take it for a spin," he said and elbowed my arm.

He slipped behind the wheel as I got into the passenger seat. He turned the key and pulled out from the parking space into an empty lot behind the dealership. Then he slammed the accelerator and the SUV raced forward, its engine humming smoothly. He swerved side to side and cut an arc like a prankster scorching a doughnut. He hammered the gas and we lunged, my stomach left behind, everything at our sides a blur as we neared the weedy border of the lot. He jammed the brakes, and the SUV lifted on its shocks, tipping its nose to the ground so that I felt as if I were being catapulted from my seat and put my hands against the dash. The tires screeched but caught, and the air instantly reeked of burned rubber.

He turned to me, the grim humor on his face hardly discernible from rage.

"The goddamn thing works," he said. "Let's quit fucking around and buy it."

That evening, in a Greek restaurant hidden from the highway by an ivy-grown wall, he asked about my plans. I explained that I wanted to do my last year of high school, then travel and write. I'd been gone only nine months, but he listened intently, as if I'd earned his respect. Or maybe he knew how easily I could leave now that I had a license. What I kept to myself was that I questioned the importance of finishing school since I didn't plan on going to college. I refused to be a dropout, but I didn't want to sell out, either. Real writers didn't go to college. I wasn't sure where I'd heard that, but it sounded right.

"And what about this summer?" he asked. "Maybe you could do some training."

"Training?"

"Yeah, boxing or something. You'd be good at it."

"That could be okay," I said warily.

"You're made to be a fighter. You're like me that way. I could've taken on the best. That's one of my regrets. I should've been professional. Instead, I fought in prison . . ."

He hesitated, his eyes on my face, as if he were trying to decide whether I was interested. I had the sense that he'd been waiting for me to get back so he could tell stories. Finally, he began to speak, his gaze becoming vague and disconnected.

"I remember this one prison in California. The inmates were fucking tough. It was after Miami, and the police had driven me there. I had some bad fights, but I could handle those guys. I really tested myself. There were never enough beds or blankets, and each night we fought over them. Sometimes, inmates got food from the outside and hid it, and if the screws—the guards—found jam or honey, they smeared it on the beds. Rats crawled over the men at night and ate the mattresses and blankets.

"Those guards," he said, "they were like a gang. They didn't look much different from inmates, and they used to take prisoners into small rooms and beat them until they couldn't stand. I'd insult them. 'I'm federal,' I said when they threatened me. 'You fuckers can't touch me. You'll all lose your jobs if anything happens to me.'

"It was true. I was in for a federal crime, and the police knew I had other crimes under my belt. They wanted to find out what I could tell them. There was a lot they could learn by making me a deal."

He paused and explained how the prison had been near LA, on the San Andreas Fault. It looked like an old brick warehouse, and with each tremor, the walls rippled, bricks swimming in their weave, dust deepening the air. The inmates stared in terror at the ceiling. My father searched for words to describe the faces of men ruined by guards, the quakes that came too frequently, even the small ones moving the walls like a tapestry beneath a breeze.

"Damn it," he said, his voice grating, "we were just waiting for that ceiling to fall."

He was staring through me. I'd forgotten how alive he could appear. The anger he'd harbored on my last visit seemed gone, replaced by an emotion I tried to identify, his gaze at times sad, at others restless.

"But the worst fight I had was in the prison where they sent me afterward. A man threatened me. He said he'd put me in the infirmary. He said it at lunch, in front of everyone. If an inmate did that, you had to act. It was a question of honor. You didn't have a choice. If someone tries to make you look bad, you have to take him down.

"After lunch, I followed him to his cell. He was a big man, but I'd been a fighter my whole life. I really could have been a boxer. I went in and slammed the cell door behind me. The doors were left open after lunch, but once you closed them, only the guards could open them again. I beat the shit out of him. I was punching and kicking him and got him down on the floor and kept kicking him and he crawled under the bed. Then I bent and took his foot and pulled his leg around the metal post of the bed frame and kicked it. I heard the bone snap. It must have broken in two or three places."

He looked at me and raised his eyebrows and sighed. The question of his life was there, in his expression. Why did that violence, that ugliness, the desire for risk and challenge, hold such sway over us?

"I guess a lot of my fights were pretty bad," he said. "One time, this guy disappeared with the money from a job we did. He was supposed to hang on to the cash while it cooled off. When I caught up with him, he was coming out of a bar. It was at night, and no one was in the parking lot. I hit him with a baseball bat. I really let that fucker have it. I don't know how many times. Then I went and changed my clothes ..."

"Why?" I asked, sensing that he was adrift and unable to make sense of his own story.

"Because bats cut the skin. I had blood all over me. I changed, then called the police. I watched while they took him away."

"Why did you call?"

"Because the parking lot was out of the way. I didn't want the son of a bitch to die."

"Did he?"

"I don't think so. I didn't check on him, but I don't think I hurt him that bad. He probably just never danced again."

He tried to smile, and I had to keep myself from looking away.

"But he could have died later," I said.

"I don't think so."

"Did you check?"

He shrugged. The story's violence had infused his posture. He sat hunched, fists against the tabletop. Again I wondered what made us need to go too far, to push at everything. I felt the impulse even now, wanting to test him. I asked a question I'd asked years ago.

"Have you ever killed anyone?"

He jerked his head back as if I'd taken a swing, and looked away fast.

"No. No matter what I did, I had principles. I wouldn't kill. And I always made sure the people I was working with understood that. One time, a guy wanted me to do a job. He told me I had to get rid of a night guard. I wouldn't do it."

"Why not?"

He lifted his shoulders, not a shrug so much as an annoyed jerk.

"I didn't want to be the guy who took away someone's father," he said. "But hurting people was hard to avoid. It happened. It had to. I never planned to, not unless I needed to keep someone from shitting on my reputation. I grew up with nothing, and my reputation was all I had. Most of the time I was just protecting myself, or someone showed up where he wasn't supposed to be."

The waitress took our plates and left, and he watched the tired to-and-fro of her hips.

"I keep that baseball bat in the truck," he said, "under the seat. I have a glove and a ball, too. In case the police ever check, it has to look as if I actually use them to play baseball. If something happened, it's the only way they'd believe it was in self-defense."

I recalled the day he'd put the bat in my hands and told me to get the money, the pregnant girl at the door. He was fifty-two now, still stuck in that old way of being. I wasn't angry at him, but I didn't know why not. I felt watchful, eager to understand not just him and everything he'd lived, but also myself and my future. Anger would just obscure all that and slow me down.

He looked me hard in the eyes and smiled, as if nothing made him happier than my return. "Come on. What the fuck were we saying?"

"What?"

"That you should train! How much do you think it would be?"

He took his wallet from his jacket and threw five twenties on the table.

"Find a gym," he said. "Just tell me if you need more cash."

Later that night, I couldn't sleep. What drew me here? Why was he the one person I had to understand—who held so much power over me? My thoughts fell back through conflicting, coexisting memories: the valley and its fields, fishing or working in the sunlight, the day we walked together through rows of trees and he urged me to step forward, to face the dead bears. When our family fell apart and we left the valley, I began to hate him. Then, briefly, I saw freedom in him, a way of being that was bigger, more alive, and I returned, dreaming—the two of us lifting immense pistols, our fists muscular, the silence a crescendo, the scene around us soon to rain down like shattered glass.

JACK KEROUAC DREAMS
ELIZABETH BENNET

We'd packed an order of salmon fillets in Styrofoam boxes and were standing in the fenced-in yard behind the store, my father, myself, and Karl, a man who did odd jobs. Short and gruff, Karl had a blond Fu Manchu, a prominent forehead, and a squint that made his eye sockets appear rectangular. His gaze wandered as he described a murder he'd heard about. A bunch of thugs had been hired to knock off a one-legged Vietnam vet.

"This guy was lively. He split wood every day. He didn't give up because he'd had his leg shot off. You could see him out there hopping around, but his wife was a lazy bitch and wanted his money, so she hired some guys to kill him. But they went too far. They could have just done the job and kept it simple, but they acted like they were in a movie or something. One of them even bought a laser sight for his gun. That was taking it too far."

His boxed-in eyes held a disturbed, glazed look, and my father and I glanced at each other. It sounded as if Karl had been at the scene.

"Anyway," he sputtered, his eyes roving and looping. "They shot that poor guy to pieces. It just wasn't necessary."

After Karl had said good night and driven off, my father and I locked up.

A truck from the Department of Fisheries and Oceans pulled in as we were leaving, and an officer got out, a man so lean that not even his uniform gave him substance.

"Mr. Béchard?" he asked in the tired voice of a telemarketer.

"Yeah, that's me," my father said with total nonchalance.

"If you wouldn't mind, I'd like to take a look around the property."

"It's all closed up for the night."

"Would it be possible to open it?"

My father shrugged and undid the padlock on the gate. Behind it, two large German shepherds began to bark and jump against the chain link.

The officer jolted, as if waking up. "Hey, can you put those dogs away?"

"Put them away?" my father repeated, lifting his eyebrows. He appeared surprised, as if the thought had never occurred to him. "My dogs? There's no place to put them."

"But how can I go in?"

"Oh, they're not mean. Just open the gate and go on in."

My father stepped aside, motioning with his hand as if ushering a royal visitor. The dogs had their forepaws in the links. They snarled, black lips pulled back from their teeth.

"Just go on in," he repeated, sweeping his hand again.

The officer contemplated the two beasts. Propped on their narrow hind legs, they stood almost as tall as he did, as if my father kept werewolves as watchdogs. The man sighed.

"I'll come back later," he said. Then he got in his truck and left.

"Jesus, can't you get in trouble for that?" I asked.

My father frowned and turned his palms up, as if my question were stupid.

"You don't think I deal with this all the time? I've bought from the Indians for years, and I've never been caught. Don't be so nervous. Those guys don't have the balls to catch me. How are they going to get me when they're afraid of dogs?"

I survived the summer by training, my father's suggestion turning out to be my salvation. Though I cut fish and packed boxes and ran deliveries, I used kickboxing as an excuse to do this as little as possible. He respected martial arts enough not to mind that I spent nearly four hours a day at the gym, hammering the bags, lifting weights, jumping rope, or running alongside the railroad track out back. When I came home wrung out, he looked up from the paper that he held at half mast before the hockey game, in case a good fight started or someone scored. He nodded, satisfied that I was doing something serious.

But as soon as my senior year began, the old tensions flared up. A few times, offhandedly, he asked if it was really worth going, reminding me that I hadn't liked school when I was younger. But I just told him I'd placed into advanced classes. Training consumed my evenings, and often, instead of returning home after the gym, I drove, exploring the countryside around the city, following roads along rivers and into the mountains. Behind the wheel, I sensed the emptiness inside me ease, emotions flooding in, the past and my hopes for the future, the stories I would live and write, as if being in motion allowed me to feel the breadth of my life.

I knew I wasn't being fair to my father. I worked only weekends, and when he asked for help on other days, I found excuses. I ran and exercised and wrote and read and drove, but by December, as his business became more demanding, his mood began to sour.

"What's wrong with you?" he said over dinner. "Do you hate working for me so much?"

"I worked today, didn't I?"

"Come on. You read the entire time you were in the store."

"It's for school."

"But it's a job. I'm paying you well." He hesitated, anger coming into his eyes, then giving way to exasperation. "I'm just saying you could help a little more. I barely see you."

I nodded and kept busy with my food. I didn't know why, but I couldn't feel sympathy for him. When we were together, I liked his stories. We often laughed and drank and ate until late, but as soon as I left, I wanted to get as far away as possible. We'd survived almost six months together, but I felt calm only when I was driving aimlessly, sometimes not returning until three or four in the morning. Tonight, he would want to tell stories, but I was supposed to pick up a girl I knew from school at ten, when she got off work.

"Maybe you could help me for an hour or two in the mornings," he said.

"Before school? Doing what?"

"I don't know. Filleting fish and readying some orders."

"I can't. I'll be tired for class and . . . and I'll smell bad." Though I knew from the novels I'd read that generations of young men had worked like this, I also knew that generations of young men had defied their fathers.

"Goddamn it," he said, though I had the sense that he was muting his anger, afraid I'd leave. "What about your truck? You're barely making enough to pay for it. You could use a bit more work."

"No way I'm working mornings," I told him. "I'll give the truck back. I don't care."

"Okay. If it's such a big fucking deal, then okay, let's just drop it." He prodded the chicken on his plate, took his beer, and sat back in his chair, rolling his shoulders and trying to adjust his demeanor. He smiled.

"You're really getting in shape, aren't you? At least you're training hard."

"That's why I'm tired in the mornings," I said.

He nodded tersely. "I bet you'll be really good. The men in my family were tough. My brothers were fighters, and my father was goddamn tough. His hands were so big we used to pass his wedding ring around and it was too big for my thumb." He held up his fist. "People said that no one north or south of the Saint Lawrence could beat him in a fight."

He looked out the window, the restaurant shrubbery yellow in the light.

"The only time he didn't win was because he was too drunk. There were a couple guys trying to beat him up, and they kept hitting him, but he didn't even swing back. He just lifted his finger like this and said, 'I'm too drunk. I'll get you all later.' It was like he didn't even notice he was being punched."

I laughed, trying to imagine this man I'd never met, whose name I didn't even know. He was laughing, too.

"You have that in you," he told me, and it occurred to me that the story might have been planned for this reason alone—to encourage me to hold steady to the path he thought best. "I'm proud of you," he said. "You're going to make a hell of a boxer."

I snuck a glance at my watch. I had to leave soon if I wanted to meet the girl on time.

"I wish I'd used my energy better," he said. "You know, when you're young, you have all that anger, and you have to do something with it. I had no guidance. I was so angry I'd drive like crazy, and if someone honked, I'd try to run him off the road. I'd stop my car, and if he got out, I'd beat him up. Fuck. I don't even know what the point of that was. Beating up strangers on the side of the road when it was my fault to begin with. I really should have been a boxer, or played hockey. I wasted all of that energy on nothing. But you shouldn't do that. You could take a year off from school and go professional. You'll never be young again."

"Yeah," I agreed, nodding. His own words seemed to have embittered him, and I could see that he was looking for a way to tell other stories, to get me interested.

He started in on a favorite, about traveling through Alberta and ending up at a party in Calgary. A woman started hitting on him, and her boyfriend came to beat him up. The guy was enormous, very German looking, and he and my father fought for a long time, throwing each other into walls, breaking everything in the house.

"I'd been hanging out with the people at the party. It was always pretty easy for me to make friends, and when I started winning, they began cheering for me."

He hesitated, giving this some thought, as if he'd forgotten something.

"They started shouting, 'Go Frenchy,'" he said, then shook his head, as if the story weren't quite as good as he recalled.

"Listen, I have to go," I told him.

"Already?"

"I have a date."

"Tonight? Sunday night?" he said and looked around the room, as if she might be there, watching us eat. "Well, you should bring her by the house sometime."

"What?"

"What do you mean *what*?"

"It's just a date."

"Okay, fine, go on your date." He sat back and held his beer and stared off, and I said good-bye. He waved halfheartedly, refusing even to look my way.

The date had come about because I'd told this girl that I drove through the mountains all night, stopping to look at the stars. When I described how I'd gone to the place I was born and parked near the river and slept there, she'd wanted to go, too. That night, I picked her up from the convenience store where she worked, and we drove to the mountains, parked, and put down the backseat and undressed. Eventually, we fell asleep, the heater on, the engine idling. Suddenly, dawn was lighting the windows. I threw on my clothes and raced to her house, speeding along the highways into the suburbs.

Then I went home to get the schoolbooks I should have kept with me.

"Where were you?" my father asked, opening the door to my room. He had on his jeans, veins dark in his face, the tendons in his throat lifted. "You come home making all this fucking noise and wake me up. I needed some extra sleep. What were you doing all goddamn night?"

I met his gaze, trying to see if his anger was for show. I knew he'd use this as a pretense to say I should be working for him, making money and not fucking around.

"Where were you?"

"I went out for breakfast. I just got back."

"Bullshit. You were with that girl all night."

"So what?"

"You listen to me," he said, his face flushed, though between his words I sensed hesitation. "You don't want to work except when it's good for you, and you say you care about school but you don't even sleep. How do you expect to get by?"

"I have good grades."

"But you don't give a shit about school," he told me in that theatrical voice of his, exaggerated, somewhere between anger and ridicule.

"I'm not dropping out."

"Then you'd better learn to take things seriously. And you can't be a good fighter without sleep. If you're going to stay up all night, you might as well work for me."

I put on my impassive face. We stood ten feet apart as he held the door, and I looked into his eyes and shook my head faintly. His scowl faded. He knew what I was thinking—that he'd been a criminal, had left home and lived as he'd wanted. Who was he to tell me what to do?

He nodded once and shut the door, but the next morning, at four, he was pounding on it.

"What?" I shouted, exhausted, having tried to make up for two nights of sleep.

He threw the door open.

"I need your help," he said, that angry laughter in his eyes.

"It's the middle of the night."

"What's the big deal? You don't sleep anyway."

"I'm tired."

"I need your help now. At the store. Get your clothes on. It's an emergency."

I sighed and flopped back onto my pillow.

"Get out of the fucking bed!" he shouted.

I rolled off and began pulling on my clothes.

Our headlights swept out across the dark suburbs as I drove behind him, the night moonless and without clouds. We pulled up to his store. Frost had sketched icy calligraphy on the cracked asphalt of the parking lot. School would be letting out for Christmas soon, and I'd spend the entire break here.

"I just got a shipment of salmon for almost nothing," he told me as soon as he'd closed his door. "But I need to get them cleaned up fast."

As he unlocked the gate, his two German shepherds came to greet us. We went into the fenced-in backyard where he received deliveries.

The lid of the large plastic crate was level with my chin, and he heaved it back. The soup of melting, bloodshot ice held hundreds of smallish salmon. Something about them didn't seem right. I reached in and pulled one out, filaments of slime dribbling from it. The fish had a bulge in its head, another in its side. All of them appeared misshapen.

"They have tumors," he said. "I got them from a fish farm. Some of the batches go bad."

"Why?"

"Who knows? Maybe it's the shit they feed them. They have those experimental foods and the hormones to make them grow fast, and they give them dyes to make their meat red. It could be anything. Bad luck. They weren't supposed to be sold. I bought them for next to nothing from a contact, a guy responsible for disposing of them."

"Like a garbageman?"

"Yeah. Kind of like that." He laughed and repeated, "Garbageman." He said we'd fillet the salmon and resell them at normal price, a transaction that was almost pure profit. I understood that he needed my help because he couldn't let anyone else see this. Though a few of his employees were ex-cons themselves, they seemed incapable of not talking about their crimes.

A clear, gold-streaked dawn lit the horizon as we worked, the fenced-in yard cluttered with waxed cardboard boxes and trash cans. We cut the fillets, often half-size, tail sections, or strips—whatever was left after removing the hard, red knots of flesh. We ran our fingers over the silken meat, feeling for lumps. Not a single fish was normal.

"Who are you selling these to?" I asked.

"Restaurants. I have a lot of orders for fillets. They'll never know the difference."

I kept checking the time as the sun clambered through the clouds.

"I'm going to be late for school."

"No you won't. Just go straight there."

"Like this?" I motioned to my work clothes speckled with fish blood and scales.

"That's how it was for me." His eyes hardened, and he threw his knife down on the plastic cutting board and clenched his jaw. "I don't know why I put up with you. I'm giving you two choices. From now on you work for me in the morning, or else I take the truck away . . ."

I nodded once, stiffly, but said nothing.

We double-bagged the tumors, bones, and guts in black plastic, and carried them to the Dumpster outside. Then I got in the SUV and rushed home to change, already late.

An Irishwoman in a housedress came to the door and showed me a Dodge Omni parked in the street. It had mismatched tires and yellow paint discolored as if splashed with bleach. Dirty boxing hand wraps lay in the backseat. It had been listed in the paper for two hundred dollars.

"It was my son's," she told me when I asked about the wraps. "He was a boxer, a good one, but he gave it up when a girl broke his nose."

"A girl?"

"A lady in the boxing ring. She gave him a right beating, and he didn't have the heart for it no more."

I hesitated, then slipped the folded money from my pocket.

"I'll take it," I told her. "I'll be back tomorrow."

It was a week after New Year's. I'd scanned the classified ads daily over Christmas vacation. Having finished high school, my brother had come to live with us, hoping to build a relationship with my father and work for him, so the pressure was off me. Still, I was determined to leave. A coldness had set in between us. When I stayed out late, he commented: "You're lazy. Look at you! How do you expect to be a boxer? You don't even sleep." Or he gritted his teeth and said, "Goddamn it, you'd better grow up!"

He'd finally realized that leniency would get him nowhere. Only his rage could keep me in line. I didn't think he was wrong, but I preferred freedom.

Sleet was falling as I picked up the license plates for the Dodge. I drove to my father's house and parked the SUV. Frosts had burned the grass yellow, and the unlit windows reflected the large wet pines along the property. I knew his schedule, but he sometimes returned unexpectedly to drop off hefty bags of dog food or the like. He was restless, his days filled with errands that seemed like excuses for him to prowl the streets in his truck. Maybe he felt the same need for movement that I did. I knew that he'd tried to appeal to me, to tell the stories I loved, but as with Dickie, I'd been looking for an excuse.

I hadn't packed anything yet. I was afraid he'd go downstairs and see my bags. In fifteen minutes, a classmate would be there to take me to the Dodge.

I got out, swung myself over the black iron gate, and ran through the door and down to my room. I rushed, throwing everything into a duffel. I sprinted back out, pitched it over the gate, and followed. I shoved it behind my seat and sat, pretending to read.

My classmate's white Toyota pulled into the lane. When he stopped, I shuttled the duffel from my vehicle to his. I tossed the keys on the floorboard and took the new plates, and I slid into his car. He did a quick three-point turn and sped away. The tires made a rushing sound over the wet asphalt, large half-frozen raindrops striking the windshield. Soon we were on the highway, the downpour slackening unevenly, falling in hard pulses against us.

An hour later, I crossed the border, retracing the windy path of my mother's migration six years before. The rush-hour ranks advanced cautiously, the parade of taillights made garish by the icy downpour. In my rearview, endless headlights appeared crystalline behind the same rain. The motor buzzed like the remote-control car my father sent when I lived in the trailer park. Each time I gained speed, I feared it might explode.

After midnight, I pulled into a rest stop on I-90, in eastern Washington. I folded the backseat and curled up in my blankets, my feet in the hatchback and my clothes serving as a mattress. The engine idled, fans beating hot air through the vents. I'd never been happier.

To avoid the cold, I cut south on I-15 through Idaho and into Utah, before turning east on I-70. I taped a notebook to the dash, and as I drove, I wrote the sloping deserts and arid plateaus, the Rockies and their companionship with a sky wider and greater than my faith in anything. It lifted peaks into its light, making new monuments of them each hour, then abandoned them into the dark, which—I told myself as I tried to sleep, staring up at snowy, starlit crags through the hatchback window—was why mountains at night are a lonely thing to see.

As the motor's vibrations cradled me, I tried to envision my life. I saw the red lines of highways on the map, stretched between cities like threads of torn cloth. I imagined a book that could hold it all together, plains and mountain ranges, dust-drab towns beyond interstates, and somewhere on the far edges, the valley in British Columbia and those nights in Virginia when I snuck out and stalked the highway, trying to fathom where I belonged on this threadbare continent. Everyone I knew should see the world though my eyes, every friend, every girl I'd ever liked: frost glittering on dry plains at sunrise, or the highway carving through rolling hills with the perfect geometry of longing. It seemed a sin to witness it all in solitude, a reason to believe in an ever-present god.

But loneliness was the trial of this landscape, my life at last like Steinbeck's novels. The interstate opened onto a solitary earth, the quiet destruction of worn-out homes, thousands of miles of violent alchemy melting away a broken people, distilling them to a few resilient loners.

The writer's life was said to be chaotic and destructive and adventurous, and I felt that by choosing this over and over again, so much of who I was would become acceptable.

The message came through my brother: my father's anger, that I'd insulted him, that he never wanted to speak to me again, that I should expect nothing else from him.

I tried not to think about it. The farther I got from his life, the clearer I was about mine. But the way I'd left had been extreme, a reminder for him of my mother's betrayal. I wasn't even sure why I'd done it—to be free or just to prove I could? When I tried to decide if he deserved it, I thought of how he had broken our family. Everything he'd built in his life seemed temporary—hopeless, even—like a few sandbags set against a dark, incoming deluge.

Again, I worked the circuit of couches and guest bedrooms and odd jobs: construction, demolition, roofing, landscaping, washing dishes. My mother had left Dickie and was seeing someone new, a thin, bald man with a Wyatt Earp mustache and such a kind demeanor I could hardly believe she'd chosen him.

The poet Henry Taylor gave a reading at the high school. He'd won something called the Pulitzer Prize, but I didn't expect much, his talk casual, his first poem prefaced with a concern for grammar. It described a horse eating grass through barbed wire, when it was spooked—by what wasn't clear—and ran along the fence, barbs gouging its neck, tearing chunks from its throat. Hearing the rhythms, I wanted to jump up and shout, to tell the horse to stop, to command Taylor to keep reading, to feel the tremendous urge for life that the horse did in the final seconds of its destruction, as it "gave up breathing while the dripping wire / hummed like a bowstring in the splintered air."

Mumbling the lines over and over, I left school and drove to the restaurant where I washed dishes. How was it done? Passing racks of dishes, I had to restrain my hand from knocking them to the floor.

The line cook with the greasy ponytail annoyed me, but I told him about the poem so I could snag half an English cucumber.

"You wanna be a writer, huh?" he said, his front tooth chipped at a nicotine-stained angle.

"Yeah."

"Well, you should read Kerouac."

"Whatever," I said. Worn-out hippies were always telling me to read Kerouac. No one who didn't look as if he'd scorched his neurons and had his skull sooted up with cobwebs had recommended him. But I nodded, devouring a plum tomato in two bites. Once, in a textbook, I'd read an excerpt from Magellan's voyages, a paragraph devoted to how, starving, the crew sustained themselves with fruits and vegetables and meats entirely new to them. For me: leek soup, arugula salad, the hard ends of French bread.

"Hey," the line cook said, "go easy on the Gouda."

"Yeah, okay." I snuck half a boiled potato from the counter and ate it in the walk-in fridge, garnished with dark olives from a plastic tub.

The next morning, I asked my English teacher if I should check out *On the Road*.

"You?" she said. "No, you should definitely not check out *On the Road*. The last thing you need is *On the Road*."

So I went to the library and got *On the Road* and *Dharma Bums*.

That weekend, I read both books, sitting on the couch at a friend's house, on the front porch, under the tree, on the picnic table, moving often as if to make myself inconspicuous. I'd have stepped into the pages: wandering, nights of camaraderie and the courting of women; the sense of innocence and hope and longing for experience. Even in their misdemeanors, the characters remained pure. They lived in the undeniable flow of life.

But what startled me above all was the working-class world from which Kerouac came, the French Canadian family in Lowell, Massachusetts, and how he'd freed himself. There was something of the observer in him, a lack of connection, a rootless quality that denied him strength. I couldn't help but think of my father's disconnected life, the emptiness into which he pulled others. And yet I knew that because of him I loved Kerouac. He'd lived wilder things, a more desperate life driven by a greater longing than anything Kerouac described—a desire I sensed when he spoke of his past, but whose source I didn't understand. No matter how I tried to forget him, I knew that his stories had first fed my imagination and made me want to travel, and that, when I myself had escaped him on the road, these stories had returned to me, ghosting my wanderings.

As soon as I finished both of Kerouac's books, I rushed through *Pride and Prejudice*. I'd grudgingly taken it from my English teacher for extra credit, but it surprised me. Unlike so many other characters in novels, Elizabeth Bennet seemed fully formed. Her rebellion emerged fluidly from the mechanisms of her society. I imagined meeting her, but her family would probably have hired me to dig a ditch, nothing more. An excruciating loneliness gripped my balls. Kerouac, too, I realized, would have dreamed of her—would have loved her fiercely, though eventually, unable to find his place, he'd have left, or she'd have kicked him out.

As I read in the library, Charlotte joined me and pushed a college guide across the table.

"Have you looked yet?" she asked.

She and I had hung out at a party and become close, though she refused to be anything other than a friend, maybe wise to my life's heedless trajectory. She'd been insisting for a week that I apply to at least one college.

"Just pick one. Everyone else has applied."

"Nah," I said and told her about Kerouac riding on the roofs of trains or living alone in a fire tower on a mountain for months, writing books.

She rolled her eyes. "Just apply. You don't have to go, but you'll have the choice."

She had long auburn hair and a classical profile, and she seemed far too good for me in the same way Elizabeth did. Rebel or not, Elizabeth would have wanted a man with at least some education. I hated the idea of it, a sort of narrow cast that would force me to write and think like everyone else, but I leafed through the guide.

"Okay, this one," I said finally. It was the strangest I could find, the most individualistic, a school in Vermont called Marlboro College.

For the application essay, I described my upbringing, my bankrobber father and occultist mother, exaggerating maybe a little. But I had no intention of going. Nothing I did could expend my energy. At times, it felt like bliss, exuberance filling my lungs so as to crack my ribs. At others, it was a virus in the blood, demanding movement and expression. The speed of my scribbling transformed words into hieroglyphs. I jotted on scraps that cluttered my car, which I now had to push-start, its alternator dead.

After classes let out, I opened its door and pushed from the side, gaining momentum, then jumped in, threw it into gear, and popped the clutch. The engine revved and sputtered, and I sped out of the lot. I drove fast, the windows down, and as I climbed a long incline, a gust blew through and carried out several scraps. The anxiety of loss startled me. I felt it in a way I never had with people. I wanted to stop and search the roadside weeds, but the car might stall and I'd be stuck. Foot pressing the gas, I drove on, grieving lost verse, as if I finally understood that the people and places in those words were gone.

The need, the desire, the disease—whatever it was that made me keep moving was unrelenting. Clear mornings, the sight of distant mountains filled me with such longing that I drove past school, wandered from town to town, or hiked. By graduation, I'd realized its alienating power.

I was living on a river in a dome tent that I'd dug from my mother's horse trailer and that my brother, my father, and I had camped in, its canvas now a Rorschach of mildew. The land belonged to friends of my mother's, the riverbank remote. I bathed naked and scrubbed at clothes filthy from construction.

My mismatched transcripts had added up, and I'd been accepted to college and even offered funding. Classes began in two months, but going seemed impossible. I didn't have enough money for the small amount not covered by financial aid, and I was in trouble with the local police, who'd fined me for driving without an inspection sticker, then without a muffler, and finally for missing my court date. My brother had told my father about college and sent me a message, saying that my father wanted to pay my way back for a visit. Though I hated my job, I didn't want to give in to him.

I opened my car door and sat. The clothes I wore had dried on a tree branch and were as stiff and coarse as animal hides. I didn't know where to go from here. I hated the idea of college, but what else was there?

I stared at the sky, the sun flashing through leaves. I punched the windshield and it split. The irreversible damage brought out my fury, and I kicked the side-view mirror off and beat on the door. I took a plastic jug with some gas in it and splashed it on the tent and lit it. I pitched much of what I owned inside. Not waiting for it to finish burning, I turned the car on. The engine backfired, sounding like a lowrider. I raced along the tractor path through the woods, half a mile to a long gravel driveway, and finally to a county road and then the interstate. I accelerated until the car shook, vibrations clapping in my ears. After an hour, the engine boomed, and I drifted to the shoulder.

When a tow truck arrived, I just signed the car over. With the sun in my eyes, I squinted off, trying to make a plan. The driver chuckled, the zipper on his overalls open to the black thatch of his beer gut, his clipboard propped against it as he wrote his name on the title.

I stuffed what I owned into my backpack and began hitchhiking to where a friend lived on a failed commune, a community built of landfill scraps, walls of mortared jars and pop bottles. But I knew the freeloading couldn't last. I'd done so much, and nothing had changed.

"Deni," my father said when I finally dialed his number collect.

How many times could I do this—keep running somewhere else?

"How are you?" he asked, trying to sound jaunty. "I heard about college."

"Yeah?"

"Yeah, so when would it start?"

"In two months. In September."

He was briefly silent. "Two months. You should come and visit me first. You're going to be busy once you start, right?"

"Yeah. I don't know. I'll probably be busy."

We were going through the motions. I'd accept whatever he offered. I couldn't see how I could get to college from where I was, with two changes of clothes and less than fifty bucks. My mother had little for herself and couldn't help me. I'd been pushing to be unattached, as far on the edge of life as possible, and here I was.

A day later, crossing the country once again felt like a solution. As I drifted west, the plains opened before me in a green unfurling of sunlight, until the jagged skyward saw of the Continental Divide warned me of change.

THE FLOOD

The lines on either side of his mouth had deepened, crow's feet at the corners of his eyes, though his dark hair didn't have a hint of gray. We were eating dinner together but hadn't yet talked about why I ran away.

"I remember one time I'd just robbed a bank," he said. "I bought a new Thunderbird with the cash and decided to drive cross-country, but I picked up this kid hitchhiking. He probably wasn't even eighteen. We were in Nevada, and I asked him, 'How long do you think it will take for the engine to blow if I drive this car as fast as it can go?' He laughed and dared me. That's back when I was still pretty crazy. A dare was all it took. So I buried the needle and just kept going. We were in the desert, and it was hot. After about an hour, the hood shot up. It sounded like I'd crashed into another car, but it was just the engine blowing. Steam and smoke sprayed everywhere. We were on the side of the road like that when a cop showed up."

My father was smiling, and I tried to figure out what had made him think of the story.

"This cop," he told me, "he was a real hard ass. You could tell he didn't believe that the engine of a brand-new Thunderbird just blew. So he said to us, 'Have either of you ever been in trouble with the law?' And this eighteen-year-old kid says, 'Yeah.' He's playing it tough and giving the cop a hard time, but I had a suitcase of cash in the trunk. I wanted to kill that kid. The cop finally took him in to check his record and dropped me off at a towing company. I realized then that I wasn't as crazy as before. I'd been just like that kid, but I wasn't anymore."

He hesitated. "That's part of being young. You have to take risks and piss people off."

I finally got it. This was his way of saying he knew why I'd left. We would never discuss it directly. But though I didn't relate to the boy and was cautious around police, I understood the wild pleasure of driving a car just to see it blow.

"Anyway, I was thinking," he went on, "before you leave, we should go fishing."

"Yeah, maybe," I said.

He dropped his gaze and nodded to himself, knowing better than to remind me of the boy I used to be, or the things I'd once loved.

Encouraged by him, I began kickboxing again. The trainer, a bowlegged Irish Newfoundlander with webs of broken veins on his cheeks, encouraged his fighters, often illustrating endurance with stories of fishermen adrift in fog or miners trapped underground who resorted to drinking their own piss. In his hip pouch, he carried a bottle of painkillers.

"Hey, do I sign you up for the tournament?" he asked, though I'd been back only one month.

"Sure. I mean, you think I'm ready?" I was pleased by his enthusiasm, but he shrugged and said, "Why not?" then wrote down my name.

The summer was passing too quickly, days sunlit and cool. By mid-August, I still hadn't made up my mind. I was supposed to be in Vermont soon. My father and I hadn't mentioned college since I'd arrived. He'd given me back the SUV and paid me too well, tossing me wads of cash as if it meant nothing. Three or four times a week, we had dinner.

"A tournament!" he said, leaning forward. "When is it?"

"In a couple weeks, I guess." I didn't want him there. Though I liked that he believed in me, I knew the truth. I got no thrill from battering others, and the best fighters in our gym lusted to hammer on anything. Besides, I'd been working on a dystopian novel, an epic of social breakdown, and often, after writing all night, I could barely train.

"I'm considering deferring," I told him to change the subject.

"What's that?"

"It means I'd put it off for a year."

"Put what off?"

"College."

He lifted his eyebrows. "You can do that?"

"Yeah. Besides, I never planned on going. I can write without it."

He nodded, his expression neutral, as if this were a conversation of no great importance.

"You know," he said, "I read in the paper one time about a really popular writer who didn't go to school. Besides, you should be a fighter, and there's this tournament."

"I might not even be ready," I told him. "It's not a big deal—just practice."

He studied me, then looked off. He got the point and wasn't going to push, probably satisfied for now that I'd dropped my plans. But I hadn't done this for boxing, and telling him, I'd felt cold, involuntarily, as if I couldn't risk sharing even my uncertainty for fear that he'd impose his own vision on me.

"If you're planning to stay a while," he said, thinking hard, eyes focused on the floor, "you'll probably want your own place and a job that pays more."

"I guess," I replied, mostly just to prompt him to keep talking.

"I know a guy with an apartment for rent, and there's a job I could get you. It'd probably be good for you to do things on your own. You want your freedom, right?"

Over the past month he'd mentioned that his stores weren't doing well. Did he think we'd be better off if I didn't work for him, or was he struggling? I tried to see how he'd benefit from what he proposed, but I couldn't. Regardless, I liked the idea of my own place, of having distance from him, writing and reading where no one could bother me. So a week later, I moved into the apartment and started the job he'd lined up at a seafood processing and packing plant, a huge rectangle on the edge of a canal just outside Vancouver.

My days started at five in the morning. Boats lagged, unloading crates of codfish under clouds of wheeling seagulls. The sun rose beyond the cargo doors as forklifts crossed the processing rooms, propane fumes stinking up the salty air.

Though I planned to put away money for travel, I immediately realized my mistake. Rent and a vehicle ate up a lot, and my job and training

left me exhausted. The date for college passed, the weather cooling, rain
replacing sunshine, and to prove I'd made the right decision, I bought a
secondhand computer and wrote every night. The more I did, the more
my emotions overwhelmed me, and the hungrier I got. Insignificant
scenes, a young man leaving a new friend, were charged with grief, as if I
were saying good-bye to everyone I'd abandoned. My stomach rumbled,
and I emptied the fridge, making 3:00 a.m. supermarket runs: orange
and apple juice, blocks of cheddar, quarts of strawberry yogurt, instant
mashed potato mix, value packs of sirloins.

"What happened?" my trainer blurted after weighing me in at the
tournament. I was one pound over the limit for my class. Seeing my name
in the heavyweight column, he took the pill bottle from his hip pouch,
popped the lid, and swallowed one.

I'd read most of the night, and now sat against the cinder-block wall
to finish *Brave New World*. Fighters from my club glanced over and shook
their heads.

When it was my turn for the ring, a redheaded teenager standing
next to me said, "Aw, man, you got the half-breed. Be careful."

I hadn't given much thought to the fight. As soon as I put down
the book, I felt disoriented, then indifferent, as if none of this mattered
and I was just biding my time. A twinge of concern made it through only
when I went into the ring. Nearly a foot taller, my opponent faced off,
half-Chinese and half-Irish judging from his last name. Almost instantly,
he was midair, spinning, driving his heel at my gut. He kicked repeatedly
as I tried to circle in. I timed his landing and struck at his ribs, driving
him back, but one of my kicks hit wrong, the side of my foot catching his hip bone, the pain sudden and intense. Backing away, I limped,
shocked to find myself here. The pain felt like the truth—that I should
be elsewhere, that I didn't care about this—as if it were true that only
by disaster, or something resembling it, could I learn what was real.

"You lost," my father said without inflection, sitting at the table, his arms
crossed. When I'd called to tell him about my foot, so swollen it barely fit
inside my shoe, he'd insisted that I meet him right away.

"I don't know what to do about work," I said, limping to the chair.

His eyes focused in, seeing the concern on my face, and for the first time since I'd returned, he leveled his look of disdain.

"Fake hurting yourself." He spat the words. "That's why I told you to come here and not go to the doctor."

"What do you mean?" I asked, trying to get my face back under control, embarrassed to have him see me like this.

"Isn't it obvious? You go to work on Monday and pretend to hurt yourself. Then you collect workers' compensation."

I was taking slow, deep breaths, willing my expression to indifference, telling myself that none of this mattered, that I could deal with it. But when I spoke, the emotion was there again.

"I'll have to spend the weekend like this," I said.

"What's the big deal? All you do is write. You don't need to walk." He waved his hand as if dismissing me, then explained how to defraud workers' compensation. "Everyone does it," he added as if offering me a joint. "I did it once when I wasn't much older than you. I was on a construction site, and I smashed my pinkie with a sledgehammer."

"Did it hurt?" I asked, wanting to take the attention off myself.

"Of course it hurt. I was trying to break the bone. You always got a longer leave for a broken bone, but my finger didn't even break. The skin just opened right up. I could see the entire bone. It hurt so goddamn bad I couldn't bring myself to hit it again."

I nodded, considering what he was proposing, that it was probably easy, though I didn't want to do it. It didn't seem necessary.

"But what if I get caught? Can't doctors tell how old a bruise is?"

"What the fuck?" He leaned close, looking hard at my face, the edge of his lip lifting. "This is nothing. You used to talk about robbing banks. Get over it."

The waitress came, and he sat back and smiled and ordered pasta with chicken. She strutted off, the menus in one hand, and again, he hunched over the table.

"Just so you know," he told me with an anger that conveyed his full disappointment, "I'm not supporting you. You want to write all day, then you figure this one out."

I shrugged. "I have enough money left over to get by for a while."

"Aw, fucking come on." He gripped the table as if he were going to flip it. "You're a minor. If you get caught, your record will be erased when you turn eighteen. Have some balls."

I nodded and rubbed my cheek. He hated that I'd lost, that I was weak and showing it, that I couldn't keep it in. And I hated it, too.

"How do I do it?" I asked, speaking softly.

He shook his head. "You want to write novels and you can't even figure out how to fool a bunch of idiots. *This* should be easy."

At the horizon, a gray line corrugated by low, uneven clouds announced the dawn.

My foot throbbed with each step, a dull prodding sensation like a blunt nail against the bone. All weekend, I'd written as the red and black bruise spread, and now, gritting my teeth, I made my way across the parking lot and tried not to think about the breaking of a law put in place for a good reason. In my novel, the dystopian society was the result of greed and war, and my actions seemed no better. But if I didn't do this now, I would look like I'd always been full of shit.

I shut out my thoughts and decided. I crossed the warehouse, empty, existing only through my senses: a gust of wet air, the hiss of water hoses and the banging of metal carts over floor drains, the weight of my rubber boots.

And then, briefly, I was alone in the gymnasium-size freezer, beneath the high metal shelves. Bing, a wiry Chinese man with liver-spotted cheeks and orange teeth, had gone to get the forklift, and I was supposed to load boxes on a pallet. I glanced around, then reached up, pulled three boxes from the shelf, and let myself fall with them. They cracked against the concrete, jostling blocks of frozen shrimp inside. I jammed my foot into the pallet's slats, then lay, looking at the distant ceiling and trying to grimace, though I just felt resigned, carrying out this task with the same indifference I'd shown the rest of my work.

"What wrong?" Bing asked as soon as he got down from the forklift.

"I twisted my foot," I told him, clutching my ankle.

He laughed. "Get up!" When I didn't, he furrowed his brow and re-peated, "Get up!"

"I can't!" I said, feigning concern.

He hurried off and returned with the boss, a short, slightly hunched Chinese man who watched everything with eyes as still and unrevealing as the lenses of security cameras.

"You're fine," he barked.

"No, I'm not. I really hurt my foot."

"No. You are fine!" he repeated as if chanting at a rally.

"I can't stand up."

"Yes, you can!"

"No, I can't."

I could see that he didn't believe me, that he could find no shock or pain in my expression.

The foreman, a French Canadian with a lean face and pale brown eyes, stepped to the front of the growing knot of onlookers. "Show us your foot," he mumbled.

The employees craned their necks. A gigantic, bearded Pole came to the rear, a man who referred to himself in the third person and who was often called upon for heavy loads. "Stan wants to see!" he announced. The Chinese before him looked like smiling children with Kool-Aid-stained teeth.

Gingerly, I removed the rubber boot. I peeled back the three pairs of socks that I wore to prevent blisters. The distended skin of my foot felt as if it might pop.

The crowd said, "Ah" and "Oh." They were speaking in Chinese all at once, very quickly, pointing as if the others might not have seen what they had.

My foot looked like a glimpse of a murder-scene photograph on a detective's desk, or something sticking out from beneath a sheet in a morgue. The crowd parted, and Stan stepped to the front and helped me up with surprising tenderness.

At the emergency room, anxiety made sweat bead on my forehead. The doctor would see straightaway that the injury was two days old. He was a gangly Al Pacino, his breath reeking of mint as if he were a teenage smoker returning home. He touched the taut skin and whistled, then poured Tic Tacs into his mouth and almost choked on them.

"Let's get you an X-ray," he said between crunching. "You're not going to be putting weight on this baby for a while."

The X-rays showed that nothing was broken, but he told me that soft-tissue injuries could be worse than fractures. I went home on crutches, with an appointment for physiotherapy and the determination to use workers' comp to finish my first real book. When I shared these plans with my father over dinner, he dropped his gaze and sighed.

"I guess you won't be training," he said.

"I'm not even supposed to walk."

He stared out the window and asked if I'd train again once my foot was better.

"I don't know. Maybe I'll go traveling then, or else I'll just write."

He nodded, but I could tell from his expression that he recognized his mistake.

Night after night, my blinds drawn, I expanded on my vision of the future, a militant world purified in a flood of biblical fire, destroyed back to its natural state, civilization ground down to a primal level, to a society of matriarchal cave dwellers.

I'd never been so happy. Society constantly hovered between fear of loss and desire for change, and I was trying to understand what it meant to believe in the world. My villains valued only themselves, their satisfaction and survival. If you believed the world was cruel and selfish, it was easy to live only for yourself. It made me think of the trailer park in Virginia, or my time with Travis and Brad, the three of us conspiring to shoplift or outsmart others, to steal whatever we could. The world had seemed a primitive place, indifferent if not hostile, willing to walk over us, and we'd just been making room for ourselves, eager to jump into the fray, to see what we could get away with.

I found myself wondering once again where my father had come from, why he'd rejected Quebec. He'd told me years before how, when he was young, he'd supported his family, working for them, keeping almost nothing for himself. In my novel, the worst character felt betrayed by everyone he loved. Was this an accident or universal?

Each time I met my father for dinner, I asked if he wanted to read what I'd written, but he shook his head and said, "I don't read novels. I don't know much about that." He asked if I'd like to go fishing before the salmon runs ended.

"Maybe later," I said.

I finished the novel the night before my eighteenth birthday, and the next morning, to celebrate, I printed and read it. Shortly before heading out the door to meet my father, I threw it in the trash.

"I'm going traveling," I told him as soon as we'd filled our plates from the buffet. I needed to live more. My book felt childish and false, lacking the ring of experience, bloated with big ideas I'd loved only in the moment of their discovery.

"When?" he asked.

"Maybe after Christmas. I'll go to California. A friend from high school is living there."

He prodded his rice with his fork and sighed. I'd expected rage or derision, but the fight had gone out of him.

"Why don't we go fishing one last time?" he asked, the lines in his face deep, as if with grief. "The salmon runs are still on. You used to love to fish. It was your favorite thing. You'd beg me to take you. It was like the world was going to end if I didn't."

The memory of myself as a child was startling, and I nodded, sad for no reason I could identify. I no longer thought about our past much, or anything other than my immediate goals.

"Sure," I told him. "That sounds okay. We can go before I leave."

He stared off. "You know, I don't regret working with fish. There's something special about them. I've always felt that."

The tenderness in his voice surprised me, his sadness, and I recalled how I'd felt about fish as a child, their mystery.

"I don't know how to explain it," he told me. "I'm not a writer. I just know I've always liked the water. When I was a kid, I could tell where the fish were out there."

"Did you use a line back then?" I asked, uncomfortable with the way he was speaking, wanting to bring our conversation back to the concrete and simple.

He dropped his gaze and hesitated. "No. Mostly a net. When I was older, I'd go fishing with a rod. But that wasn't for money. It was just to be in nature."

"No one fished with lines when you were growing up?"

"Of course they did, but we mostly used nets." His gaze faded out, growing distant the way it did before he told a story, and I felt relieved to see the sadness leave his expression.

"We had a small wooden boat," he said, "and I used to go with my father on the Saint Lawrence. I'll never forget this one time. We'd just put down anchor when we saw two giant fins coming across the water—the biggest fins I'd ever seen. Both turned at the same time. It was like they belonged to the same fish. They came right at us. It's hard to believe, but these enormous black and white fish, they started jumping over the boat. I was wearing a red Canadiens sweater, and my father knew that fish often go after the color red. You could even catch some fish with just a red string tied to a hook. He pushed me into the bottom of the boat and started swinging his oar at them. But as soon as I was out of sight, they left. This must have been around 1946. He'd been fishing the Saint Lawrence since he was a boy, but he'd never seen anything like that. There were rumors that a fisherman up the coast had gone missing and his boat had washed up with large, sharp teeth stuck in the wood."

He looked down and stabbed his fork at small shoots of stir-fried broccoli.

"A journalist came and saw us afterward, and there was a newspaper article about it. They told us that the fish were *épaulards*—killer whales. Years later, I saw a picture of the same fish, but when I read about them, the book said they were rarely in the Saint Lawrence. One time at Stanley Park I asked a woman at the aquarium, and she said that killer whales sometimes wander out of their normal territory and become more aggressive because they don't have enough to eat."

He took a bite, then pushed his food around slowly.

The whales interested me less than my grandfather, whose name I didn't know. When I was a boy, my father's few stories about his village always involved fights, drinking, and religion. I'd pictured weathered shacks slanting from a ridged, windy sea, or men in church, each holding a foaming tankard. He'd described a bar where a local tough, for a drink, would jump and kick the low ceiling with both feet, leaving sets of sooty boot prints on the boards. I'd stared at our own ceiling, trying to imagine how I could do the same.

"Why did you leave?" I asked.

"What?"

"Quebec. Why did you never go back?"

"There's nothing for me there."

"But you still have family, don't you?"

He waved his hand. "I've been gone too long . . ."

"Why did you leave in the first place?"

"It was backward. The church ran everything. They kept the people poor."

"You think it's still like that?"

"No. It isn't. It's changed. But there's no reason for me to go back."

I remembered something I'd read when I lived in Virginia. Assigned a history report for school, I had chosen Canada because I thought it would be easy. I studied *les coureurs de bois,* the hardy trappers who went against fur laws and lived in the wild. The book said that because the early French population of Quebec was largely composed of men, there was a great deal of intermarriage with the Indians.

"Do you think we have Indian blood?" I asked.

"What?" He looked up from the food that he was prodding more than eating. When I told him what I'd read, he said, "I don't think that's true." He picked up his water and emptied it, then put down the misting glass and sighed, the skin loose at his throat as he lowered his chin.

"The older generations were hard people. You wouldn't understand. You've had it easy. When the winters were bad, the men would leave their wives and children with the food and they'd go into the woods to live with nothing but their guns and tools. They'd just hunt and find ways to survive. That way they didn't take away from what the family had."

I was going to ask about my grandfather, but he was staring past me, above the buffet, squinting as if struggling to make something out. I turned. Over the kitchen door, a plastic sign showed a cartoon pig rolling in food: Take What You Can Eat, and Eat What You Take.

He shook his head.

"What's wrong?" I asked.

"They had the same fucking sign in prison." He shoved his plate back, spilling rice on the table. "If people are paying, it shouldn't be there."

Without looking at me, he got up from his chair and left.

When I was six, at a time when his business was growing rapidly, he told me that a man who owed him money had agreed to give him anything we wanted from his house.

"It'll be like going shopping without having to pay," he explained to my brother and me.

He laid out the plan. We would carry cardboard boxes into the house, and my brother and I would pillage the bedroom of the man's son while our father did the kitchen and living room. My mother refused to go.

"It's wrong," I heard her tell him.

All the houses on the street were a lot newer than ours. My father knocked loudly and turned the handle, opening the door and calling inside with a playful voice, as if a good friend lived here—"Anyone home?"

"Hey, André," the man said, sounding tired. Bald but for some carroty fluff, he slouched, hands in his pockets. "Go ahead. Take what you want."

My father perused the kitchen, putting a few pots in his box. He snatched a lamp and said, "Hey, this is nice!" The man watched from the corner, and I sensed an intention to humiliate in how my father dismissed objects. He poked at some oven mitts and made a nasal sound to indicate no. He opened drawers and didn't bother closing them.

"Go on upstairs," he told my brother and me. "Take whatever you like."

I wanted this to be one of our wild adventures, but I knew it wasn't, that laughing now would be wrong. My brother and I climbed the stairs and hesitated at a doorway. Toys covered shelves and the floor, and a big boy with red hair and freckles blocked us and crossed his arms.

"Stay out of my room!" he shouted, but his father hurried up the stairs and pulled him down the hall by his elbow.

My brother and I went in, filling our box with G.I. Joes, Star Wars toys, and the new Gobots. The loot extolled on TV was finally at our fingertips. We took it all and went out to where my father was putting boxes in the truck, already having loaded a mini pool table. The boy was sitting on the steps, staring off, and I realized how he must feel.

I took a Gobot from the box and offered it to him.

He stared at the blocky figure in my hand, then glared into my eyes.

"Keep it, you fucking frog!"

I didn't know what he meant, but I recognized an intention in his insult that was deeper, more direct than profanity.

Years later, after my mother had left my father, during our first week of school in Virginia, my fifth-grade teacher announced that we'd be watching a video about racism.

She wheeled the TV to the front and put in a tape. The narrator told the story of a neighborhood where the English and the French didn't like each other. We saw the lives of two boys, one from each background, and at some point the French boy, with his gang of friends, jumped the English boy on his way through an alley and took his money.

"You frog!" the English boy called him.

When the video ended, I sensed all eyes on me. I'd known I was in trouble the moment it started. In a school where black and white kids fought in the halls, it seemed strange that the video would be about French and English Canadians. She'd wanted to teach the other students about where I came from, and now she asked how I felt about it. "It sure wasn't easy to get a video about Canada," she said, "but I finally found one!"

When I didn't respond, she added, "You don't want to say anything?"

"No," I told her.

Later, on the playground, a group of boys came over, shoulders rolled forward and hands half-lifted as if to begin throwing punches.

"Hey, frog!" one of them called, then hesitated. "Are you a frog?"

"No." I tried to think fast. "The frogs are from somewhere else."

"Oh," the boy said, he and his gang clearly disappointed.

After dinner on my eighteenth birthday, I couldn't stop thinking about my father's omissions. Where had he come from? Why had he left? I no longer wanted stories about prison or his ambition to pull the big job and throw it all on the betting table; I wanted to hear those brief, muted recollections of the life he'd fled.

The highway curved beyond our headlights, following the mountain. As he drove toward Squamish, he told me how he and my mother had lived out there, in a cabin near the river. He'd made some speed and sewed a sample into the seam of his jacket, but on his way into Vancouver to deliver it, he'd realized the police were following him. He drove to a garage and sloppily painted his van green, then hurried home but came to a highway checkpoint.

"This cop, he had a sense of humor. He asked if I'd been drinking. I said no, and then he said, 'I liked your van better when it was blue. Have a good day.' Without that tip, I might not have acted so fast. He saved me. I had my laboratory and two guns, and that night I went into the woods and buried everything under a fallen tree. The next day the police arrested me. They kept me for a few days, but they had no evidence. When I was being released, the officer who gave my stuff back started going through the box. He began feeling along the seams of my jacket, and I realized I'd forgotten to take out the speed. I pretended to be furious and shouted, 'Are you going to keep me here another day? Give me a fucking break! You guys arrested me for nothing!' This guy just looked at me and said, 'Okay.' He pushed everything off the counter and let me pick it up. He'd been seconds from finding the speed."

"Do you think we could go to where you buried the guns and dig them up?" I asked, thrilled at the thought of it—the foray a mixture of old passions: crime and archaeology.

He nodded, watching the road. "It's been twenty years, but I wrapped everything in plastic. Maybe I can find the place. We can look later today."

Until then his face had been creased with fatigue, his skin slack, but he brightened at the thought of us unearthing his old guns and laboratory.

"If we can find the house," he went on, "we can buy a shovel at the hardware store."

We followed a gravel lane and parked at a high embankment clearly bulldozed in place years ago to keep the river from washing out the roads.

Standing before the headlights, we attached our reels and threaded the rods. He squinted, taking his time tying the hook on, finishing long after I had. Seeing him, I remembered a night at the reservoir when I was a child, the workings of his hands as he threaded the line. He'd muttered and reached in the truck window, and the headlights came on. He'd crouched before the bumper, his hands moving in the beam, scars across their knuckles, the blunt fingertips pinching and pulling. I'd stood in the light falling past him and looked at my own hands, the soft pads, the pink rounded fingertips and my few pale scars. The memory startled me with a sense of loss, that the years between that moment and now had been a mistake, that I should have lived a different life. I took a few slow breaths and stared off until the emotion passed.

When he was ready, we climbed the embankment and followed the shore. He stepped carefully between rocks and driftwood, his head bowed. Something had changed in him, his movements slow.

"Are you okay?" I asked. I'd noticed Tylenol bottles in the truck but had thought nothing of them.

"I got in a fight the other day."

"What?"

"With some idiot. This guy—you've met him, Tom Alding."

"That guy?" The man was tall, not burly, but well over six feet and solid looking.

"Yeah. He tried to sell me bad salmon. We were in the store, and I smelled one. I don't know if he took me for an idiot. I guess he really needed the money. I told him no way, and he grabbed me by the neck and pushed me backward over the counter. It hurt my back."

"What did you do?"

"I hit him. I punched him in the face and got him by the hair and kept hitting him until I had him out the door. Then I kicked him in the ass, and he fell off the porch. He had the nerve to say, 'Take it easy.' Jesus Christ, the guy pushes me and then he says, 'Take it easy' in the middle of a fight. I went in and got the baseball bat from under the cash register, but by the time I returned he'd run away."

"You keep a baseball bat under the register?" I asked.

"You didn't know? I have one in all my stores." Then he grit his teeth and said that his back hurt and he hadn't been able to sleep. He conveyed this with no self-pity, speaking harshly as if still at odds with the other man.

Dawn lightened the sky above the wide river, and its water, broken by boulders, shone silver like a long rippled fabric running on toward the mountains.

"I'm fifty-four," he said, watching the current. "I shouldn't be fighting at my age. It's stupid. All of this is stupid."

I nodded. I didn't like seeing him weak. It shook me in a way I couldn't explain, but I knew he'd hate me if he saw me feeling sorry for him. I realized that if I let myself worry about him, it wouldn't be as easy to leave, so I tried not to think about it, and just breathed the air off the river.

Gradually, as we began to fish, he moved more naturally. Chum salmon weren't in season, and we were trying for the rarer, smaller coho, whose meat was better. Though we occasionally hooked a large chum, we let it go and competed to see who could catch a coho. In the late afternoon, he shouted and laughed, and I walked along the riverbank to join him.

The salmon's gills pulled for air, and I crouched and looked at the markings.

"It's a small chum," I told him.

"No, it isn't. I work with fish all day. You don't even like them."

"It's a chum," I repeated, gliding my finger along the scales. "Look here."

He drew his face near, lips pursed with anger. The salmon opened and closed its mouth and snapped its tail against his hand. He reached into his jacket and took out a pair of glasses.

In the lenses, his eyes appeared large, like toys, blinking slowly. He crouched and stared, then straightened and folded the glasses and put them away.

The salmon struggled, drowning in the air, and he picked it up and carried it to the water. He eased it in and released it, then rinsed his hands and shook them dry. He told me that we should go and look for where he'd buried the guns while there was still enough light.

We followed the river in his truck. Warm air blew in the vents, and the cab smelled of the mixed, hard odor of his life, a briny animal scent of dogs and fish and cologne. A few unlit cabins stood in the woods, and we slowed at each one as he scrutinized it, frowning, before we continued on. The embankment was soon gone, replaced by stretches of scattered stone along the river that shone violet in the sunset.

He took the road slowly, gazing out, all around us naked branches reaching against the luminous sky. I'd come here with him once when I was a boy, just he, my brother, and I, and we'd camped in the same dome tent I later burned. We got up at dawn to fish, and as the sun rose, he told us that we should do this every fall. I agreed. None of us could have imagined how much our lives would change.

It was getting dark. We'd driven for nearly an hour along gravel roads, pausing at washed-out flats where the water had risen in the past and uprooted trees.

He pulled the truck onto the shoulder.

"I don't recognize anything," he told me. "There was a big flood some years back. Everything's different now. Even the roads."

As soon as the waitress brought his beer, he took a long drink and sighed. He said he should have spent his life in nature.

"That's all I ever really cared about. Everything else was bullshit."

"No, it wasn't," I said. "Come on. You've lived. You've really lived."

He shrugged. "And what the fuck do I have now?"

I hesitated. "Have you ever thought about getting in touch with your parents?"

"My parents?" he repeated, as if he'd never had such things.

"What were their names?"

He cleared his throat. "I left Quebec to give myself a new life. Too much time has passed now."

He finished his beer, drinking more quickly than was normal for him.

"What would I go back to?" he asked. "I quit school when I was in fifth grade. Every morning, I used to ride along the coast looking for wood that fell off barges. I fished or I worked in the fields, planting potatoes or digging them up. When I was sixteen, I started logging on the north coast. I was younger than you are now, and I spent all winter in a camp with grown men. At your age, I was working in uranium mines and on high-rises, whatever I could find."

He called for another beer and told me that if his body hurt it was because he'd worked too hard as a child. "It stunted my growth. My shoulders hurt. Everything fucking hurts. We used to read by candle-light and now my fucking eyes are ruined. Why in the hell would I go back? I worked and sent my money to them, and they didn't even give me an education."

He stared past me, his cheekbones and forehead pronounced, cast-ing shadows.

"Maybe I could write your stories," I said, as if I had nothing else to offer.

He took a drink and put the bottle down and nodded.

"Sure. I'd like that. My stories deserve to be told."

"They do. But I don't know anything about your childhood."

He shrugged. "There was work. There was some fighting. There was a lot of church. I hated the church. I remember my first confes-sion. I was a little kid, and when I told the priest I hadn't sinned, he said that everyone sins and it's a sin to say otherwise. So I had a choice be-tween telling my sins or saying Hail Marys for lying. I made up little sins, being jealous of my brother or angry at a friend. But it was bullshit. We worked. We did nothing but work on the farm, and that fucking priest made us invent sins. We didn't have toys. All we did were chores. We got up and fed the animals and picked up wood or worked in the fields. When was there time to sin? Maybe if it weren't for him I'd never have started breaking rules."

He hesitated, nodding to himself, his gaze distracted.

"My older sister used to walk with me to church in the morning. It was about a mile. The road was just above the gulf, and it was cold. We weren't allowed to have breakfast until after confession, so we'd walk to church, then home, then back to the village for school. My sister wanted to say her Hail Marys quickly so we wouldn't be late, but the priest caught us leaving. He yelled at us and made us stay. The nuns at school would hit us on the hand with the strap if we were late. So we both got punished that day . . .

"But you know, that fucking priest, he lived in a big house behind the church, and he had a live-in maid. That's what people called her. His maid. Everyone knew he was screwing her. But if a girl went to confession and said she was having sex, he'd yell at her so everyone could hear. That happened to . . . to some girls I knew. I wanted to kill that son-of-a-bitch priest . . ."

He sighed. "These kinds of stories—you want to hear them?"

"Yeah, I do."

"There's one I'll never forget. One Sunday that priest preached against adultery. A man and woman in the village had left the people they'd married and were living together, and the priest told us to pray and call down the fire of heaven on them. I snuck out of church and ran to their house. I went right to their window. I'll never forget it. They looked happy. There was no fire. I kept waiting for it to come down and burn them, and I was worried I was too close to the house and might get burned up, too. But when the fire didn't come, I knew that fucking priest was a fake. After that I never believed another word he said."

He finished his beer. The waitress was bringing our plates, and he called for another.

"Remember how we used to talk about just living in a motor home and fishing? That's what we should've done. This business, everything, crime, all of it, it's bullshit."

He ate slowly, searching out bits of chicken with his fork, then paused.

"Our best years were in the valley," he said.

I didn't know how to respond. He gazed off for a moment, then looked at me.

"Promise me something."

"What?"

"When I die, promise me you'll do one thing."

"Okay," I said. I couldn't recall if I'd ever seen him drink like this.

"Promise you'll bury me in the mountains on the edge of the ocean."

I nodded. "All right."

"No. Fucking promise. I haven't asked fuck all of anybody and I haven't gotten fuck all. So promise."

"I promise," I said, though I had no idea how I'd take his body into the mountains. "Why are you talking about dying, anyway?"

"People die. Sometimes you're here and everything's okay, and then the next day you've lost your health and money, and no one gives a fuck about you and you die."

"Are you worried about dying?"

"I'm just saying that sometimes it happens. Money's always a problem. The economy is shit. It's never easy. Life doesn't get better."

"But your health is okay."

"Of course it's okay. My grandmother lived to a hundred. I'll probably live to a hundred, too." He stared at me, his eyes suddenly clear and unguarded. "I never thought about that. Maybe you'll be too old to climb into those mountains to bury me. You'll be an old fart. Maybe I should die young. You can drive me into the mountains and bury me overlooking the ocean. I'd like that, but you'd have to be young and strong. I wouldn't be able to wait until I'm a hundred."

"It's probably illegal," I said.

He shrugged. "Yeah. A lot of things are illegal if you get caught. You figure it out. If you can't get my body, just use the ashes. I won't be angry at you."

"Okay," I said.

"I don't like this *okay* bullshit." He asked me to promise one more time, and I did.

He drank another beer as we finished the meal in silence. I felt that I'd never seen things so clearly, the strangeness of my family, how hard it was to make sense of him. He'd been the person I'd stood against, measured myself against, declared my freedom from. I didn't know how to see him weak.

He noticed me watching and narrowed his eyes, glaring, letting me know he was still awake, that I'd better not count him out too soon.

Getting up, he swore and grabbed at the table.

"I'm too drunk to walk," he told me with a smirk and drove his elbow hard into my ribs. "Yep, I'm too drunk to walk. Looks like I'll have to drive."

We met a few more times before I left. He told stories after late dinners. Snow flurried across the parking lot, and his eyes almost closed as he gazed through the window. He described the boredom of work camps, a day when polar bears maundered through a mining town, a night so cold his axles froze, though he'd left the engine running as he slept.

"Crime," he said, "was better than anything I'd known. If you saw where I came from, you'd understand. It felt like the only way out."

I dropped him off one evening when his truck was in the garage. He went through the metal gate, and five large shepherds ran across the yard and gathered about him anxiously, lifting their heads as he moved his hands, touching each of them on the nose until they calmed. He stood still, gazing on them as they sat or stretched out at his feet.

Though I'd soon be free, I no longer felt the need to run. I simply craved the highway, its lightness and sense of loss, as if the divine could be found only by leaving, by losing myself in the country. Yet even as I thought this, I couldn't imagine my father's future. I refused to let myself feel anything, afraid I might stay, so I just watched, seeing, studying as if for later, as if I knew that he'd soon be gone and only these memories would help me understand. In the big dogs' wordless allegiance, in the way his presence calmed them, I sensed his need for one thing that would never leave or betray him.

My mother's talk of destiny came back to me, the hope and necessary destruction I'd found in her words. But nothing in our futures seemed as perfect as our lives in the valley. I stood at the window as dogs loped across the fields, followed by a man. They raced away from him, toward an invisible point, leaping and falling over each other, then rushed back as he continued through the rows of trees with the same steady pace.

Once, he'd taken me to sloping mountaintop pastures. He wore his rain jacket and sou'wester and walked the rows, pruning trees. I huddled in the green pickup as fog blew past, silhouetting him and masking all but the snap of the machete. When he came back, his clothes were soaked. I asked why, and he tousled my hair and said it was the clouds. "What clouds?" I asked. He said that what was all around us wasn't fog. Later the clouds broke and sunlight raced over the damp trees and grass. Beneath us the valley opened, a swath of green marked with specks of color, the road and streams intertwined like sleeping snakes.

The day I left for California turned out bright, sun flashing on snowmelt.

We met where I was having my SUV serviced for the trip, and he drove me to get lunch.

"It's good that you're going to travel and go to college," he said, squinting in the light through the plateglass windows. "I'd have done the same thing if I could."

"I can come back and visit," I said.

He smiled and looked down. "Who knows? Who knows with this fucking life?"

"No, seriously, I'll come back."

"You don't know that." He sat with his shoulders curved forward, appearing fragile.

As he drove me back to the garage, we followed a red convertible in the traffic.

"Look at that guy," he said. "It's not that warm."

The blond driver was bundled in a jacket, and his alert posture made him appear nervous. The four-lane road had a broad median, and he pulled into the left-hand turn lane in front of us. The oncoming traffic passed in packs, and there were several openings that he didn't take. With each gap, he lifted his head and inched forward. The car looked almost new, its red paint brilliant and its tires a solid black.

"Goddamn it," my father said, "doesn't he see he's had plenty of chances to turn?"

Traffic surged past again, and two more openings came and went. My father lowered his window and leaned out.

"Turn!" he roared, the tendons in his throat standing out. "Turn, you son of a bitch!"

The driver hit his accelerator, and an oncoming sedan braked and rammed his fender, crumpling the hood and scattering shards of plastic and glass over the road.

"Jesus Christ!" my father said. He swerved back into traffic and sped away. He glanced at me. "I didn't mean for him to turn *right then*."

My heart hammered as I looked back at the crushed, diminishing cars, wondering if anyone had been hurt. They vanished from sight and we stared forward, neither of us speaking. Then we glanced at each other and began to laugh.

We were still chuckling and swearing under our breath when he dropped me off. We shook hands, and I told him I'd call, and he said I could always come back if I wanted.

I just nodded, and he started his engine and pulled his truck next to me.

"Hey," he said. "Do you know I'm the number one driver in Vancouver?"

"What?"

"That's what everyone tells me. Whenever I drive by, they say, 'Hey, you're number one,' and they do this." He showed me his hand and lifted his middle finger.

He laughed and jammed his accelerator, spraying slush and oily grit from the asphalt. I covered my face as he scorched a half circle. Then, as if to say that he was the one leaving, he raced into traffic, cars braking and swerving, and soon his truck was gone from sight.

part v

IMAGINARY FAMILIES

My father and I spoke little over the next year. I traveled to California and stayed with a friend and four other young men in a two-bedroom apartment, writing when I could and working for a temp agency renovating a Sears. We slept on couches around the TV and climbed chain-link fences at night to swim in pools. But the friend started a fight over a girl and I left, though I would have regardless because the next day we were evicted.

When I told my father on the phone, he asked me to come back and help at his store. Instead, I headed east, looking for jobs in Utah and Colorado. I wended my way across the continent, and by April ended up in Virginia, where I worked construction until the first semester of college began.

By then I was grateful for it, having struggled to write another novel and realizing how little I knew, how much I wanted the time to study. I loved the readings and discussions. With each novel, I felt myself filled with language, erasing the old patterns words could take, creating possibility. I reread *Absalom, Absalom!*, searching through threads of identity, the ambition that grew into a man, hiding the initial wounded impulse of a boy.

When I thought about what I might write, I envisioned a great novel just as my father might have imagined the big job. The novels I loved most grew from awareness of family: talk between generations, the shared, conflicting wisdom, parents and grandparents rooting forward-gazing children. Novels seemed the product of that tension, between parents and children, between those they loved and struggled against.

As I embraced these novels, it occurred to me increasingly that I knew next to nothing about my father's past. That absence, the dim history that had shaped him, refused to let him become whole.

During our rare phone conversations, I asked again about his family and why he'd lost contact with them. As usual, he evaded the questions, saying that too long had passed, that he had nothing in common with them anymore. When I asked about Quebec, he told me how backward it was, how poor they were. And then he changed the subject to his business. It was struggling, and he asked if I'd come back and help. But I was happy, and the desperation in his voice made me wary.

Talking to him, I was unsure of what to feel, as if he were a stranger. My life and ambitions were now so different that I no longer knew where he fit. Only when I wrote did emotions surface, did I feel his absence and worry about him.

The summer after my freshman year, I again worked construction in Virginia. He and I spoke, and he asked if I wanted to visit him, but I said it was too far. I feared I wouldn't make it back to college. My life had an equilibrium, a shape, at last, and I was afraid to disturb it.

Silence settled in the rooms. Through the window, autumn air seemed vaguely sweet, flavored with the decay of leaves. The only sound was the dull tap of the few remaining moths against the screens.

A week earlier, I'd moved into an attic apartment on the mountain road leading to school. Two professors rented it to me, and since the house phone didn't reach my door, I waited for them to leave so I could call my father. I watched their car's taillights disappear down the curve of the driveway. It was strange to think that at fourteen I'd broken into a house, but now I was so desperate for this life that I was cautious in every way. I didn't want the professors to overhear my conversations, the casual talk around crime.

I called collect. I'd tried twice that week, but the line had been busy. Now it rang repeatedly. I was about to hang up when he answered, his voice so hoarse I hardly understood it.

The operator gave my name, and he accepted, then asked, "Who's this?"

I repeated it loudly.

"Hey, Deni. Is that you?" He coughed and cleared his throat.

"Are you sick?"

"A little."

"It's nothing serious?"

He coughed again. "Just a minute. I need to clear my throat."

The phone clunked down. From a distance, there was the reedy sound of a faucet, and then his cough, thick and wet. *Sick* was a word my father never said. Once, when I was four or five, my mother had told me to leave him alone because he was sick. He'd been sitting in his chair, looking focused and furious, as if refusing this weakness.

"Are you okay?" I asked when he picked up the receiver again.

"Yeah . . . I'm fine. I was expecting you to call."

"I've tried, but your line was busy."

"I've been taking it off the hook."

"What kind of cold do you have?"

He fumbled with the receiver and said only, "I've been a little sick lately."

"Should I let you go?"

"I just woke up. It takes a minute to get going."

He coughed a few times, then breathed loudly, saying nothing as I talked randomly about the classes I'd enrolled in.

"Do you think you'd want to come back," he interrupted, "just this once? You could take a few months off."

"I can't. I'm already enrolled."

Absentmindedly, I turned the lamp off, the house dark but for the porch light, the furniture faintly silhouetted.

"How's the market doing?" I asked.

"Not good. There's new management running the building."

"Shouldn't that help?"

"No, the manager's a fucker. He raised the rent." He drew a slow breath, then went on in a faint voice, describing store owners leaving, just walking away, and how the manager used to work for "that dictator in the Philippines." "Marcos," he added uncertainly.

He paused and swallowed a few times, sounding a bit like a person rearranging dentures. "I'm not intimidated. They're overcharging and bullying people, but I can handle it."

"You can keep the store going?"

He started to cough again. His receiver rasped against his shirt.

"Sorry about that," he said. He sounded drunk, slurring his words.

"You were telling me about the new manager."

"Yeah. He's a big guy and people are afraid of him, but that doesn't work with me. He tries to play games, and I put him in his place." He hesitated, panting softly into the receiver. "I'm getting fed up with that damned store. I guess I've been thinking a lot about success."

"Success?" I made a noise in my throat to let him know I was listening.

"I've been thinking," he said—"I've been thinking I haven't accomplished much. I don't like failure." He suppressed a cough, then talked about not being able to cross the border to do business, and how that affected him. "But it's good to see you going in the right direction. I know you'll get somewhere. We both like to accomplish things."

His breath remained short and labored. Abruptly, he said, "I guess I'm thinking of letting the store go. I might have to declare bankruptcy again. I'm thinking of doing something else."

"What would you do?" I asked, surprised by my own vague sense of irritation—the possibility that his problems might affect me. No other emotion came to me, and I realized how wary I still was.

"I'm thinking about it," he said.

"Traveling might help," I suggested, searching for a solution. "You could hide some money for after the bankruptcy."

"That would be dishonest," he told me in this new voice.

I didn't reply, and after a few more breaths he said, "I've had my good years. Vancouver is my home . . . I could have gone back to Quebec twenty, even ten years ago, but there's nothing there for me now."

Neither of us spoke. I didn't know this voice.

"Besides," he said, "money's not good to have when you die."

"Are you dying?" I asked and was almost relieved by his anger.

"It's just a way of saying things. I'm talking about when it happens. There's no point trying to do anything else. It's too late. I don't have the experience."

When I didn't respond, he said he should let me get to bed since it was three hours later on my coast. Then he hesitated. "Do you think you could call me more often?"

"Sure," I said, but then he quickly changed the subject.

"I was driving by your school the other day. You know, the one in Abbotsford. I sell to some people down there, and I was thinking about when we used to go fishing. Then I started thinking about how you came back. Things were hard, I know, but you came back."

I didn't say a word. He coughed briefly and continued.

"I should let you go so you can get rested for school. I just want you to know that what you're doing is best. If I could have, I'd have had more education. I got a high school diploma once . . . when I was in prison. I guess I wanted one. But it was with the name I used when I was arrested, so it doesn't really count."

Again we were silent.

"It must be late," he said. "You should call on the weekend so we can talk longer."

I frowned and closed my eyes. "It is the weekend."

Between breaths, he asked for my number in case he needed to call. I told him, and he repeated each digit, two correct before he had me repeat the next two.

"I'll call you," he said. "I'm planning on moving, so I'll call you after I do."

"When will you move?"

"I haven't found a place yet, but something will turn up."

"Why don't you just stay where you are a bit longer?"

"It costs too much."

I asked where he would keep his shepherds.

He hesitated. "They're at a friend's house. Anyway, I should let you go."

I couldn't imagine him without his dogs. Was there something he hadn't told me? I made myself speak to keep him there. "You know," I said, "I want to write your stories. I've thought about that a lot."

He cleared his throat again. "That would be all right. Listen, I should let you go. It's good to hear from you. Don't worry about me. Just give me a call if you want to talk, okay?"

"All right," I said. "Okay."

"It's been good talking to you," he told me, his voice superficial, as if we'd done business. He hung up before I could say good-bye, this a habit of his, to hang up quickly.

I held the receiver until it began to beep, then put it down and just sat, emptying my mind, refusing to worry about him. I got up and went outside, and stood in the dark beneath the cooling September trees.

For me, Quebec was no more than a list of facts: Jacques Cartier's voyage to the Saint Lawrence in 1534, Samuel de Champlain's trading post on the site of Quebec City in 1608, the declaration of New France as a royal colony in 1663. Gaspésie, the peninsula where my father grew up, was thought to be named for the Micmac word *gespeg*, "the end of the earth."

He'd told occasional stories of his village: on election day, men in suits arrived and gave each fisherman five dollars to let them cast a ballot in his name; or, when he was a boy, his uncle and aunt in Montreal asked to raise and educate him since they couldn't have children. He dreamed of playing hockey in Montreal, but his father refused: *"T'es un homme, pis on a besoin de toé."* You're a man, and we need you.

My grandfather had ten children, but he'd called my father his ace, proud of his strength and diligence. My father always knew he'd refuse to let him go. They'd stood on the shore, the sea, as I pictured it, gray as lead, the far coast hardly darker than the low cavernous sky, as if the sun were weaker in 1947, or in that part of the world.

On the uncle's visit, he gave my father a thin metal chain, like a necklace. My father, who was eight, tied it to a wood chip and pulled it through the sawdust on the barn floor, imagining it was a train. When it fell off, he searched, raking his fingers through the dirty sawdust even where he hadn't been. He described how he'd looked again the next morning, the barn dark, bands of light between the boards. The hogs had begun to grunt, thinking he'd come to feed them.

"That's how pathetic that life was," he explained. "That something like that could matter."

As I wrote these notes, I felt a vague sense of anger, a tension behind my eyes like the onset of exhaustion. Since these stories weren't of crime, I'd given them no importance. In a restaurant, he'd offhandedly mentioned his uncle, and I'd thought little of it. But this was among the few childhood experiences he'd shared, and I let myself wonder briefly how my life might have been had he not hidden his past, had I known his family and the place he'd grown up in. As I tried to write his stories, I felt his inchoate longing as if it were my own, the regret of a missed opportunity, and I was certain that this boy's rage was in him still. It had been his first chance to escape, though I still didn't know what he'd left behind.

I sat next to the window screen, the telephone on my knees.

His breathing was barely audible. I'd told him about my plan to turn his life into a novel, but he talked about the market. He wasn't in the mood for stories.

"I'm pretty tired of this business. Sometimes you just get sick of things. I'm sick of working every day. It shouldn't have to be like this."

"What are you thinking about doing?"

"There's a lot of stuff I haven't told you. A while back I hurt myself. I took a pretty good fall off a freezer. I was trying to fix a light, and I fell on the concrete. Since then there hasn't been much I can do. I can hardly pick anything up. I think I've ruined my back for good. I forget I'm not young anymore. I feel that way, but I guess I'm not."

I waited, but he didn't continue.

"You sounded pretty bad last time we talked," I said, trying to find words for the feeling I had. "I was worried. You sounded like . . . like you didn't want to live."

He was silent, and I listened for the soft motion of his breath.

"Don't say anything to anyone—not even to your brother or sister. I didn't want you to know. I thought maybe you couldn't handle it. If I tell you this, will you not tell anyone?"

I had to swallow, lifting my chin, before I could speak.

"All right. I won't say anything."

"I didn't want to tell you, but near the end of the summer, I decided to kill myself. I think I'd known I would for a while. I sold a few shepherds as police dogs and gave the rest away. It was the first time since the pen that I haven't had shepherds. I don't think I realized until then that I would do it."

I held my eyes closed, then blinked and stared beneath the tilted-back shade of the lamp, letting the light wash in. How had he come to this so quickly?

"I bought heroin," he went on. "I read in the paper that people were overdosing on China White, so I went and got some. I bought enough to fix ten people, and I took it all. It put me in a coma for more than two days. When I woke up, I was so sick I couldn't get out of bed. I was blistered all over. I went to the doctor, and he told me that our bodies move when we sleep, that way the blood doesn't settle. I guess I didn't move. I had blisters all over my thighs. One of them covered the entire heel of my foot. I could hardly stand."

"Was that when I called?" I kept my voice steady, surprised at how empty my mind was, how still everything felt around me.

"I was pretty sick," he said. "I spent two days in complete darkness. It wasn't like sleeping. It was like I was gone. I think I was afraid afterward. I don't remember. I went to the doctor and told him. He put me on medication."

"You're still on medication?"

"It seems to make things a little better."

My throat felt dry, my chest constricted as if I wanted to cough. I asked if he was going to try again, my voice calm. I didn't want him to think I was too weak to hear this, but I was surprised at my steadiness, that I didn't feel more sadness, just empty, unmoored, vaguely disoriented.

"I don't know," he said, his voice sounding far away. "I don't know if it's worth risking that there really is a God."

"You haven't given up on God?" I asked, hearing how I sounded more startled by this than by his talk of suicide.

"I gave up on the Catholic Church. I don't think God's part of the church. Sometimes I think he has nothing to do with it."

"Have you been going?"

"No. I went a couple times, but there wasn't anything there for me."

"Do you think," I said, searching for the words to make him reconsider, "do you think you can get through all this?"

"Not without wanting to. People in my family live a long time. I don't want to live that long, but I'm afraid to kill myself. I should have died."

"Isn't there something else you can do if the store doesn't work out? You could go on a trip or something." Saying these words, I felt pathetic.

"The store is only part of it. I'm sick of working on things that don't give anything back. It's too hard. It might not have been so bad if everything had turned out differently. If I'd seen you guys grow up. That's the one thing I'd change. It wasn't right for your mother to take you like that. She used my past to do it. I still remember when I called her in Virginia. She threatened to call the *po-lice*. She said it like that, like someone from there. She'd been gone two weeks. But I'm not mad at her, not anymore. I got over that. I just would have liked to see you grow up."

Not a word was spoken for what felt like a minute. Against my ear, the conscious silence felt too intimate. I didn't know how to speak to him about this.

"I'm not proud of the things I've done," he said. "The other day I read about some guys who robbed a bank, and it made me angry. Those kind of people don't appreciate hard work."

"Still, you did some pretty amazing things."

"I don't think you can understand. You've had chances I never did. If I could, I'd switch with you in a second. But I missed my chance. The things I did in my life went against the world. But you're on the right path. I just want you to know that."

He paused, maybe trying to make sense of his own words.

"I always saw so much of me in you. But I'm not proud of the years I spent inside, and I'm not proud of the things I did. If I could go back, I'd change everything. I've damaged a lot of lives. I see the world around me, and I'm not part of it."

I realized I'd been interjecting affirmative sounds at his sentence breaks, but now I stopped, angry. I needed to say something to change his mind, but we had never talked like this. I wanted to get off the phone. I wanted to put it down—to hang it up so slowly and neatly that he wouldn't know until the line went dead.

"You shouldn't be ashamed," I forced myself to say, my throat dry. "Most people couldn't have lived your life."

He hesitated. "Maybe. I don't know."

"I want to write your stories. Will you tell them to me?"

"There's at least one book in my life," he said. "That's something, I guess."

The silence stretched on. Squirrels scraped in the leaves outside and bickered near the bird feeder. In the distance a dog barked. I rubbed my eyes and pressed my fingers into them, phosphenes pulsing along the lacy glitter of capillaries, the white glow my mother had once called the light of the soul.

"What would you need to know for a book?" he asked. "Where would I begin?"

"With your childhood."

The novel I imagined would contain the world he revealed: a gray stone church, wind-beaten houses, fishing nets strung between eaves, the families, children filing behind parents on Sundays, snowdrifts against walls, footpaths shoulder deep; later, wagons mired to their axles in the spring thaw—or the day when the power company came and installed glass globes that burned without heat or smoke.

He and I spoke regularly after that night. I called him when my landlords were away, or from campus. Sometimes he paused from storytelling to ask me to drop out and come back, saying he'd never needed an education. But each time I refused, he grudgingly went back to describing his past.

As a child, he'd been aware of words, he said—those in English that they used in French, as if car parts had no names in his language. At the store, there were labels that meant nothing, sold nothing, with letters that had lost their places. He got his favorite, Eagle Brand condensed milk, as a treat. *"C'est du Eagle Brand, ça!"* one of his siblings had said of the car an American tourist drove past on the dusty coast road. They all nodded in agreement, laughing.

The sense of mystery that I wrote into this new world was mine. I saw it as if through a child's eyes, each detail lit by my longing to know more. But in his words, I felt deeper emotions: the loyalty to parents, the love and rivalries of siblings, and the desire to make things your own, your own ideas and passions, your own adventures. I wrote to bring myself close to the edge of all that, seeing not just his family but my own, the place from which the road away began, and I knew that we'd been leaving since long before I was born.

My anger surprised me at times, rising suddenly as if released, giving me an animal restlessness, consuming the hours when I tried to sleep so that I finally returned to my desk.

In my notebook, I wrote the Saint Lawrence whose frigid waters I'd never fished. I wrote days at sea without having known the flash of cold when my hand strays too far on a net line, becomes nothing more than knowledge, until pressed inside my jacket as if to melt.

One of his earliest memories: he stood at the window, watching the pasture as a man crossed it toward the house and climbed the stairs. He recognized him and called to his mother, telling her that Grandpapa was there. She opened the door, but there was no one, just the empty stoop, wind blowing over the pasture. Her father lived across the Saint Lawrence, a day of sailing or a flight away, and she explained this to her son. But an hour later, she received a telegram from the village saying that her father had died.

Though my father had been born on the north shore, in a village run by a Jersey cod company, soon afterward his father had moved them back to Gaspésie, to the family farm. His mother never fully accepted the new village, telling him that he was better. She made clothes for her children and claimed that the garments in the shops were inferior.

While she maintained appearances, his father, a burly, dark-skinned man who loved a fight, had him and his brother, Bernard, put on boxing gloves and square off in the living room. "That's my ace," my grandfather would say of my father, stoking the rivalry between the boys.

My father had done this with my brother and me as well. I was bigger, but my brother had age on his side, and after he punched me, I went berserk, flailing. When our mother commanded us to stop, my father looked stunned. I understood it now, that he was seeing the past.

Spring through fall, my father worked. He saw himself as a man and hated the winters, when the coast froze and fishing stopped. Men from the village signed on with logging companies and were flown north until spring. But my father stayed behind with the women and children. Winters were chores, feeding the animals, mucking the stalls, bringing in firewood.

On November 12, 1953, he turned fifteen. Sixteen was the legal age to sign on with the logging company, but he lied. His father let him, eager for the extra earnings.

Each hour, my father grew more anxious. Any work would be better than living trapped in the small house with his mother and siblings. He readied his bag, his work clothes, his boots. But at the landing strip, the priest stood with the recruiter. He called my father over and berated him for lying. He'd been the one to record my father's baptism in the church register, and he'd brought his birth certificate as proof.

The plane left, and my father walked along the coast, a wasteland of folded sheets of ice. He'd always hated Curé Félix Jean, who ruled the village like his own kingdom.

Locked in rage, he stared over the Saint Lawrence to the ragged horizon. He couldn't bring himself to go into the house, couldn't think of any motion or action that might satisfy him.

"I wanted so badly to get out, to leave," he said over the phone. "That's all I could think of. I had no idea what I'd do when I was gone. I just needed to go."

Where did such longings reside in us, passed on through blood or stories, through a father's distant gaze as he tells his son of far-off places? It seemed to me then, hearing his words, that a father's life is a boy's first story.

I woke in the dark, sensing my mind at work in my sleep.

It was only 1:00 a.m. I dressed and quietly went out along the wooded driveway to the unmarked asphalt. My breath misted as I walked. Chimney smoke rose against the moonlight, casting fleeting shadows over the road. The glittering stars seemed the source of the penetrating cold, a million points of ice.

How much had I changed since I was a boy? If I wasn't discovering something, restlessness took over. Maybe crime had been his cure for this just as writing was mine, or learning about his past, unlocking his secrets. Was everything we lived just for the thrill of being alive, of pitting all of yourself—intelligence and strength—against something so tangible and challenging that you felt yourself fully real?

The forest opened to the college grounds, silent but for my steps. I went in the campus center, turned on the hall light, and unfolded the metal chair next to the pay phone.

"Hey," he said and accepted the call. "It's late there."

"Yeah, I couldn't sleep. I was thinking about the stories you told me."

"Which ones?"

"Just about your family. I still don't understand why you never went back."

He didn't answer at first, then, in that way that made each new conversation feel like a beginning, he said, "I wanted my own life. My father was strong. He was a big man, and people respected him. He worked hard and could fight. But that's all he had. When I was sixteen and finally went to the north coast with him, I remember how he warned me. A

frozen tree could split and kill a man, or during *la drave,* the drive, when
they ran logs downriver to the Saint Lawrence, men got injured. But I
just wanted to work. I wanted out of the house. I didn't care.

"One night, there'd been a hard freeze and then snow, and in the
morning we left camp for the river, where we'd tied a boat of supplies
to the shore. On our way there, we saw a new camp of loggers. They
were English. I was surprised. The English owned businesses or came as
tourists, but I'd never seen them like this. There were just four of us, and
they invited us to eat with them. The food shocked me. They had beef
and sweet sauce and canned peaches and a kind of melon I'd never seen.
We ate everything we could and even put some in our pockets. I noticed
that they were laughing. I didn't understand at first. I thought they were
happy, but then I realized they were making fun of us."

He hesitated. "I'd been proud to be on the north coast, but I understood something then. I saw that others didn't respect us at all."

Could this really be why he'd gone so far away? Respect had always
been important to him, but I didn't believe he'd needed to leave his family and culture behind to become someone new.

The next morning, I would write what he told me next, the details
outlandish. He and his father and the other two men continued to
the river, kicking a path through fresh snow. The quiet of the north
loomed from the frozen earth, palled between the trees. As if to break
the silence, one of the men spat and uttered the racial epithet for the
English—*"Maudites tête-carrées!"*—Damned square heads!

The trail curved along the river, the expanse sheathed in fresh
ice, cleared of snow by the wind that had followed the storm, scoured
blue in places. Here or there, narrow, dunelike drifts rose from the surface, like the unstrung coils of a serpent. The small boat was frozen in
place, loaded with bags. They stomped on the ice. It wasn't thick but
it would hold them, and they carefully emptied the boat and decided to
pull it free and drag it to shore.

My father had still been thinking of change, that it would come
through work, each job a step further from home and closer to a new
life. He wanted to put his rage into something, to show his strength, and
he grabbed hold next to his father and pulled, startled at the ease with

which the boat nearly lifted from his hands. The river rushed at his feet. No matter how he tried in the years that followed, he could never recall slipping, and even his father next to him did not see him disappear. But somehow he sensed the absence. He dropped the boat and sprinted. The shadow of his son fluttered against the blue, darkest where the wind had driven hard against the river.

The first jolt was too sudden for my father to feel. Then the cold clamped down, stars in his eyes, the air forced from his lungs. He refused to gasp and tried to make sense of what had happened. He struck the ice, but the mark was no bigger than his father's heel above him. The effort pushed him deeper, so he stopped moving, let himself skid along the belly of the ice. He wanted to breathe. Hurry up, he thought. The cold cradled him.

He knew from having seen his father drag nets and boats from the sea and wrestle an unbroken Clydesdale to the ground that the feet stamping whorls above him were not a vain attempt for the sake of conscience. His father didn't consider failure as he ran, the shadow of his boy stretched out at his feet as if it were his own. The figure below was of perfect calm, perhaps death, legs loose, palms so close to the ice that in the moment he dropped his body to strike, he could see the perfect outline of the hand, each finger.

The sky roared upward, tilted into sight. Clouds hung hard against the horizon, ink stains against the sun. His father lifted, so great the pull that buttons skittered and froze upended.

"*Réveilles-toi!*" Wake up! his father shouted and shook him to his feet. He struck him on the arms and back, pushing him to run. My father raced to the camp house, swept it, split the firewood, his clothes steaming as if a flame burned inside him. He loaded the iron stove, but when he held his hands above the griddle, his father shoved him back into motion. "*Dépêches-toi!*" he shouted.

That night, eating dinner, my father swallowed his mouthful of potato and asked what had taken his father so long. The men laughed and slapped the table.

"My ace," his father called him and told the others that his son was charmed. But a rage lingered in my father, that he'd needed to be saved, that he still saw his father as insufficient—strong, yes, he was known all along the south shore for strength—but this wasn't enough. He was French Canadian, trapped in this little world run by priests and owned by the English. If Anglophone loggers ate such good food, then what did the rich ones eat?

Speaking haltingly over the phone, he told the story of his near death like a tall tale, a myth of ancestral strength, and I listened, sensing his past, an absence larger than his life. The story couldn't be true. He told it like this because he was trying to make it contain the world he'd lost and the feelings he couldn't voice.

At the camp-house table, as he daydreamed, his father bragged to the others about his charmed son, the boy who'd seen the ghost of his grandfather climb the stoop and doff his hat good-bye before vanishing like a moment of bliss.

When I said good-bye, the horizon had gone pale, washed with a violet light, and in the pearling air, the vivid reds and yellows of the turned maples came into focus, as if they lay just beneath the surface of water. At the roadside, frostbitten mullein leaves clustered around dead stalks. I walked along the road, too much energy in my body—anger, sadness, guilt.

He'd spoken for hours, prompted by my questions. At times, he sounded old and dreamy, and I was unsure of his chronology, the sheer number of places he'd worked, but I rarely interrupted.

In our silences, I knew that we both asked what the point of his wild life was if not the joy of being alive, in motion, moving toward something new. And why did I need to put these pieces together, living what he had, letting myself feel that loss, the rage that makes us search out a new life, the guilt of leaving others behind? I claimed the past from him as if jealous, planning how I would write him, how I'd make him clear. Why had I refused to visit the previous summer? I couldn't go back, but I could listen for hours, finding what we shared in his words. And yet his loneliness was palpable in the way he tried to keep me there with his stories.

Work, as he described it, proved a passage out, but he did not love it. At a uranium mine, to protect his lungs, he had to drink two glasses of milk before going underground. His first week he gulped them down, but he saw no pleasure on the tin-colored faces of the older men. Miners were paid for how much they brought up, and he ran all day, pushing the barrow along the track. He bragged that he earned twice or three times more than anyone else, but a month later, the occasional cough brought coarse, sooty phlegm into his mouth. The odor of milk was enough to make him gag. He thought back to his uncle who'd wanted to adopt him, and seeing the consequences of that loss, his rage burned, stronger even than on the day his father refused the offer. The desire for a better life ached in his gut.

He sent money home and visited at Christmas, playing floor hockey upstairs in the house with his younger brothers. When Bernard was around, he and my father struggled to speak, both still feeling the wounds of their rivalry. Their mother greeted my father with show, kissing his cheeks and telling everyone how much money he'd sent home. His youngest siblings were getting the education he hadn't.

"What's your problem?" my grandfather asked him.

"What?"

"This attitude."

"*C'est rien.*" It's nothing, my father said, unable to dispel the distance between them, his fury and desire to leave and never return. How long would he keep working and sending his money back when they'd given him nothing?

His next job was on a skyscraper in Montreal. He liked the high wind and could even drink milk again. He made fun of those afraid of heights and ran the beams.

Passing an Iroquois worker on a girder, he stepped on a bolt someone had left out and his ankle twisted. He liked the Iroquois men who were braver than his own and whom he copied when he hooked his heel on a beam and leaned down, his feet holding him in place as he set a rivet. The man grabbed his shirt and leaned back to counterbalance him. They hung in place. Then the Iroquois pulled them upright and let him go.

My father tried to calm himself, but his rage came on worse than before, the wildness, the desire to keep running the beams without boundaries, fearless, unencumbered.

"What's the point of this?" he asked Martin, a friend he'd made. The two would meet in a bar, drink, and discuss the future, but the conversation rarely got past work—jobs that were maybe a little better, but not so different—or the dowdy bar girls.

"It was . . . it was shit work," he told me. "There had to be something better. I didn't know what. I couldn't imagine what another life might look like. I was just looking . . ."

On the skyscraper, at the end of each day, the bolder men ran to the corner and grabbed the flared edges and slid down story after story until their gloves were hot and their feet hit the ground. But that payday, as they ran to the corner laughing, my father just behind Martin, he saw his friend's pant leg catch on the end of a rivet.

Maybe it was the newness of friendship, the high, clean air, or simply the joy of being paid, of ending a long day, the sun flaring hard against the horizon, their nimble, overconfident running, and then his friend's silent, fragile, insignificant dive to stone.

The next morning, he hammered his sledge against a jammed beam. He'd begun to sweat. He struck three more times, then flattened his hand against the iron, reared, and drove the sledge down. The flesh of his pinky split like a bean pod, revealing white, knuckled bone. He cried out, the sledge flipping down through the steel ribs. He grabbed the girder and gasped. He felt as if he might weep, as if only now, with this pain, he could finally give voice to his hopelessness. He'd wanted the better compensation for a broken bone, but he couldn't bring himself to strike again.

For a few weeks, he rented a room on Montreal's Plateau and often sat on the fire escape teaching himself English from a book. He'd bought an eight-track and listened to rock 'n' roll. He went to a few boxing matches, frequented bars, and tried liquors whose labels were as foreign as the logos on the sides of trucks he'd watched pass as a kid. He held his bandaged finger before him like a symbol of nobility.

When he was almost out of money and nearly healed, he ran into Gaétan, a wolfish man from the high-rises who had a gift for making men laugh two hundred feet up while standing on a twelve-inch I beam. They talked about the poor pay and Martin's death. Then Gaétan admitted he'd quit his job and said he was moving that afternoon. He asked if my father would help.

"You drive," he said and directed him into an alley behind an apartment building and told him to wait. My father wondered how Gaétan could afford to live there or own such a nice car or why he'd insisted on putting the ragtop down, when clothes started falling from a balcony—silk dresses and pinstriped suits, a small wooden chest that bruised the upholstery, a jewelry box with a mirror that shattered. Rings tumbled along the floorboards.

When Gaétan swung down from the fire escape, my father was furious. But Gaétan was already in the car and said, *"Dépêches-toi!"*

My father hit the gas, and they raced off.

As he drove, Gaétan showed him a Judy Garland record. *"C'est du quoi ça!"*

My father didn't respond. When he reached the east end, he parked and got out and began walking, insulted to have been used like this. Gaétan called after him that if he wanted to make real money, he could ask for him in the bar.

My father left Montreal, afraid to be tied to the robbery. He took a job on a dam up north. He was there for several months. Sundays, he skipped Mass to go fishing, and just before sunset he sat on the scaffolding and smoked, staring off toward the West.

But within a month he had an accident. He'd been working at the top of the dam, pouring concrete into the wooden forms along its rim. He stood on the wood, guiding the sluice behind the truck. The sun was rising through mist and clouds, sometimes pale yellow or silver white, at times blinding. Bulldozers shifted mud and rock below the dam. He heard a cracking sound and grabbed the wood beneath his feet as the form he stood on broke free. The wall of the dam was rushing past, and he gripped the two-by-four frame that skidded like a sled along the concrete cliff, nails striking sparks.

He reached the shallow water below, crouched, his heart eerily calm, his mind empty, as if he'd been made to do this and nothing could be more natural. When the men along the rim saw that he was still on his feet, they began to cheer, and at first he couldn't understand why.

The next morning, he packed and took his final paycheck. At the post office, he divided his money and sent half to his family. He began hitchhiking west with what remained.

Travel was recent in my life, the thrill of setting out still familiar. There was the first breath taken as the journey began, the expansiveness in the lungs and heart. His words recalled this for me, the freedom of movement, the hunt for simple needs — food and places to rest — and above all the realization of how asleep we are, animals in our own cages, feeding ourselves indifferently. As we explore, meals and beds are not promised but won, coming into our lives with a power like revelation. He crossed the continent, amazed at the endless variety of earth and people. He saw the Native American man trapped on a rock in the river, and he understood that he wanted to live for himself and forget the dead.

He traveled aimlessly west and then, as his money ran out, back east. He arrived in Montreal penniless.

"Gaétan introduced me to the man who taught me safecracking. I was good at it. I liked the challenge. Safecracking's not for idiots. It takes concentration. It was like a game. I'd test myself. I knew I was good. But he didn't pay much. We'd steal a thousand, and he'd give me a hundred. I wanted to go out on my own. I told him I wasn't making much more than in the mines. He's the one who set me up."

The night he broke into the sporting-goods store, he huddled in the doorway — wet streets, coronas beneath hooded lamps, no sound of footsteps. A long car with finned rear fenders passed, throwing up lines of spray. His hands were tight in his pockets, his chin to his collar, heart and mind still. He began to understand this strangeness in him, that he was at home only in uncertainty, in that place where possibility and danger extended about you like a naked plain.

Then he exhaled, the sound loud in the darkness, surprising him. He turned and slid a flat bar from inside his coat and jimmied the lock, cracking the casing. Inside, he waited until his eyes adjusted. He crept past racks of hockey sticks, shelves of ice skates and helmets, all colorless in the dark. At the back, his hands hunted over the panels of a door.

With a stab, he locked the bar and levered it. Slivers of wood crunched beneath his boots, screws trilling on the uneven floorboards.

In the next room, past the desk, he found the safe. As he knelt, the doorway flared. He rushed out. Blinded by the brightness, he slammed into a shelf. Balls fell and bounced across the floor. Each window was a brilliant grid, red and blue eddying behind the keen light.

He never described being arrested, only prison, the inmates no tougher than the men in his village, the constant tension, the almost-sexual sizing up as he passed cells and brushed shoulders. He hated the thin cots that smelled of sweat, the exposed toilet and the cracked sink stained from the drip of rusty water, the blood on its rim after that first fight, when he struck a man's head against it then let the weight of the slumping body pull the knotted hair from his fist. He hadn't foreseen that the inmates would explain his arrest, saying he'd been set up, patching theories as they pressed spoons into lukewarm potatoes.

"That was my school," he told me.

Through talk and stories, the inmates taught him to pick any lock, to crack the hardest safes—they carried him beyond prison, to jewelry stores flush with daylight, to banks, and like a final secret, through steel-ribbed concrete vaults.

Behind his voice, there was the clear sound of pouring rain, its steady beating on his roof. Outside my window, in the moonlight, the first snow flurries lazed in the wind.

"Did you see your family again after that?" I asked.

"One more time," he said. "One time after that. But I wasn't the same. I realized that I couldn't stay. Too much had changed."

He was quiet a moment, his breathing barely audible against the rushing rain.

"I used to dream of going back rich. I realized how easy it would be. I learned everything in prison. I made a plan to go straight to the top. I would do the big job and take the money and go home. I never thought about what I'd do after that."

"Why not?"

"I guess I knew I wouldn't go back. I knew I'd never be satisfied there."

"Would you go back now?"

"No. Too long has passed."

"What if we went back together?"

He hesitated. "That might be okay. The two of us. That could be all right."

"Where do they live?" I asked, trying to sound patient, to mask the anger and resentment that came more and more frequently.

But he was silent. I wanted to insist, to tell him that it was my past, too, but I didn't. From the pause, the way he cleared his throat, I knew he would ask me to come back and work with him. He did so often. I would say no, so I didn't ask.

CURES FOR HUNGER

My father's birthday was the day before mine, and I decided to call after midnight so it would be both of our birthdays. He liked finding similarities in us and, during a previous conversation, had told me that every eleven years our ages were inverted: fifteen and fifty-one, twenty-six and sixty-two, thirty-seven and seventy-three. He also said he'd come across a book on astrology in a bookstore and read some—only out of curiosity, he added, as if to keep from sounding ridiculous. He'd noticed that we were Scorpios and tigers, and he wondered aloud if this meant anything, though he changed the subject before I could respond.

Leaves had fallen, winter had come early, the radio calling for a light snow. I pushed through the campus-center door and dialed from the pay phone, but he didn't answer.

What if he really was going to kill himself? Was college so important? The continent protected me from his life, though I hated myself for thinking this. Nothing but stories held us together, our conversations nearly devoid of the present.

"Sometimes I don't know what it was all for," he told me one night. "I was trying to get away, but I never really knew what I wanted to get to. I was too busy just trying to get away."

Other times he laughed, recalling his wildness. I sensed in his words the drive to do something dramatic and impossible for others—to take action and say, "This is mine. I did this." The impulse seemed true to me, to leave a mark on the world before you could think about whether that mark was worth making. Even as I wrote, I was trying to figure out what I hoped to find, why I was composing this.

An hour later, I called again, wanting to fall into that momentary grace, our shared attraction to a life that denied nothing, that made holy the imperatives he could not begin to understand, so that I could do the same, write it with an equal fierceness.

I called over and over from the pay phone and gave up only after 3:00 a.m., when that brief, diminishing time, which I'd wanted to gift to him, had passed.

Two years in prison. He felt like a gambler who'd lost half the money in his pocket and was desperate to win back what he imagined was his. The lost years meant that his return home had to be dramatic. He couldn't go with nothing to show. He hadn't called them and didn't want to see them until he was rich. Only money could justify his absence.

Prison taught him the nature of the self, the way it can be shaped and hardened. He learned to like the adrenaline, to thrive on the thrill of a fight. He craved the world—all that he'd take for himself when he was free. Longing carved out an empty space within him. He felt gutted and learned to like this, too.

After prison, as he headed west and left Quebec behind, the plans he'd made began to come apart. Rage and a nameless desperation rushed him forward. Someone only had to bump into him in a bar and he'd fight. He pulled armed robberies, but the cash was never enough. With the intention of going straight, he took a few jobs, mining and construction, in the Yukon and Alaska, but they only confirmed his belief that without crime he'd never escape the life he'd been born into. It was his wildness that repeatedly put him back in jail, for fights or reckless driving.

After his release, he got a new social insurance card and a license with the name Gaston Tremblay, then crossed to Montana. He'd made friends in bars and prison, and they robbed a few banks. Drunk, they went into country tourist shops, guns ostentatiously tucked into their belts. They put on clothes and hats, filled their pockets with candy bars and beef jerky in front of the clerk, then walked out, waving good-bye. They ate dinners, then tore hair from their heads and threw it on the plates and said, "I'm not paying. There's hair in my food!" They once fought an entire kitchen staff and finally ran out when the chef began swinging a cleaver at them.

Eventually they were arrested for robbery, and he did a year and a half in a prison where local teenagers took their mufflers off and drag raced outside the walls at night to wake the inmates. He'd lain in bed hating these kids, that they saw him as nothing more than a criminal who deserved punishment, that they didn't know what had brought him here, what he'd been running from. And yet he knew that in their place he'd have done the same and laughed over it. His stupidity and that of all people sickened him, and each morning he woke, waiting, impatient, a child again in his father's house, counting the months until his freedom.

One January afternoon, as he walked in circles in the yard, smoking diligently, he heard the tremulous voice of an old man announce, "I own the world. I tell you, I own it all."

My father turned to the man who stood in the cold with his arms spread. He shook his head. "No, you don' own world. Everyt'ing excep' Quebec."

According to my father—who told this proudly, as if he'd met a celebrity—the man was one of the last living members of the Karpis-Barker gang. He had worked for Fred Barker and Alvin Karpis, though now, when asked about their exploits, he talked about his childhood. "Oh, those days fishing brown trout in the spring, the warm spring!" He lifted rickety hands to show the size of the big one his dad caught. He had a tremendous nose and hit it each time he slipped on the ice, so it was frequently bandaged. Guards and bruisers alike loved him, and even the meanest inmate, Joe Yates, who'd knifed his obese cell mate with the sharpened rusty shankpiece of a boot, would take the old man's elbow to walk him over patches of ice. The guards had contrived to have a fake checkbook printed up for him, and he was forever buying things.

"How much is Quebec? I'll buy it off you."

"One hundred million dollar."

The old man pursed his lips. "How many zeroes?"

"Eight."

He wrote out the check clumsily and tore it off and handed it to my father.

Hearing this, I laughed, and in that moment, I felt there was hope, that I could ask about his family again, about going back. But he was still thinking about the check, and he told me that he'd gotten the better deal. He cursed the Catholics, the backwardness of Quebec, and finally, that night, when he stopped speaking, I no longer had the courage to ask.

After Montana, he crossed the border and changed his name again. He tried to be calm, businesslike in his crime, but the wildness still took hold. He pulled a few jobs in Edmonton, but worried that the police were onto him. Then his partner ran with the money.

"That time," my father told me, "I almost got it for good. It's crazy how things work out—the chances I took. It's like I was charmed. The cash was from a small job, but you let a guy fuck with you and everyone will take you for a sucker. So I went to his girlfriend's house and asked if she wanted to get something to eat. It was winter, and there'd been more snow than usual. Snowbanks practically blocked out the sky. As soon as she was in the car, I started driving at least a hundred miles an hour. She was begging me to stop, and I said I would if she told me where her boyfriend was. She claimed she didn't know. She swore she'd tell me if she did. She said she hated the guy, and she said some bad things about him—that he had a little dick. Stuff like that. I was going to stop. At that point I believed her. Just then we came over a bit of a rise. I barely had time to see the car accident on the road. It was almost funny. One of those funeral cars—a hearse—had hit a milk truck. All I could do was put my car into the snowbank. We went right into it, right into a field. The snow was so high we couldn't open the doors. The engine was still running, and the heat was on. The antenna had broken off so the radio didn't work. It took the police three hours to get us out of there. She and I made up during that time. We got along pretty well. Then we had to go to the station to file a report. There were always lots of wanted photos on the wall, and there was an old one of me, but nobody seemed to notice."

I could picture the fear on their faces, the car slamming into jewel

blue dark and sudden calm. The headlights still shone, a faintly luminous core before them, like a diamond somewhere out there, buried in
the snow. He turned up the heater and adjusted the vents. The engine
chugged, the sound seeming to come from deep below them.

I love this image, two people captured in ice, held within stillness
and cold light, like characters caught, set together in a flash of the imagination. Memory holds us until we are ready to see. Speaking, he knew
his words had the charm of impossible odds, the close call, the signature
of magic that reminded him that his life was truly his own.

He returned to Calgary and pulled a job with two men he'd met in prison.
But he'd seen his own wildness in them and should've known. Escaping,
they hit a patch of black ice and went over an embankment, the police
a mile back.

The car rolled, and when it stopped, he was underneath, arms and
legs broken and gasoline soaking his chest. Vehicles pulled off the road,
and their drivers stood, talking and smoking, though my father tried to
draw air into his lungs to tell them not to. One of his partners had struck
his head on the dashboard with such force that he'd been scalped, his
bloody skull exposed, his hair hanging from the back of his head. For
the first time, my father was relieved to see the police arrive. The judge
gave him a lighter sentence because God's hand had been swifter than
earthly justice.

The day he got out of prison, the paddy wagon dropped him off in
an alley, and the officer gave him five dollars. Then my father went to
a dive hotel. He'd stashed money in the ceiling vent of the room where
he'd been staying when he was arrested, and that afternoon he bought
a battered truck without brakes from a farmer.

He was ready to cross the border for good. When he'd been in the
prison hospital, he'd known it was time to change. This wasn't the life he'd
been after—a tiny cell or, when he was out, a seedy hotel room or a rundown house in the suburbs, enough cash from robberies to get by. Lying in
bed, he'd thought of America, so close, like the beating of a woman's heart.

Each failure promised a new beginning, proof that his will was strong and nothing could extinguish his fire. Was he driven by the desire to risk everything, to lose everything, to be stripped—of language and culture, of name and family—to his essence, as if there might be a self as absolute and free as the soul? Only then, when all else had fallen away, could he sense the transformation that he craved, the possibility of stepping into another life.

He drove his brakeless truck to Tijuana. I knew his need for exuberance, for release, the impulse to freedom the same as that to fiction, the liberty to remember his life as he chose. He sometimes offered descriptions with an impetuous edge to his voice, as if seeing what he could get away with, still testing the limits of the possible.

His trip to Tijuana was no more than this. He drove there the way others stretch. He was warming up for a change, a new type of crime, but first he needed to taste his freedom, to enjoy the emptiness of the highway sky and see the many shapes the earth could hold.

He pulled a string of robberies along the West Coast and claimed to have robbed at least fifty banks and as many jewelry stores at gunpoint. Wanting to look respectable, he got a nose job to repair the damage of fights and years in prison. He triangulated his life between LA, Las Vegas, and Salt Lake City, where his girlfriend thought he was a traveling businessman. All that time, he was contemplating the details of the Hollywood burglary, the big job, the one that would set him free and allow him to go home with pride.

But there was still the recklessness—casinos and resorts and a night when, drunk and standing on the hood of a moving car, he fell off and broke his arm. He robbed a jewelry store with it in a cast, but, back in the car, couldn't get his gun out of his pocket. He asked his partner's girlfriend to take it out, and she accidentally pulled the trigger and blew a hole in his pants.

"We were lucky the bullet didn't hit the gas tank," he told me, then described another time when his partner forgot his gun in a jewelry store, having put it down to fill his bag. Nobody wanted to go back, but their fingerprints were on it since they'd all used the same guns.

"I was scared that time," he said, "going into a place I'd just robbed, with a bunch of people who were pretty angry and had one of our guns. I went in with my gun pointed, but they hadn't even picked up the one we'd left. They all got right back down on the floor."

He paused, "You know, I understand why you want to write. I get it. I know why you're doing what you're doing."

I just cleared my throat and nodded, stupidly, as if he could see, and he began telling me about the big job again.

"When I pulled it, I thought everything would be easy. I thought it was my way out. I couldn't know my partner was going to be stupid and set fire to the surveillance apartment. When his girlfriend and I got to the house in Nevada, we drew the blinds and dumped the money on the living room floor. The pile of stacked bills came up past my knees. I thought I'd done something so big, so perfect, I'd never have to worry about anything again. I thought I'd fooled life."

I was trying to understand what this had to do with writing, but before I could ask, his voice grew faint.

"It wasn't what I thought. Those big dreams don't work out. Nothing's as easy as it looks." He hesitated and said, "That's when I finally went home. I knew the police were after me, and I wanted to show my family how rich I was. But I couldn't stay. I was already on the run. It's the only thing I regret. What I did to my mother. She didn't deserve it."

I'd become used to his contrasts, enthusiasm then regret, the way he spoke like an old man, tired of life, then suddenly shifted to anger, as if facing his choices once more. Then he would sound hopeful, as if again planning the big job: LBJ giving his speech, the truck in the alley, the jackhammer to blast through the vault so he could slide inside. But the grain of the concrete pointed in, hooking on his clothes when he tried to get out, and he had to undress. How did he feel, wriggling naked from the vault, over the jagged edges—a rough birth but one full of promise, not the disillusionment I might have expected?

When his partner didn't show up, he knew the police would come looking. He bought a Chevy convertible, new silk clothes, and dozens of gifts for his family, then drove to Quebec, crossing the continent and border, passing Montreal, following the rugged coast home, the Saint Lawrence growing wider until he could barely see the other shore. He felt as if he were returning to some wild outer region on the edge of the world, and yet the wildness in him was greater than ever, and he'd been transformed like a man gone off to war.

I don't think he knew why he was returning, whether to prove something or soothe his guilt, or just to have an audience for his success, to fill that longing all children have to please their parents, to show their strength.

His sisters and brothers ran outside as soon as he parked.

"*Maman, Maman!*" they were shouting.

His mother kissed his cheeks. There was no recrimination. He'd called over the years and sent letters with lies, but there had been gaps, his time in prison. He realized that the feeling he'd always had, that he'd been her favorite, was right. She would forgive anything.

Bernard was there, in boots and work pants, arms covered in tattoos. His own nose had been flattened, and he teased my father about the new nose and asked if he was a Hollywood star.

My father said no and lied that he had a transportation company in the US.

Bernard snorted, jealousy and uncertainty in his eyes. "*Une compagnie de transport?*" He wiped his mouth and turned away.

A few days later, my father took his mother to visit her sisters on the north coast. She hadn't seen them in years. He chartered a small airplane, and in the spring sunlight, she gathered with her family, children milling about as he stood with the men, saying little, just practicing stories about his imaginary company.

When they returned, Bernard teased him about the presents, calling him a good boy, "*un bon 'tit garçon.*" My father ignored him, and Bernard spoke about the merchant marines, the brawls in port cities. He was glad their father had taught him how to box. He wanted to go drinking, to see my father fight again, but my father was afraid of drawing attention. He said he didn't fight anymore, and Bernard just nodded, watchful.

My father talked about life in the US, how he'd chosen not to become an American citizen since he didn't want to be drafted for Vietnam. Bernard asked what he thought of the province now that the priests had lost power and Le Front de libération du Québec was planting bombs in Montreal. But my father just shrugged.

"You don't really have a transportation company, do you?" Bernard said.

"Of course I do," my father told him and walked away.

Expo 67 had begun in Montreal, and my father planned to take his two youngest brothers. The day before he went, he invited his father for a ride in his convertible. They argued. He didn't say why, only that he'd never liked his father. Even when I asked, again frustrated with him for all that he hid, he refused to give a precise answer.

"We never got along or had much to say to each other," he told me, then pressed on with his story. In Montreal, he walked past a police station to look at the wanted photos. His was there. He knew he shouldn't stay any longer, and yet he couldn't help but stare and feel the weight of his errors. He hadn't stripped away anything, become light or free. There was no frontier left that he could cross to start again. His crimes had followed him through so many fake names and temporary addresses, making their way home.

During a heavy snowfall, I called him from home and asked if he remembered the card he'd received at the post office when I was a boy. He'd stood in the sunlight, staring at the flowery card. I asked what it was, and my mother joked that it was from his other family.

He didn't remember the card, but his response was surprising. "Maybe it was from the girlfriend in Salt Lake City. She had a son."

"A son?"

"She was pregnant when I went to prison, but she never visited me. She sent photos. The boy looked a lot like you used to. But then she married another guy, and they had a kid. I saw a picture of both kids. The other one was really ugly. Anyway, I stayed in touch for a while after I was deported. But I realized there was no point in it. The kid had never known me. He had another father, so I let him live his life. Maybe she sent the card. I don't know."

"You never wanted to meet him?" I asked, trying to accept this, that I had another brother. I closed my eyes against my anger.

"No, he was named after the fake name I used back then," he said, as if with that name he hadn't been the same person, and so this wasn't his son. "But that woman was pretty angry. When I was in prison, she found out that she hadn't known my real name, and she changed the kid's name to her new husband's. Is there really such a thing as a fake name? I mean, we make them all up. One's as good as another, right?"

He was silent, as if recalling what he'd felt then. I gazed out the window, the snowstorm ending now. Clouds thinned, the white forest lit by the moon.

"You know, I was reading about angels the other day," he went on, his voice growing soft. He described an article about a Florida couple who met a beggar in front of their house. The beggar asked for food or money, and they gave him a sandwich and twenty dollars. A month later, a black man with blue eyes came to their door and gave them a winning lottery ticket. He said they'd lost it. They never bought lottery tickets and told him so, but he showed it had their names on it.

I was having a hard time listening, still thinking about the brother, but there was nothing to feel about it, no space even for regret, and so I tried to hear his story about angels, and when he'd finished, I said it sounded a little sketchy.

"It was in the newspaper," he told me. "They don't put bullshit in the newspaper. This is all true stuff."

He talked about miracles, ghosts—the time when he was a boy and saw his grandfather. Years later, after my mother had taken us to the US, he'd seen his own father standing at the foot of his bed one morning, hair and skin so dark he seemed a figment of the dawn. Light was just coming through the windows. It was his father as a young man.

"I'd hated him," he said, "but I felt at peace then. I blinked and he was gone."

Though I tried to listen, I was thinking of something else.

"Is André your real name?"

He was silent, then cleared his throat and said yes.

Later, after we hung up, I just sat, tension in my throat and chest. I could get used to anything, I realized, the silence of my rooms, the pain of what I was trying to accept. My head was becoming cluttered, and it might feel good to talk to someone else. I'd been studying too much and had little contact with other students. My mother and I didn't speak often, and I'd been distant from my brother and sister for years.

I put on my hiking boots and a few long-sleeve shirts, then went out and jogged a forest path that was no more than a white trace through the trees.

Cold air stung my lungs, and I gained speed, enjoying the slip and plunge of my feet as they sought purchase on the hidden earth. The moon shone over the evergreens, the white shelves of their branches, the naked maples limned with snow.

I found a rhythm, and as I moved, I saw dozens of characters, stern or hopeful faces. Who were they—the men who'd taught him crime, or his partners, his girlfriend, the inmates he'd fought, his family, Bernard and the others whose names I didn't know? I was furious with my father for all that he'd kept from me, and for all that I couldn't bring myself to say. I wanted to ask him more about these fleeting faces, to find the words to put them on paper, to reveal his past and make him human, infuse him with a breadth of fallibility and simple need.

After his arrest in Miami, he had one opportunity to escape. He'd refused the plane in hopes of this, preferring the trip cross-country in the police car, the two cops taking turns behind the wheel looking more miserable than the convicts in the back. There was my father and occasionally one or two others along for a leg of the ride, shuttled between jails just as my father was being returned to California so he could stand trial. They ate at diners, used public bathrooms, all the while handcuffed and guarded. After lunch one day, my father took a paper clip off the counter from next to the cash register while one of the cops paid.

In the backseat of the cruiser, he sat in the middle, the convicts on either side holding the edge of a newspaper so they could all read. Using it as a shield, he began picking his cuffs. The convicts looked concerned, but with the radio on and the windows cracked, my father was able to whisper that if they ratted him out he'd kill them in their sleep. Both on his side of the law and not uncurious about what kind of show he might put on, they didn't.

He got his cuffs picked, and as they were slowing through a Southern city with high wooden sidewalks and packed dirt roads, he hopped over the convict at his side and threw open the door. He sprinted and jumped onto the sidewalk and raced along its boards. The car skidded to a stop, and then the cops were out, too, running behind, pointing their guns but unable to shoot because my father ran as close to pedestrians as he could.

He was nearing a corner when a man tripped him and he fell from the raised boards, the wind so badly knocked out of him that he could only stare at the sky.

"That man," he said, "he stuck out his foot like he was some kind of hero."

The anger in his voice was fresh, and he no longer sounded far away, or old. He didn't describe what the cops did. He always skipped getting caught. An old lady spat at his feet as he was led away. "May the Lord have mercy on you," she said. That much he did tell me.

He was eventually sentenced to seven years and sent to a prison in Tacoma. On his first day there he went to the warden and requested his own cell. He was told that only murderers got their own cells.

"Do you want me to kill someone?" my father asked.

Later, he was taken to a single on the top floor.

In the pen, he perfected his English and learned some Spanish. He strengthened his resolve with fantasies of what he would do when he got out. He'd train dogs. He'd raise a family and teach his sons to fish. But on the days when visitors were allowed, his girlfriend never came. To pass the time, he got a diploma, and when the teacher explained the expression *tabula rasa* and asked for an example, he answered, "Like my criminal record each time I change my name."

There were many stories cast in the thin gray penitentiary light. One inmate stabbed him suddenly in the shoulder and he managed to snap the man's arm before his own went numb. And the story of the fight in which he shattered the man's leg he told again, as if trying to make sense of that strange amalgam of strength and powerlessness, how one captive could destroy another. The man had been bragging that he could beat my father up, so after lunch my father followed him into his cell and slammed the door, the lock falling into place. The damp knuckles, the kicks, the bruised and broken ribs and split lips were so common there, and in the end, the man was down, clutching his side, his eyelid and cheek clouding his face. He tried to crawl under the bed to stop the beating. My father stooped and took his leg as if to move a log. He folded it against the metal bedpost and kicked. Then he sat on the toilet as the man screamed and wept beneath the bed. He listened to the running footsteps of the guards, unable to open the door himself.

His telling of this story was almost gentle, as if he couldn't understand how a man could be made to suffer such pain and humiliation.

His punishment was two weeks in solitary confinement, in the Hole, a cramped space where he could barely stretch out. His clothes were taken away, and he was given loose overalls. There was no cot, only a large Bible with a disintegrated spine, and to sleep, he spread its pages on the damp concrete. A slit in the door allowed guards to peer in, and a larger one near the floor was for bread and water.

He exercised, doing sit-ups and push-ups, and became obsessed with perfecting his kicks, trying to hit the ceiling. He was given one full meal a week, on Sunday, and when a guard opened the door and another carried the tray in, my father was ready. He unleashed his perfect kick, catching the tray on the bottom and sending the food into the guard's face. The man fell backward and scrambled out, and the other guard slammed the door.

Moments later, the warden called through the slot, "Two more weeks!"

Living on bread and water, my father kept practicing kicks, angry with hunger as he stretched or exercised, his muscles taut. He hammered his body with his fists, then leaned back and struck the cement ceiling with the ball of his foot.

"I didn't want to be pathetic," he told me. "I didn't want to be grateful and stuff all that food in my mouth. It looked like a good meal, and after I kicked the tray, the cell smelled like good food. It drove me crazy. But I didn't want those fuckers to think I'd thank them for feeding me like that. So I enjoyed myself. I made it a game. I did nothing but push-ups and sit-ups and stretches. My body had never been that hard."

I knew the wild light in his eyes, the joyful madness that had driven him into so many reckless situations just to test himself, to know that he could win. He didn't want to fall asleep. He would keep his fire. It was better to stay hungry.

The next Sunday, when the guard opened the door, he kicked the tray again, faster, with more strength. Though the guard was ready, the food still splattered. The warden stormed back into the basement.

"Another two weeks, you son of a bitch," he shouted through the thin rectangle that several times a day framed a bored, indifferent eye rimmed with red.

But a few days later my father was released back to his cell because higher powers had interpreted his actions as a hunger strike, and no one wanted to risk that he might die.

Several months passed, and he learned that he was to be deported to a prison in British Columbia, where Canadian taxpayers could feed their own criminal. He was waiting for the transfer papers to arrive, but shortly after he told the other inmates, one of them spread the word that he was planning to kill my father. It was the first death threat my father received in prison. Though the man might have been bluffing, trying to sound tough because my father was leaving, my father had no choice. He told me the rule: if a man says he's going to kill you, believe him and kill him first. He sat up all night in his cell, readying himself.

"I didn't want to have to do it," he said. "I got lucky. My transfer papers came through the next day, and I was sent from Tacoma to Vancouver. If they hadn't, I'd have killed him. Prison's about honor. That's all you have. If someone says he'll kill you and you do nothing, you'll be killed. Someone will do it. You'll become a target."

His voice was severe, his breathing loud and ragged.

"You know, I dreamed that stuff forever. I've seen a lot of bad things. I saw that guy get scalped in the car wreck. He came out of the backseat and hit his head on the dash. It peeled his scalp right off his head. I guess I got it worse. I ended up under the car. There was nothing good. Nothing worth remembering. The pen was terrible. There were men in there for raping women and biting off their nipples. We spit on them. They couldn't be put in with us, because we'd kill them. When we served food in the line, we spit on their food and on them. We just kept spitting until they were through. I was in there for honorable crimes. I was respected."

He stopped speaking, just breathed hard. I couldn't help but wonder what of his past he was leaving out. What was the truth? He'd served little time relative to everything he'd done. My frustration only grew as he spoke. I was sick of this, of how little we could actually say to each other.

"Shouldn't the sentences have been longer?" I asked, trying to stay calm.

"No," he said, his voice hoarse. "Most of my crimes they could never pin on me. But police want to make deals. They need to close cases. They agreed to reduce the charges if I claimed a few robberies and gave them some information. Criminals always take advantage of the police bureaucracy like this."

"Did you have to tell them about your partners?"

"No. It was never anything serious. They just wanted to close cases."

The intensity of my anger surprised me. It was the conversation itself, that we were discussing this—like this—that I had no tenderness, no way to voice sympathy or sadness. I knew with absolute certainty that he'd hate me if I did, if I made him feel weak. What was the point of all this talk? So he'd stay alive a few more days and I could put together his fractured life, writing it just to see and feel all that we'd lost? What else was there than to test limits, to keep sharing adventures? Not even the truth mattered.

"So you never ended up killing anyone?" I asked quietly, at first not sure what I wanted, then realizing that I'd said this to hear his remorse, his pain, to see if I could make him admit even once all that he'd ruined.

He didn't answer right away, maybe surprised that I'd asked again after so long.

"It's—it's complicated. Sometimes on jobs, things happen. But I never went in planning to. I never wanted to take away someone's father. I made that my principle . . ."

I listened, waiting for him to finish.

"I should let you go," he said. "It must be late there. We'll talk to-morrow. Okay?"

"Okay," I said, but he'd already hung up.

Pages turned and I had a sense of understanding, like a surge of adrena-line, but just as suddenly it faded. I searched through sentences that blurred, pages turning faster and faster, the dark ink of words washing over my face like rain.

Wind drove against the walls, rattling the windows, and I woke. There was the distinct sound of icicles breaking in the eaves, falling along the side of the house.

I got out of bed and sat at my desk. I stared at the dark pages of my notebook, their empty outlines. How much of his life had he invented? Had his shirt clung to his back, itching, his shoelace too tight on one foot as he walked to the bank and pulled on the mask? Had every sound outside his window at night made him think of men watching, ready to dismantle the world as it turned in his head? Would I see myself in the rain, a baseball bat bumping my leg as I walked—or a tailgate crusted with ice and fish blood as I tallied illegal pounds, the dip toward the skyline as the sun unplugged the night and drained it away to show the filth that lay beneath, the river's edge like solder beneath the mist, beyond the trees—and find something redeeming?

His stories of crime didn't haunt me, just simple images: a day I fol-lowed him through the rows of pines, his hands half-open against his jeans as he walked, and I asked why he didn't cry or if he'd ever cried. He'd told me that I shouldn't, and I wanted to understand how it was possible not to cry when angry or sad or hurt. He stopped. "I don't cry. Men don't

cry," he said. "I have work to do. Go back to the house." I flushed, too furious to speak, tears coming into my eyes, embarrassing me and making me
hate him all the more. I turned and started walking away, but he'd seen my
face and he called for me to stop. He was looking at me as if confused, as if
a thought had just occurred to him. He stared, his brow furrowing, cheeks
lifted. Was he struggling to say something? I stood, waiting, and he said,
"I'd cry if something happened to you, so be careful, okay?" And then he
smiled, as if this were a joke, and we both laughed. He waved and I started
back across the fields toward the house.

Why hadn't this world lasted? Was it his restlessness or the constant fight in his eyes, as if he was most himself when trying to overcome someone or something, or to set himself free? And yet he'd tried,
transforming himself into a businessman, opening seafood stores and
selling trees, and at one point he could even boast the largest Christmas
tree lot in BC's lower mainland. But he'd always seemed to be leaving,
uneasy in any one place, and when he told stories, I'd felt, from the way
he laughed or the eagerness in his gaze, that he'd soon be living these
adventures again.

Once we went fishing in the Nicomen Slough, near where I was
born. He let me row downriver as he set up the lures. Then we drifted
and fished. The sky was a field of gray, and the wind churned the water,
small waves slapping the boat's hull. When needles of icy rain fell, he
began to row. We'd drifted far, the bridge a thread of shadow. I didn't
think we'd get back. He put the rods in the bottom of the boat and
pressed the oars rhythmically. I huddled into my lap as the wind swept
spray into our eyes.

After he put the boat in the truck and tied it down, we walked to a
diner across from the landing. He sat at a booth and I went to the bathroom. My numb fingers couldn't get the button back through the stiff
jean, so I held them under hot water, too proud to tell him. When I came
out, my hands burning with renewed sensation, he had two coffees
waiting. He'd never let me have coffee. It was a light chocolate brown
and, in my mouth, creamy and rich. He watched me with pride, and I had
a sense of all that he knew and how similar we were. The storm blew

against the windows, and his fingertips fluttered the edge of a napkin as his eyes focused beyond the glass, on something far away.

He called just before midnight, having forgotten the time difference. I apologized to my landlords and switched to the phone in the living room. I asked if he was okay.

"I'd like to disappear sometimes," he told me.."I don't want to weigh you down with this, but after your mother took you away, I planned to kill myself. I didn't because I worried that you'd think I was a coward. But you understand it's not cowardly?"

I swallowed a few times. What was he asking me?

"I do," I said.

"I was afraid if I told you, you'd be upset and it'd interfere with your school."

"I want to know. It's important."

He cleared his throat and asked, almost childlike, "Do you think it's wrong?"

I wished I could see his face, read the intention in his eyes. How could I make this decision—how could I tell him to give up or go on suffering, waiting?

"You have to understand that it's not cowardly," he told me, "what I want to do."

"I do," I said, absent of emotion, set adrift.

"I worried that if I told you, you'd be upset . . ."

"I wanted to know," I said. "It's important."

I moved my lips as if to speak but hesitated, and he sighed and said, "I was thinking maybe you could take some time off. You could come out here and help me, and maybe we could get the market going again. In the summer, we could rent a cabin somewhere and do some fishing. We could get a motor home and just travel and fish."

"I can't do that," I said too quickly. "Listen, I really can't—I don't want to work in your business."

I shifted the phone and rubbed the hot lobe of my ear, digging my fingertips into the skin as if to wake myself. I wanted to ask him how he'd thought his life would end after all he'd done. But I said nothing, and he told me, "I understand. But maybe in the summer . . ."

"I don't know. Maybe." I wished I could pause and answer more carefully, but I couldn't imagine going back. I liked who I was becoming here. I'd worked so hard for it and didn't want to get stuck in the life he'd created. Still, I silenced my thoughts and forced myself to stay calm and keep the conversation going. I said, "I've been writing all of your stories," but I couldn't bring myself to tell him that I wanted to hear more. He'd already shared so much in a short time, urgently, as if only when he finished could he die. And yet I knew that we'd never finish, never come to a place of real failure, or that of our shared pain. I wanted to be angry at him for what he was, for what he hadn't been able to be, for us, for our family. To do this, to believe he was wrong, I would have to renounce what I most loved.

"Good," he told me, after a pause, softly. "I like that you're writing them."

I thought of all he'd described, journeys that never quite linked up, and how badly he'd wanted a new life. Had he learned to live for the pleasure of hunger alone—for challenge, for winning, for escape? Could this be it? Hunger for the unattainable, for what you will never have and what will never disappoint you. Hunger for solitude, where no matter how you grapple with yourself, you will always be victorious. Hunger for intensity, a sensation like the seed of all fruit stripped of its colorings and shells, made the same, so that whatever has been lost can be gained again in something else, so that nothing is desired for what it is, only for a fleeting moment of connection, of recognition, before it has been expended and cast away. Hunger for truth, for love, for God, for a single thing that we can trust because it does not seem of this world. Hunger for the perfect pleasure of wanting, a hunger that lasts so long it can no longer be cured in the ways we are told it should, by the simple joys of life.

He spoke as I carried the phone to the window. The moon lit the clouds. The unreal past was there, winters returning, blown across the yard in gusts and flurries.

THE LONGEST HIGHWAY

After classes let out and five months after his death, I drove to Virginia
to work construction and thaw myself in the sun.

I was house-sitting for a friend, and one evening I visited my mother
where she lived near the Appalachians. Large, thick-bodied moths battered the windows with powdered wings, startling our reflections as
we sat at the table. The sweltering dark came through the screen door,
crickets chirping, the faint, distant echolalia of night birds.

"I want to talk about André," I told her.

"I don't think about him anymore," she said. "It doesn't do any good."

"I want to hear how you saw him—what you remember."

Her eyes were pale blue, the skin around their edges slightly pinched
as she scrutinized her hands, strong and tanned from garden work. She
rubbed one along her arm. She'd never been a storyteller, reticent in that
Scottish way, and only through casual disclosures had I come to understand her: her anger at the US during the Vietnam War, the time she'd
seen Jimi Hendrix play in a college basement before he was famous, or
the Guatemalan boyfriend she'd had in DC in the sixties, a man from a
powerful political family who'd wanted her to move to his country. She'd
shown little need to speak of her past, so if I wanted to know something,
I had to insist.

She began to tell me the usual things: that my father knew how to
live off the land, offering her the life she longed for. They traveled and
fished, their freedoms mirroring, his from jail, hers from her Protestant
upbringing. But when he got involved with the men from his past, she
became afraid. He left with them, and she didn't want to know what he

was doing. She felt she could hardly step outside their cabin. She'd go to the door and the horizon would fall away, the sky empty and colorless and unfathomable, a void echoing her distrust and uncertainty.

When I asked about his crimes, she sighed.

"God, it's hard to admit to myself that I was so stupid."

"You were young," I said. "Besides, it wasn't what you signed on for."

"No, it wasn't. But it's still hard to accept."

I asked for details of his drug dealing: the rifles and speed, the laboratory.

"Well, he had some guns, but I never saw them. He kept everything from me. And he didn't have a laboratory. Maybe that's what he called it, but it was more like a kitchen. He cooked some stuff on a hot plate. It was definitely a kitchen, nothing fancy at all."

Only when she became pregnant did he stop. Her pregnancies were among the happiest times of her life. She loved how her body thrived. Other women she knew complained, but she found it easy, feeling alive and calm, and she believed he'd turn his life around.

"He was extremely intelligent. It was amazing sometimes to hear his ideas. And as soon as he got into business, he was successful. Within five or six years, he had several seafood stores in and around Vancouver. He had a knack for business, and as far as I knew, everything was legal. I kept his books for him, and I saw what he was buying and selling. If there was anything else going on, he did a good job of hiding it.

"I suppose," she said and hesitated, "I suppose when I left him I'd finally accepted that he'd never change. He'd never be satisfied. But he was so charismatic and convincing. Most of our friends criticized me. Nobody could imagine that he was doing anything wrong. That's why I stayed with him so long. All those years I thought he'd become a better, kinder person, because that's how he seemed. But it was as if he had to destroy everything, as if some part of him had to make his life as bad as it could possibly be so that he could have something to fight. And even then he managed to look good to others. I don't know how he did it."

"I want to find his family," I told her. "Did you ever meet them?"

"No. I talked on the phone with them once, but we barely understood each other since I hardly spoke French and they had almost no English."

"Why did he stop talking to them?"

"He told me French families were invasive, that they'd be visiting all the time. That was the reason he gave." She hesitated. "After we met, we drove cross-country. We went through Quebec, right past where he grew up. He kept saying how backward it was. We stopped and ate at one of the fry stands they had along the road." She described the Saint Lawrence, the windy coast and how they'd parked to walk along it.

"He called his parents from about fifty miles away. He told them he was in Vancouver. That night we drove through the town where his family lived and didn't stop."

By the time my parents met, he had his German shepherds, one black and tan, the other black with a silver flare at the throat. He'd received early parole and lived in a van, traveling and fishing, sleeping under the stars. He couldn't satisfy his longing for freedom.

When he'd spoken of meeting her, saying, "I ordered ham and eggs and left with her," I hadn't understood what had brought them together. But maybe it's fair to say that there are simple needs, empty spaces that must be filled.

Twenty years old, she'd left the draft dodger she'd fled to Vancouver with, and, loving Canada, stayed. She met my father and they traveled, but eventually he needed money and went looking for men from his past. He began making speed for a friend.

"That friend . . . ," he'd told me, "he was the guy who got his eyes burned, the one who set fire to the apartment in Hollywood. He still couldn't see too well. I felt sorry for him. He had this idea, for the speed. He had the recipes and ingredients. I thought I could help him out."

The story lacked ballast. How could he, a man who'd brutalized others, forgive so easily? But the friend had been in his life for years, he explained. He'd been a partner in many crimes. Perhaps my father had his sentence reduced by making a deal with the police, and so maybe he had a different view on disloyalties.

He never described the period following this clearly. When my mother got pregnant, he quit crime, not wanting another child born while he was in prison. He believed that a family would hold him in place and give him satisfaction. To make money, he began buying and selling salmon. He still had to check in with his parole officer and had received permission to visit his son in the US, but he decided to break contact and never went. He called his mother a few times in Quebec, but decided he needed a fresh start.

"I wanted my own life," he told me. "Too much had changed."

But his words didn't ring true. That was the week before exams. I watched myself study. I was withdrawn. Daily, I walked the road to school and on occasion drove my uninsured SUV into town, usually after midnight, to the twenty-four-hour supermarket, the streets empty beneath cold Christmas skies, colored lights on a few leafless trees.

It was always late when we spoke, his voice loud while I kept mine hushed. He told me that life was a joke. He'd been raised without education and given direction by criminals.

"I robbed those banks in my early twenties," he said. "I was a kid. A fucking kid. I'd do anything to start over. I wish I could've been you. You were always so full of hope."

I'd heard enough about crime, but if I asked about his family, he'd just tell me that too much time had passed, that there was no point in going back.

"Still, I never lost heart," he said. "I always had the nerve. I remember the last bank I tried to rob. I was with a guy who'd pulled a lot of jobs. I'd seen him rob other places. But we walked around the building, and he couldn't get his mask on. He kept saying, "Not yet." After we passed the door the last time, he told me he couldn't do it. He was sweating and shaking. He didn't know what the point was anymore. He told me he just wanted his life to be simple. We were in the alley, and he asked to be let out. That's how it was. You could do it for years, and then the nerve just went out of you."

I think of songs, of men in prison longing for motion, envious of the rumbling of trains, the inescapable sun above the road crew and the passing cars, the staring children or the naked shoulders of girls. The man couldn't bear the thought of damp nights in jail, the sun caged in windows. He said he wanted out because he had a baby coming, as did my father, whom he'd turned to because he knew him to be reliable. They both had women waiting.

Now my father hesitated, as if he were searching for words.

"I let him off," he said finally. "But I never lost it like that. I only stopped because you guys were born. I wanted a family and didn't want to go back to prison."

Hearing him, I had the impression that he was bothered by his life since, that the one thing he'd wanted, a family, had failed him and he should have stayed in crime. But the truth was becoming clear to me. The banks and jewelry stores had been easier for him. He was still that boy afraid of wintering in the house, of being trapped in a normal life.

I wish I could hear him tell this again, not those easy crime stories in dim restaurants, the chairs upside down on the tables and the two of us the last in the place, but the way he tried to paint his power as he let his friend off. He spoke of a man so afraid, so uncertain of what the world had given him, that when he stopped and let the static hum along the phone line, I wasn't sure who he was describing.

The valley returns in simple impressions: patterns of light across the kitchen floor, the shadow of mountains outside, cool air through the door and our mother calling us to eat, the smell of dark bread and the hot elements in the open oven. Or the misted stillness, the sense of safety next to him as we crossed fields, the warped boards of the fence, its posts obscured by yellow grass.

The days I spent with him are among the clearest. I studied his face when he spoke—his dark, expressive eyes and large beard. His breath smelled of coffee. He was often lending small amounts of money, and once, standing outside his store as sunlight filtered past the three pines he'd planted there, I asked him why. He told me it was worth a little money to know if you could trust a person. I considered the wisdom in this and began lending nickels at school.

Those years, he built dog pens, put up fences, sold trees, and established stores. He hadn't been sure he'd enjoy this work, but the skills his father had taught him came back quickly—the fish on this coast not so different, his hands moving the knife on their own, working him past the soft boundaries of memory. Often, it seemed he was challenging himself to do as much as he could, satisfied with the authenticity of the life he was building, affirming his strength, finding new ways to grow, to challenge himself.

One morning he came out of the house wearing a sports jacket, a briefcase in his hand. Our mother sat on the steps, watching us play. Wind rustled the leaves of the tree near the porch, casting a shadowed map of branches and sunlight across his face. He tugged at his sleeves, and she looked up. I watched, sitting on my bicycle, one foot on the ground, and she laughed. It was a laugh of pleasure and surprise, but he flushed and walked to the truck and got in. She'd longed for an existence in nature, but his desire had been to become the businessman in the stories he'd told his family, to transform himself one more time.

"Maybe I could have gone back," he said, "if things had turned out differently with your mother. I could have shown them my family and business. They'd have understood that. But even then, it was complicated . . ."

"What was?" I asked, knowing now that nothing ever would have been good enough for him.

"I'd been gone a long time . . ." He hesitated, then spoke with an anger out of proportion to his words. "I remember when I went back, it was poor. I didn't want to be part of that world. And my brother, he was always getting in fights. He had a flat nose. I wanted to move on . . ."

After my mother left, he'd stayed in bed for weeks, hardly eating. He got up only to use the bathroom or drink water or continue the calls he made to her or her parents. In a drawer, he found the address of a psychic she'd seen, a woman who'd told her that Vancouver would be destroyed in an earthquake. He made an appointment, wanting his own prophecy. The woman said she couldn't talk about my mother, but told him that his middle child would be the first to return. It wouldn't be soon. That was all she could say.

When he finally drove downtown, his hands shook, nausea grabbing at his throat as he turned with the traffic. He sideswiped two parked cars but didn't stop. His store was unlocked and abandoned. He'd eaten a carton of fries, but he threw them up when he opened the door to the melting ice and rotting fish, the bluebottle flies flecking the display windows. The power had been shut off, and a reddish, jellylike fluid seeped from beneath the door to the walk-in freezer. The rancid, humid air was overwhelming, and he stayed only long enough to see that no money was in the register. A wino's rusty shopping cart had been parked in the back room. Letters from creditors had piled on the floor. An eviction notice was posted on the door.

He sat in the minivan he'd bought a few months before, new on the market then—perfect for deliveries, he'd told everyone. His leather briefcase lay on the passenger seat and again he had a vision of filling it with fish. He'd take it to the bank and buy a safe-deposit box and put the fish inside. He realized that he'd spent years fighting banks or prisons, trying to get at something locked away or to keep from having himself locked up, in a prison or a house or a life that was too small.

Back home, as he lay in bed, the phone rang constantly. He had too many creditors and no money for taxes. The life he'd built was less substantial than he'd thought, and what he did next was more in keeping with his youth than those seven or eight years of relative success. After he stored a few of his possessions at a friend's house, he went home and got some gasoline, a rope, and a knife. He poured the gasoline on his head, made a small cut at his throat, and managed to tie himself up. Then he struggled free and called the police. When they got there, he told them that men had come to his house, bound his hands, put a knife to his throat, and dumped gasoline on him and threatened to set him on fire. He'd confessed to where he kept his stash of money, and they'd taken everything. The police filed the report of stolen earnings, which he sent in the next day with his tax papers.

Then he loaded a backpack with food, a can opener, and a bottle of whiskey. His creditors would be looking for him, and he knew that everything would be repossessed. He hitchhiked until he was dropped off at an entrance ramp of the TransCanada Highway. The moon was rising, and it was the hour when he'd normally return home to the comfort he'd struggled against. He wasn't far from a place he recalled, where the wide median was heavily forested, and where, just beyond the nearest exit, there was a convenience store. He waited until no headlights were in sight, then crossed the pavement. The median was two hundred feet of forest. He pitched his tent in a deep, comfortable gully out of the wind. Even the sound of traffic seemed remote. He had a good sleeping bag. A little snow had fallen, preferable to the damp.

"No one expects you to disappear on the median of one of the world's longest highways," he told me. "Your creditors will think you've changed provinces or gone across the border."

He said that when he was in the city, every now and then he still ran across men who were amazed to see him. "We thought you were dead," they'd say. "You just disappeared."

And that night, unable to sleep, he did consider dying. He wished he could see his mother one last time and apologize for decades of absence and the grandchildren she didn't know existed. He asked himself what life he'd been made for, or if he was better off like this, here, alone. He lay with the bottle of whiskey as snow began to fall again, and his breath condensed into beads of moisture that speckled the canvas roof and froze.

But this wouldn't be an ending. He'd dreamed that a family and business would put his old life behind him, though my mother still tells me that he was never able to change in the one way that mattered— that she'd left him because what made him who he was couldn't change. It was too strong or too broken, strong in the way that injuries become strengths through endurance, that fractures mend hard within the bone.

As he lived on the median, the strength within him had to abandon a dream and find another shape, not quite new, but still testing and searching, incapable of not surviving. I imagine his tent pitched in the evergreens, in that wide descent of stony earth, an echoing culvert below. I've traveled enough to know the solitary emotions of highway nights, but I can't imagine that loneliness and rage. As he lay there, tremors passed through the earth, semis carrying raw tonnage from the interior along the highway that cut through the continent's vast wilderness, from Vancouver to Quebec, connecting the lives he'd abandoned.

"I was thinking about my mother," he told me. "I loved her. I was her favorite, and I felt that I'd hurt her."

"You could go back now," I said, hesitant to interrupt his story, to challenge him or reveal that I was losing sympathy.

"No. It's been too long. I can't."

"What was her name?" I asked.

But he was silent, and then he told me that it was late, and said good night.

The windshield wipers barely kept up with the rain as I pulled into the gas station and parked next to the phone booth. The forecaster was announcing an unusual storm: a cold, blustery precipitation that would turn into sleet and freezing rain after midnight. I'd be home soon. I had driven to the UMass library for research, and only the mountain road remained. Classes had let out for finals, and I hadn't talked to my father in a few days, but the night before, he'd left a message with my landlords: *your father called.*

I ran through the rain to the phone booth and dialed collect, the connection bad. The operator's voice gave way to static marked by loud clicking. The line rang, and I waited for his accent, his quiet *h*'s and heavy *r*'s. When he answered, he sounded far away.

"Just a minute," he said, and his end of the line went silent. Then he was back, his breath rasping. "I've changed my mind," he told me straightaway. "I've decided I'm going to keep the store going. There's no point in giving up now."

I took a deep breath, not sure that I believed him. "I'm glad to hear that."

"This winter will be tough," he said, "but I've gone through worse."

"That's great. I was really worried about you. I was afraid I wouldn't hear any more of your stories."

"You know," he said, "when I was little —" His voice broke, whatever assurance he'd had instantly gone. "Things weren't good. I just want you to understand that."

"What? Yes. I understand that."

"I know I've made some mistakes, but I just want you to understand I've been angry for a long time. I keep thinking I'm not angry anymore, but then, you know, it doesn't take much. It doesn't take much, and I'm angry again. I was thinking about my uncle the other day. If I'd gone to live with him, I could have played hockey. I could have finished school. But my father needed me to work. And that was that. I was so angry. I remember, I saved every penny I had to buy a rusty pair of ice skates. But then I didn't have a hockey stick. It was stupid."

He tried to laugh but broke into a dry cough.

"When I was a young man," he said, "I thought if I'd been born English, everything would be all right. We had nothing but our family and the church. I didn't believe in the church, but I thought a family was the most important thing in life. I don't know why I hated one and not the other." As he spoke, he paused to take long ragged breaths. "I should've hated both. I just used to think I'd have kids someday and everything would be different. But . . . but you're a lot like me. I think that's true, don't you?"

"In some ways, maybe."

"I think in a lot of ways. You used to be pretty serious about crime."

"I just liked the stories," I told him, suddenly exhausted, unsure of what to say.

"I want you to do things better than I did. I don't want you to ruin your life. If it weren't for you, I never would have talked about that stuff again. You could have been like me, but it's not worth it."

"I wouldn't have," I said, trying to bring reassurance into my voice.

"You don't remember how you were. You would have."

"But I won't," I told him, my frustration back, tired now, a feeling like surrender.

"Okay. Well, don't worry about me. I'll deal with the store. I'll deal with all that."

"You're not going to let it go?" I asked, knowing he would, my body beginning to ache, ribs and throat sore, the pressure of sadness against my chest, the way even the premonition of grief bruised, so that the injury would seem to have always been there, just beneath the skin.

"I don't know," he replied, his voice hoarse. "I'll deal with it."

The connection crackled as lightning jarred the sky.

"Is there a storm out there?" he asked.

"It's the first lightning I've seen in months. I doubt we'll get much more."

"You shouldn't be on the phone. You might get shocked."

"I'll be fine."

The rain began to fall harder.

"Do you want to call me back in a couple of days?"

"These next two weeks are going to be crazy. I have finals. We can talk for a while now."

Raindrops pattered over the booth's windows as headlights passed on the road.

He was silent, then offered, "We could get a cabin up in Squamish. I meant it, what I said before. We could do a little fishing, and I could tell stories."

"You know I can't. I don't even like to fish anymore."

He spoke softly. "It was never about the fishing. It was about being in the mountains. It's just nice to be on the rivers. Sometimes you don't catch anything."

"I know."

"But you can't take a little time off?"

"Not right now," I said, my own anger rising, as if all that couldn't be said, held within me, had turned into rage.

The rain had become loud, sleet and the occasional hail rattling the panels of the booth. The line hissed and cut out, and when his voice returned, it echoed.

"Is the storm bad?"

"Yeah," I told him.

"You know, if you're ever going to write this stuff, you'd have to write it the way it was. I'd like that. It's not that I'm proud of having been a criminal. I'm not. I'd have given it all up to watch you guys grow up."

The line crackled again, and I said nothing. I couldn't tell him that in his heart he'd never stopped being a criminal, never given up that destruction and let himself just be a father or an ordinary man. He spoke, and I tried to silence my thoughts and listen.

"But crime," he said, "crime wasn't always good. I didn't rob because it excited me. It wasn't something I even wanted to do at first. I knew if I did it, I'd survive. What's strange is I never thought about what happened to people when I wasn't there, other than maybe my family. But you know, later, I felt bad for that guy in the jewelry store. I wished I hadn't gone in there. In the paper he said I was over six feet tall and had black hair and eyes. He said I was the coldest-looking bastard he'd ever seen. I had to think about that. It's one thing to rob a place, but it's another to hear the person you robbed telling how one time the place was held up when his little girl was in there, and how he didn't want to give up on his business because of criminals. I can't remember everything he said about us, but we laughed when we read it. Later, I wondered what he felt like, if he would shoot the next person who tried to rob him or die over a bag of rings."

Thunder banged through the earth. He sighed, speaking softly, and I had to focus to hear him.

"When I gave up crime, fish was the only other thing I knew. I wanted to have a family."

The wind slammed down, hail rattling off the top of the booth and drowning his voice. Cars pulled off the road, hazard lights flashing. The line was breaking up, and he repeated something I couldn't understand. Water streamed through the corners of the panels. I yelled that I'd call him back later, but suddenly the hail and wind subsided into the crackle of static. I stared through the wet glass into darkness and passing headlights, and for some reason I recalled the working of his hands, the night at the reservoir, as we stood above the shore and he rethreaded the line on the fishing rod. He reached into the truck window, and the headlights came on, and he went to stand before them. His hands moved in the beam, scars across their knuckles, the blunt fingertips pinching and pulling.

I closed my eyes. We were silent, as if waiting through that lull, no rain or wind, as if gravity had lapsed.

"I wanted to see you grow up," he said. "Your mother was good with you guys. She treated you really well. I'm sorry things didn't work out the way they were supposed to."

His voice was different, softer, and he spoke quickly now. "You know, I was there to deliver you. I'll never forget. You were born at home, but you had the umbilical cord around your neck. I had to blow into your mouth and press your chest until you started breathing. When I held you, you lay across my hands. I knew we'd be the closest. I always felt there was something special because of how I held you when you started breathing."

The storm was building and fading, striking at the windows. The line gasped with static. My eyes were still closed, and I saw the slow, strange working of his hands again, the fishing line invisible in the dark and against the light.

"You're not going to come see me, are you?" he asked.

"I don't know," I told him too quickly, instantly wishing I'd taken the time to consider. "Not right now."

"I know. What you're doing is right. I'm glad you're strong. I've ruined my life, and you should . . . you should focus on yours. But you'll be okay?"

"Okay?" I repeated.

"Are you sure you can deal with it?"

I didn't speak, and as we listened to the breaking static, I thought of what I could tell him, what emotion I could give voice to that wasn't strength.

"Will you be okay?" he asked.

"It's . . . it's your choice. I can't ask you not to."

"You can deal with it?"

"Yeah, I'll be okay."

"It's what's best," he said.

Sleet pattered across the panels, making his voice distant. I shivered, realizing how cold I was.

"When I'm dead," he told me, "you can contact my family. My mother's name is Yvonne. I'm sure she's still alive. I'd know if she was dead." He was quiet a long time. "She lives in a place called Matane, in Quebec."

"Matane," I repeated.

"Promise me you won't try to find her while I'm still alive."

"I promise."

"If you contact her, tell her you're Edwin's son."

"Edwin?"

"That's what they called me. She's the one I miss. I wish I could see her one more time. I lied to her a lot, and then I stopped writing. I used to send her postcards saying I was in Mexico or on my way to Alaska. One time, when I was logging, I saw a guy get crushed under a tree. He cried and called for his mother. I didn't understand."

Neither of us spoke, and I tried to think of what I could say, how I could talk to him differently, in a way that would change all this.

"There was a time," he said, "when I could've gone back, when you guys were little. But it's too late now. How would I explain everything? I have nothing to show."

I stared through the dirty glass of the phone booth, at the smear of headlights above the road. Something fell in the static behind his voice.

"Listen, I should go. I should go," he said. "It's late. You should get some sleep."

He said good-bye and hung up before I could speak.

I got in my truck and pulled onto the road, taking my time going up the mountain, rain gusting past the headlights. My mind was silent. I turned into my driveway and parked and went inside to my apartment.

I sat and touched my face to my hands, my elbows to my knees, and breathed.

EPILOGUE

That spring a public accountant in Vancouver called to explain that my father had owed tens of thousands in back taxes and the government would confiscate and auction what they could, which wasn't much—two wristwatches. A month later I received the rest, a small box of photographs with *Air Mail, Par Avion* stickers on it, the customs slip stating *No Value*. Inside were pictures held by blue rubber bands: photographs of our family and of himself. These were all he had while he sat in the single chair in his house, telling me his stories.

My favorites were those of him, the flash of superiority in his dark eyes, his bold stance before the camera. One showed him young, leaning on the tailgate of an old pickup, heel cocked against the hitch, his lean brown body taut as he laughed. Another had him holding a baby. His arms bulged and the baby cried. Behind him, a German shepherd looked out the window, its dark nose invisible against the black glass. And then, years later, he posed before a decorated Christmas tree, his beard shaved to a mustache, his face lined. He wore a gray sports jacket and a white shirt. His jaw was lifted, with an expression of Old World pride, a look that said to the photographer, This is the shot you want.

That year and the next, silence hummed within me. I burned my old writing, all except the notes from our conversations. I wanted stillness, lightness—as if by losing everything, I could, if only briefly, feel complete. I wrote and studied, trying to compose him in a novel. In my need to write, I recognized his longing to speak—the urgency of his telling, to make us understand each other and bring us to a place of forgiveness. I wanted to know what in him had been capable of leading his life, just as he'd been trying to understand the life he'd lived, and the simpler one he'd wanted but been incapable of. The more I wrote, the more I became clear, my words, my way of telling a story, the further he receded. He eluded me— the landscape of his youth, the people who'd helped create him.

Gradually, after two and a half years, the silence subsided. I began to read in French often and dreamed in it as I had years before. Memories returned, forgotten emotions in the sounds, the language and culture I'd taken for granted. I'd say *foulard* and within the word was a flash of cold and the bliss of a parent who knelt to tie my scarf and fit it into my jacket. It didn't seem like him, but as I read, the sound of words remembered for me: my grammar book with the ducks on the cover, the exercises we repeated: *je suis, tu es, il est, nous sommes.*

I wrote the letter, saying that I was the son of Edwin, the name a stranger to my pen:

Chère Yvonne,
  Je sais que vous ne me connaissez pas et que le contenu de cette lettre va être surprenant et même parfois difficile à lire . . .

A week later, a man called, his gravelly voice so familiar that I had a moment of confusion, the impression of dreaming, of a night conversation from two years before. He told me that he was my uncle, and we spoke about my father and the family, their happiness that I'd written, the questions they had. When I explained how my father died, he asked that I not share this with my grandmother. She was past ninety and, though strong, deeply religious; the news would be devastating. I agreed to say he'd died of cancer.

I set out for Quebec, driving through Maine and into New Brunswick, then north toward the Saint Lawrence, into a rolling landscape of weathered stone. Late August showers blew through, dark patches in an otherwise clear sky. The landscape revealed little about its inhabitants: scant villages, Lac-des-Aigles or Saint-Esprit, hardly more than a gas station, convenience store, and a few houses lining the road. The land climbed until the horizon dropped and far below, the Saint Lawrence extended like a plain of stone.

The fear I'd been harboring—that I'd discover a family of thugs—was quickly dispelled. I met my uncle first, the youngest sibling. He'd been a boy when my father left. He was my height, well dressed, wearing glasses, his eyes and hair dark, hints of my father in his jaw, though otherwise a very different man, as I would learn—gentler, kinder. He was a successful businessman and introduced me to the family. From time to time, he paused to say how happy he was, that they'd never known what happened to my father.

"*On est bien content que tu nous as écrit. On n'avait pas de nouvelles d'Edwin.*"

My grandmother was ninety and lived in her own apartment. When I entered the room, her gaze didn't leave me, searching my face even as she stepped quickly past the others. Her green eyes focused through her glasses. She gripped my arm and studied me.

"*Mon dieu, mon dieu,*" she uttered and said I looked like my father—"*comme il a l'air d'Edwin.*"

The next four days were visit upon visit, conversations that lasted into the morning, tears and questions. The family hadn't seen him since 1967, exactly thirty years, and the last time he'd called was around 1973. They remembered him saying that my brother had been born. A large framed photo of my father had stood on my grandmother's television for decades.

I asked her what he was like as a child, and she gave this some thought.

"He didn't cry," she said, "and he was the only one who didn't sing when he worked."

My father's older sister showed me other photographs, the stark cabin on a barren stretch of northern coast where he was born, the shot from the water, past immense stones. And at last there were pictures from when he'd returned home, a dapper young man, his jacket pulled back at the side, hand on his hip, like a land baron posing for a portrait.

Seeing pictures of the family and clapboard house, I struggled to connect this world to the man I'd known. My grandfather Alphonse had died years before, and my father's brother Bernard as well, but no one said much about him. There were the stories I already knew about how Alphonse had made my father and Bernard box in the living room.

"They were hard men—your grandfather, and Edwin and Bernard," my uncle's wife told me. She suggested that I ask my uncle about Expo 67, my father's last visit. "It disturbed him," she said. "He doesn't like to speak of it."

After dinner I did ask, when my uncle and I were alone. He drank his beer and gave this some thought.

"I saw them start a fight. Edwin and Bernard. Not with each other, but with everyone else in the bar. It really shocked me. They'd taken me to the expo. I was dressed in my best clothes and was wearing a tie. A man accidentally spilled his drink on Edwin's arm. I just sat there. I couldn't move. I've never seen violence like that. Edwin started it, and Bernard joined him. They hit anyone who got in their way. They broke everything. They . . . they destroyed people."

He appeared to consider this.

"You know, your father used to call me. I was pretty young then. He said he'd been in prison because he accidentally killed a man. He said he punched him and the man fell and hit his head on the edge of the sidewalk. He wasn't old enough to go to prison so he was sent to a detention center in the prairies. He told me it was boring."

Though I didn't say it, I wondered if this story had been my father's way of justifying his absence, of making his years in prison sound accidental. It may also simply have been one of the many things for which he'd been incarcerated.

We sat quietly at the table, the rest of the family watching TV in the living room.

"How did Bernard die?" I asked.

He looked at me, his eyes impassive behind the steel frames of his glasses, as if to see who I was required not close study but simple patience.

"*Il s'est suicidé aussi*," he said finally. "That's why we can't tell your grandmother the truth about your father. For her to know that another of her sons took his own life would be too much. She drove everyone crazy trying to get Bernard's ashes into the cemetery."

The next day, I had lunch with my aunt, and she told me about my father's last visit. We sat in the dining room, the afternoon cool and blustery through the open windows.

"He was driving a convertible and had on silk clothes and brought presents for everyone. Each time we talked, he laughed and said nothing was stopping him. He was going straight up. But he and your grandfather got into an argument. They'd gone for a drive in Edwin's new convertible. When they came back, your grandfather got out and spit on the floorboards. Edwin was furious. No one knew what had happened. Edwin had been his favorite. He'd been everyone's favorite. He was the one who decided he hated us. Not us. We loved him. We always wanted him to come back."

Maybe my father blamed my grandfather for their poverty, their entire way of life. I tried to understand how my grandfather's violence could have shaped his sons. She explained the rivalry between the brothers, Edwin and Bernard, their eagerness to better the other, to win their father's admiration.

"Bernard," she said, "used to tell us that he was lucky he'd learned to fight. *Ton grandpère* would put gloves on Edwin and Bernard, and the family watched as they fought. Bernard was a lot bigger even though he was two years younger, but Edwin was fast. *Il était malin et orgueilleux* — clever and proud. He always found a way to win."

"What about Bernard? Tell me about his death."

She hesitated. "He was a difficult man. He drank too much and was aggressive. He didn't have your father's charm. Edwin was easy to like, and that must have been hard for Bernard."

She explained how between voyages as a merchant marine Bernard would occasionally show up at her door, drunk and wanting to talk.

"Once," she said, "he told me he'd seen your father. He said he'd found him in prison. I didn't believe him. He said Edwin was in a prison in Tacoma . . . *Y était en prison,* he said. *Chus allé aux States et je l'ai trouvé."*

She'd not have believed anyone else, but Bernard, Edwin, and Alphonse were different. "There were men in the family like that, who could go anywhere, do anything."

He'd described to her how he found him and told him that everyone would know he was a criminal—that he'd go back and tell *Maman.* She'd asked how long ago this was. *Plus de cinq ans,* he told her. More than five years.

My father had claimed he never had a single visit in prison. Why hadn't he mentioned this meeting with Bernard, one brother having found the other in a world of impossibility? Were there kind words between them, and did old resentments come up later? Or did Bernard arrive wanting to punish my father for his last, splendid visit home, the way he lavished the family with gifts as the others never could have done?

Tout le monde va savoir, he'd told him. They're all going to know.

What could my father have done behind the wire mesh and Plexiglas? How did they say good-bye? And when he returned to his cell, he must have believed he could never go home.

But Bernard then told my aunt another story, a stranger one, more recent, from that year. He'd docked in Vancouver and gone to a popular market near the downtown, called Granville. He'd seen Edwin behind the counter in a fish store. Edwin had a large beard and pretended not to know Bernard. He claimed he didn't speak French. My aunt described perfectly, as Bernard had described to her, Granville Island Market and my father's shop there, even my father, with his beard, as he'd appeared those years.

But Bernard never told their mother any of what he knew. When he spoke to my aunt, it was with anger but also pity. He hadn't told the family as he'd threatened.

"It made sense," she said, "why your father called a few times. He must have been trying to find out what we knew. He told me that things were difficult, that he didn't have much money. Normally, the family would have offered to help. He wouldn't have needed to ask. That's how we were. But we'd seen him so rich we couldn't imagine him poor. And he was too proud to ask . . . Only now that I've seen the photos of your childhood, I understand how poor you were. We would have helped. He should have asked."

I recalled our years in the valley, how he started businesses and worked constantly to build a life. His effort had hidden the bitterness of loss, the intention that whatever Bernard told the family would no longer matter. Was it possible that he'd gone against his nature and built that life, one so close in so many ways to his own childhood, only to prove his brother wrong?

As for Bernard, he told only my aunt. Shortly after that conversation, he called from Montreal and she answered. He asked to speak to his mother, who was at the table for dinner. He told her that he loved her and shot himself in the heart.

What had my father thought, seeing Bernard across the counter in Granville? The year our father opened the shop would have been the same that Bernard died. Maybe he believed that some things could never be fixed. Or he couldn't undo what he'd resolved through pride and strength: to disappear rather than let his family see his failure. But though Bernard was the one person who knew of his crimes, he no doubt also loved him as the rest of the family did, this his older brother, after all. Perhaps he wanted to say he'd never made true on his threat.

Even now I try to grasp this, the two suicides acted out in each other's absence, in the ignorance of the other's solitude and pain—two brothers walking past each other like strangers.

Nights, unable to sleep, I rewrote drafts of my father's story. I struggled to give it a shape that made sense, to see other versions of his life, to resolve questions that he'd left unanswered.

Gradually, I realized there were too many fabrications, too much fantasy. I found myself peeling back the fictions. I craved to see the characters clearly and wondered how much of what I was writing was true— not just my embellishments, but his own exaggerations and those of his family. There was so much chronology I could never iron out, so many jumbled facts. He often told his stories slightly differently, depending on his mood, on whatever truth he sought in his past at that moment. From my family, I learned the word *agrémenteur,* slang for "storyteller," a play on words: *agrémenter,* "to embellish," and *menteur,* "liar." I wasn't as interested in the facts behind his stories, the prisons themselves, or the police records. The memories of fictions and fantasies are as real as memories of any other experience. But still, there was so much I wished I could ask him. I tried to recall his voice through the phone, his silences so intense that I could hear each leaf's rustling fall to the frostbitten ferns outside the window.

One afternoon, my uncle and I drove along the windy coast to the southwestern edge of Gaspésie. We stopped at the old farmstead where my father had grown up, where my grandfather had been raised. A rutted dirt track rose from the main road, the overgrown land making a steep ascent to higher fields. Far below were what my uncle called *les islets,* a few weathered ridges just out from the shore, where my grandfather and his father before him had fished. My aunt had shown me the place in old photos, nets pulled up from the channel, the scattered fish a bright shade of gray among the rocks.

We walked from the farmstead, where nothing—not a sign of house or foundation or barn—remained, to the stones of an old seawall against which the steady gulf wind broke.

We drove to the nearby village of Les Méchins: ramshackle houses in a few lanes next to the stone church that had been the focus of many stories, where Curé Jean, the priest he'd hated, had preached. He died during my father's last visit, in 1967, a topic of some speculation.

At the cemetery, we stood before the graves of Alphonse and Bernard. I considered how quickly this part of the world had changed, how a generation gap could make my father's youngest brother the businessman he'd wanted to be. But I knew it wasn't that simple. There would be no easy answer for why my father had chosen his life.

My uncle began telling me that I should consider staying, maybe getting a job, but when I said nothing, he let his words trail off, and we just stared at the headstones. I knew that I hadn't yet satisfied my hunger for experience, and that soon, in his eyes, I'd resemble the brother he'd lost. In my travels, I'd come to recognize the loves I shared with my father—of chance and the pleasure of risk, of loss and solitude, and of our hungers themselves, not the need to cure them, but the joy of living with them, of the way they fill us and carry us forward. I recalled being a teenage boy, entranced by his stories of adventure. I'd sneak out at night and stand by the highway, letting the rigs pass close, their wind against my face. I wanted to find him in my own risks, to feel all that he had, to arrive at the dark edge of another life, so that, when I turned back to my own, it would shine.

My uncle and I stood within sight of the church, both of us silent. The wind from the gulf was strong, so relentless I could imagine a man going mad living and working here. Briefly, I leaned back into it and felt it hold me in place.

AUTHOR'S NOTE

I wrote the first draft of what would eventually become this memoir in March of 1995, when I was twenty, only three months after my father's death. Unsure of the story I wanted to tell, I wrote it quickly, during my college's spring break. I had yet to consider the difference between fiction and memoir, and at the time I called it a novel because I wanted to be a novelist.

During the two weeks when I hammered out the draft, I couldn't have imagined that seventeen years of rewriting would follow. While working on another novel and numerous smaller projects, I rewrote the memoir dozens of times, convinced it would never be published, that it was a story I had to write for myself. For about ten of those years, I consciously chose to make it a novel, changing numerous details, though keeping the core facts, and when I decided to rewrite it as a memoir, I realized how the repeated telling of any story separates it from the original event and gives it a life of its own. My father, after so many decades of telling his own stories, might have experienced something akin to this, and I spent years digging through the layers, trying to reconstruct the past and find what I wanted to write.

I have often been asked if it's all true. I describe the scenes that involve me as accurately as possible, but a memory is a work in progress, and it's hard to know how much the ensuing years have shaped what I recall. During the editing process, the time line has occasionally shifted, and some events have been told closer to each other for the sake of continuity. This seemed favorable to adding irrelevant or repetitive detail. As for my father's stories, he told so many that the transcripts from any given year might be in the thousands of pages. As I got older, he told them differently, revealing or possibly adding minor details to make them more interesting to me. Through his family, I have confirmed much of what he told me about his youth, though their own versions occasionally vary. Given that I became less interested in the banks he robbed than in the influence of that knowledge and those stories on me when I was young, I have not gone to great lengths to verify the numerous details of his criminal record. Furthermore, he lived and was incarcerated under several different names, not all of which I know. I have tried to obtain his criminal record in Canada, but an individual must be deceased for twenty years before it can be released. One of my late aunts told me that she had read it years before, having convinced a friend of hers in the police force to get it. She refused to say much on the subject, confirming only that my father had committed numerous crimes and been to prison several times. On the subject of his criminal record, she did say, "*Il ne faisait rien à moitié.*" He didn't do anything halfway.

I also tried a more direct approach than writing to the government, and went to a police station in Quebec with his death certificate. The officers on duty told me that they most likely had nothing on file, then checked and appeared quite shocked. Though they said that there was definitely a file and that he'd done a lot, they insisted that they couldn't share the information. Instead, they asked me several questions, as if concerned that I might be like my father. They finally said that I would have to go through the government.

Last, I have occasionally changed some of the characters' details in order to protect their identities, and, for the sake of my brother's and sister's privacy, I have intentionally said little about them except where necessary.

ACKNOWLEDGMENTS

I would like to thank the following organizations and people for their support over the years: the Anderson Center at Tower View, the MacDowell Colony, the Edward F. Albee Foundation, Ledig House at Omi International Arts Center, the Jentel Artist Residency Program, Canada Council for the Arts, and the Conseil des arts et des lettres du Québec; T. Wilson, Laura Stevenson, J. Birjepatil, Janice Kulyk-Keefer, Judith Thompson, Constance Rooke, Patrick Holland, Harry Lane, Ray Klein, Tracy Motz, James Arthur, Robert Olen Butler, John August Wood, Joanna Cockerline, George Grinnel, Robert Hedin, Heather Faris, Graham Moore, Arthur Moore, Joanne Cipolla, Tristan Malavoy-Racine, Kevin Lin, Leza Lowitz, Greg Foster, Julie Buisson, and Austin Lin. I would also like to thank Mark Anderson for helping translate the quotation from Aristotle's *Politics*. I am grateful to my brother and sister, Marc-André and Ré Lise, for their permission to be included in the memoir, to my family in Quebec for their stories and friendship, and to my mother for decades of encouragement. I am deeply indebted to everyone at Milkweed Editions, to Allison Wigen for so meticulously coordinating many aspects of the production, and to Daniel Slager, for his brilliant and rigorous editorial guidance. Lastly, I would like to thank everyone at Goose Lane Editions, especially Corey Redekop, Colleen Kitts, and Susanne Alexander for their enthusiasm and support.

DENI Y. BÉCHARD was born in British Columbia to French Canadian and American parents and grew up in both Canada and the United States. He has traveled in over forty countries and done freelance reporting from northern Iraq and Afghanistan. His articles, stories, and translations have appeared in a number of magazines and newspapers. His first novel, *Vandal Love*, won the 2007 Commonwealth Writers' Prize.

Interior design by Connie Kuhnz
Typeset in Anziano
by BookMobile Design and Publishing Services
Printed on acid-free 100% postconsumer waste paper
by Friesens Corporation